Maturity and the Quest for Spiritual Meaning

Edited by

Charles C. L. Kao

Contributors

Harrell F. Beck	Arthur J. Dyck
James W. Fowler	Margaret Gorman
Merle R. Jordan	Charles C. L. Kao
Richard F. Lovelace	John L. Maes
Walter G. Muelder	William R. Rogers
John H. Snow	Krister Stendahl

UNIVERSITY
PRESS OF
AMERICA

Lanham • New York • London

Copyright © 1988 by

University Press of America,® Inc.

4720 Boston Way
Lanham, MD 20706

3 Henrietta Street
London WC2E 8LU England

British Cataloging in Publication Information Available

Library of Congress Cataloging-in-Publication Data

Maturity and the Quest for spiritual meaning / edited by Charles C.L.
Kao ; contributors, Harrell F. Beck . . . [et al.].
p. cm.
"This book is the outcome of two symposia, 'Maturity,
Spirituality, and Theological Reconstruction' and 'Maturity in
Ministry,' sponsored by Maturity Studies Institute, Inc."—Pref.
Includes bibliographies.
1. Christian life—1960–   —Congresses. 2. Spirituality—
Congresses. I. Kao, Charles C. L., 1932–   . II. Beck, Harrell
F. (Harrell Frederick), 1922–   . III. Maturity Studies Institute.
BV4501.2.M367   1988
248—dc 19   88–9607 CIP
ISBN 0–8191–6972–2 (alk. paper)
ISBN 0–8191–6973–0 (pbk. : alk. paper)

Acknowledgments

No book is a single-minded work. This book is no exception. As I look back, I cannot help but to express my gratitude to all the participants at the Symposium on Maturity in Ministry and the Symposium on Maturity, Spirituality, and Theological Reconstruction, particularly the speakers, respondents, and panelists for their intellectually stimulating, spiritually vital, and professionally beneficial contributions. (Unfortunately not all of their contributions can be included in this volume.) They are Prof. Harrell F. Beck, Prof. Carole R. Bohn, Prof. Harvey G. Cox, Jr., Dr. David Danner, Prof. Arthur J. Dyck, Dr. Justus J. Fennel, Prof. James W. Fowler, Prof. Margaret Gorman, Sr. Mary Hennesy, Prof. Stanley Harakas, Prof. Homer L. Jernigan, Prof. Merle R. Jordan, Prof. Gordon D. Kaufman, Prof. Richard F. Lovelace, Dr. John L. Maes, Prof. John McDargh, Dr. Anthony Miserandino, Rev. Jacques Monet, S.J., Dr. Walter G. Muelder, Prof. J. Robert Nelson, Prof. Sharon Parks, Prof. Lucien J. Richard, Dr. William R. Rogers, Dr. Victor F. Scalise, Jr., Prof. John H. Snow, Prof. Krister Stendahl, Prof. Daniel B. Stevick, Prof. J. Earl Thompson.

In support of Maturity Studies Institute which sponsored the symposia, several individuals kindly contributed. They are Rev. Thomas Finley Brown, Dr. Paul C. Clayton, Rev. John D. Elder, Prof. James W. Fowler, Mr. Kenneth Kao, Dr. and Mrs. Herbert Ng, Dr. Oliver Powell, Rt. Rev. David E. Richards, Dr. Victor F. Scalise, Jr., Prof. Krister Stendahl. I am deeply grateful for their symbolic vote of confidence and support.

In preparation for the symposia, I had the pleasure of talking with a number of leaders in the academic community and the church in the Boston area. They candidly shared some of their ideas, personal experiences, and wisdom. I also had the pleasure of receiving written responses to my personal letters, sharing maturing experiences and concepts of maturity in ministry and other professions. I am very grateful to them for their valuable contributions, although they are too many to be listed here.

Over the years, those whom I invited to serve as advisors (Prof. Robert Freed Bales, Prof. Harvey G. Cox,Jr., Prof. Merle R. Jordan, Dr. William R. Rogers, Prof. Krister Stendahl, Prof. Orlo Strunk, Jr.) and consultants (Prof. Arthur J. Dyck, Prof. James W. Fowler, Prof. Margaret Gorman, Prof. Homer L. Jernigan, Dr. Robert Kegan, Dr. John L. Maes) have been very helpful in providing opportunities for personal dialogue, intellectual stimulation, and moral support. To them I express my hearty thanks. Likewise, I am indebted to my longtime friend and executive associate Dr. Victor F. Scalise, Jr., for his unwavering support and practical help. He made available the place for the symposia, the Harvard Club in Boston.

Last but not least, I express my profound gratitude and appreciation to my wife and son for their strong support and frequent encouragement sharing my burden and joy of carrying the project to its completion.

—Charles C. L. Kao

Contents

Part III Maturity and Meaningful Ministry

Contributors

Chs. 1, 3 **Charles C. L. Kao, Ph.D.**, founder of Maturity Studies
Institute and author of *Search for Maturity* (1975) and
*Psychological and Religious Development: Maturity and
Maturation* (1981).

2 **James W. Fowler, Ph.D.**, Professor of Theology and
Human Development, Director of the Center for Faith
Development, Emory University Candler School of
Theology, and author of numerous books, such as *Stages
of Faith* (1981) and *Faith Development and Pastoral Care*
(1987).

4 **Harrell F. Beck, Ph.D.**, Professor of Old Testament,
Boston University School of Theology and former
President of the Massachusetts Bible Society.

5 **Krister Stendahl,** Theol. Dr., is Bishop of Stockholm,
Sweden, and former Dean and Andrew Mellon Professor of
Divinity at Harvard Divinity School. He is author of
numerous books, such as *Meanings* (1984). This chapter
is composed from his lecture at the symposium on
"Maturity in Ministry," personal interviews, and written
materials.

6 **Richard F. Lovelace, Th.D.**, Professor of Church History,
Gordon-Conwell Theological Seminary and author of
Dynamics of Spiritual Life (1978) and *Renewal as a Way
of Life* (1985).

7 **Merle R. Jordan, Th.D.**, Associate Professor of Pastoral
Psychology, Boston University School of Theology, and
author of *Taking on the Gods: The Task of the Pastoral
Counselor* (1986).

8 **Margaret Gorman, Ph.D.**, Adjunct Professor of Theology
and Psychology, Boston College, and editor of
Psychology and Religion (1985).

9, 11 **John L. Maes, Ph.D.**, Director of Danielson Institute,
Boston University, and Professor in the faculties of
Theology, Education, and Liberal Arts.

vii

10 **Arthur J. Dyck,** Ph.D., Mary B. Saltonstall Professor of Population Ethics in the School of Public Health and member of the faculty of Divinity, Harvard University, and author of *On Human Care* (1977).

12 **John H. Snow,** M.A., Professor of Pastoral Theology, Episcopal Divinity School, and author of numerous books, such as *On Pilgrimage* (1971) and *The Gospel in the Broken World* (1972).

13 **William R. Rogers,** Ph.D., President, Guilford College, and former Parkman Professor of Religion and Psychology, Harvard Divinity School and Graduate School of Education. He is co-editor of *Nourishing the Humanistic in Medicine* and author of "Interdisciplinary Approaches to Moral and Religious Maturity" in C. Brusselman's *Toward Moral and Religious Maturity* (1980).

14 **Walter G. Muelder,** Ph.D., Dean Emeritus of Boston University School of Theology and Professor Emeritus of Social Ethics. He is author of numerous books, such as *The Ethical Edge of Christian Theology* (1984).

Preface

This book is the outcome of two symposia, "Maturity, Spirituality, and Theological Reconstruction" and "Maturity in Ministry," sponsored by Maturity Studies Institute, Inc. The following chapters are papers originally presented at these two symposia. They share an underlying concern, i.e., the quest for meaning and maturity. Life must have meaning. Otherwise it ceases to be tolerable. Those who suspect that life has meaning are bound to be haunted by a sense of futility. If life has any meaning, it must owe that meaning either to something within or to something beyond life itself. Christian faith affirms that life owes its meaning to God's purpose in history for God is the source of life, and life is meaningful because it participates in the divine will in history. God's purpose antedates creation to the goal in which all things will find their final fulfillment and consummation. Despite differences, these papers all make this basic affirmation. Human search for meaning and maturity has to do with this final consummation and fulfillment, which provides direction for spiritual growth and content for theological reconstruction as well as rationale and motivation for Christian ministry.

The word "meaning" and its derivatives have many different usages: "(1) I mean to help him if I can, (2) The passage of this bill will mean the end of second class citizenship for areas of our population, (3) Once again life has meaning for me, (4) What is the meaning of this? (5) Keep off the grass! This means you, (6) That look on his face means trouble, (7) 'Procrastinate' means—to put things off."[1] In this book, we shall focus on number 3. Unlike other philosophical discourse on "meaning," it is the religious dimension of meaning-making that this book is all about.

It is no surprise that meaning of life has to do with religious faith. Religion is human search for ultimate meaning. Bishop Krister Stendahl, a biblical scholar, names his collection of essays *Meanings: The Bible as Document and as Guide*.[2] Albert Einstein once contended that to be religious is to have found an answer to the question, What is the meaning of life?[3] We live in an age in which science and technology change not only living circumstances but also meaning of life and attitudes toward life. In that process, our faith in our tradition has been changed also. The change is religious.

Furthermore, it is no surprise that meaning of life has to do with human suffering because life has something to do with suffering. As observed by Dr. Victor E. Frankl, the founder of logotherapy, "To live is to suffer; to survive is to find meaning in the suffering."[4] Suffering reminds us of the victims of concentration camps, of the bloody wars and terrorism, but in fact, suffering permeates every corner of the earth and ever human being everywhere at one point or another in life. If there is any meaning in life, there must be a purpose in suffering and in dying. Each human being must find it for himself or herself and must accept the responsibility that his or her answer prescribes. Frankl was fond of quoting from Nietzsche, "He who has a *why* to live can bear with almost any *how*."[5] In this one finds the capacity to transcend one's own predicament no matter how grim the circumstances may be and to find an answer to the question, What is the meaning of life? In this the will to live is not lost. Blessed are those who have the will to live! Once lost, it seldom returns. Then the future is doomed. The struggle is spiritual and theological, and it is the core for Christian ministry. Out of this struggle one becomes more mature.

The meaning of life differs from one person to another, and from moment to moment. Therefore, the meaning of life is to be defined individually according to the situation. Life does not mean something vague, but something very real and concrete, because life's tasks are very real and concrete. Every person has a specific vocation or mission in life to carry out concrete tasks in order to find fulfillment. The discussion in this book can only serve as a conceptual guide in understanding the dynamics of meaning-making and its maturation. The true meaning of life is to be discovered in the world rather than in this book or even within each person's own psyche. Life is always directed to something or someone other than oneself. The meaning of life is discovered in the encounter with something or someone, in creative works or deeds, and in dealing with unavoidable suffering.[6] Suffering ceases to be unbearable at the moment one finds its meaning.

This book is divided into three parts. Part I focuses on foundations of meaning-making in terms of faith development and spirituality, spirituality and theological reconstruction, maturity and spirituality in the Bible. In beginning this part I shall discuss the psychosocial dynamics of maturity and maturation in the life of meaning-making in terms of what I call the Triune Dynamism of differentiation, integration, and transcendence. Part II deals with the life and crises of meaning-making, particularly in the contexts of family life, midlife crises, spirituality and suffering, spirituality and ethical decisions. Part III discusses the ministry for meaning-making and maturity in counseling, in preaching, in teaching, in person-centered administration, and in political action. The book concludes with a brief epilogue summarizing a few excerpts from two panel discussions, "Toward a Mature Theology" and "Maturity in Ministry in Ecumenical Perspective," which shows the unfinished tasks for the community of faith that require further exploration.

—Charles C. L. Kao

x

Notes

1. Paul Edwards, ed., *The Encyclopedia of Philosophy,* vol. 5 (New York: The Macmillan Co., 1967), p. 233.

2. Krister Stendahl, *Meanings: The Bible as Document and as Guide* (Philadelphia: Fortress Press, 1984).

3. Viktor E. Frankl, *The Unconscious God* (New York: Simon and Schuster, 1975), p. 13.

4. Frankl, *Man's Search for Meaning* (New York: Simon and Schuster, 1959), p. 9.

5. Ibid.

6. Ibid., p. 115.

Part I

Foundations of Meaning-Making

I. Christian Maturity in Psychosocial Perspectives

Charles C. L. Kao

Shortly after World War II, a little book called *The Struggle of the Soul* was published, in which the author, Lewis J. Sherrill, made an intriguing observation on modern civilization and its relation to maturity:

> The individual in the present world is caught between two fires. On the one hand modern civilization requires that the individual be a person of extraordinary strength if he is to thrive in the midst of that civilization. For in proportion as our civilization grows more complicated, more difficult to understand, and more resistant to rational control, to that extent the individual is the harder put to it to find or make his place in society as a self respecting personality. . . . And yet, on the other hand, modern society is producing, in vast numbers, persons who are rendered deficient because they cannot achieve precisely that kind of strength and maturity which our civilization demands.[1]

Decades later, in the late 1970s, a similar and yet quite different observation was made by a few academicians in science and technology. Elting Morison (Kilban Professor, Emeritus, MIT) quoted what Huxley said at the dedication of Johns Hopkins University, in raising the value question at a panel discussion on "Modern Technology: Problem or Opportunity?" when the American Academy of Arts and Sciences met in Cambridge, Massachusetts. Huxley challenged his audience, and more fundamentally modern civilization: he "really did not care how powerful America was in terms of iron, coal, steel, and all that, the essential thing is, what are you going to do with all these things."[2] Similarly Harvey Brooks (Benjamin Peirce Professor of Technology and

3

Public Policy at Harvard) said, "It seems to me that because technology opens up options, it takes a strong value system to control the choice of options; and so, where technology is disastrous is where it enters a culture or a social situation with a weak value system and very little sense of collective welfare."[3] Technology is attractive, but it invites a "Faustian bargain."[4] If Huxley were here today, I imagine he would say: "I don't care how powerful you are in terms of computer technology, nuclear power, laser beams, and all that. The essential thing is, what are you going to do with all these things?" This is a challenge to our maturity.

1. Maturity?

The task of defining maturity is complex and difficult. Maturity is culturally conditioned: it has something to do with social norms, moral values, and religious beliefs that constitute a mythos for the development of personal character and the maintenance of social order. No one can live without it.

In American culture, and in other cultures as well, the popular notion of maturity is aging. The basic assumption behind this notion is: old people are mature, and mature people are old. In traditional Chinese culture, children are taught to "honor the old" and "respect the wise." However, such an assumption is only a partial truth, and in some cases, it is questionable and cannot be fully proved, either by popular observation or by psychological investigation. This assumption is challenged by the old saying we occasionally hear, "There is no fool like an old fool." It is also challenged by the psychologist Gordon W. Allport, who points out that a person's chronological age does not warrant his or her maturity.[5] The old are not always wise, nor are they perfect. What is crucial in determining a person's maturity is not quantity of time but quality of time, not *how long* he or she has lived, but *how* he or she has spent the time; what matters most is *kairos* and not *chronos*, for *chronos* is a clock time passing in monotony, but *kairos* is a time charged with meaning and purpose and insight and value in touch with the eternal. The accumulation of years in life does not necessarily lead to the possession of wisdom or the formation of character. Therefore, aging is an inadequate definition of maturity.

Even so, age can be a significant indicator of a person's maturity, for wisdom has rarely crystalized itself in the inexperienced, immature person. The wisdom that is a sign of maturity should not be confused with the insight and perceptive sensitivity of the creative child. The creative child's insight differs from the mature adult's wisdom in that the latter has gone through the test of time, whereas the former has not. The test of time involves suffering and pain in life as well as validation of one's beliefs, aspirations, and ideologies over the years. Thus, the popular equation of aging with maturity contains some truth, even though it is too simplistic, inaccurate, and sometimes dead wrong.

The concept of maturity can be approached in two ways: (1) as a state of being, (2) as a process of becoming. As a state of being, "maturity" signifies full growth, full development, and perfection, an ideal state. It is like truth, goodness, and beauty to which one can aspire but seldom achieve. Such an approach to maturity tends to dominate the lives of the people living in a traditional society whose coherent value system is upheld as social norms and personal ideals and whose policy is to perpetuate the status quo and to transmit its value system from one generation to another. Such a culture is idealistic, and such a society may be static.

Maturity as a state of being is inadequate for the people living in our ever-changing society. Thus, another approach is needed. In response to my request for a definition of maturity in a survey of three hundred professionals in various parts of the country, an eighty-one-year-old retired writer writes, "Well, I looked into the dictionary and found that maturity means 'ripe.' No, I don't want to mature. I want to change and I want to grow until I drop." Semantically, "maturity" is derived from the Latin word *maturus*, which means "ripe." Such a traditional concept of maturity is no longer popular, because we live in a society in which "change is king." Today, "pluralism" is a popular word, and "progress" has a powerful attraction. Consequently, the dynamic approach supersedes the static approach, and the tendency is to see maturity as a process of becoming and to equate maturity with maturation. In this way, maturity is to be understood as a direction, not a destination.

However, the truth of the matter is: maturity is both a state of being and a process of becoming, and in the strict sense, it means the degree and quality of maturation at a certain stage of life.

2. A Psychological Perspective

Although the focus of this chapter is Christian maturity, we who live in this scientific and technological age cannot ignore what modern psychology says about maturity. It is not irrelevant to our discussion. Psychology, by its investigation of mental processes and behavior, does provide us a significant perspective in our probing of the dynamics of maturity in ministry. It is an effective tool in our conceptual analysis and interpretation of the dynamics. But to determine what this psychological perspective is is not easy.

A brief survey of psychological literature reveals that diverse terminologies are used and concepts advocated. Some are related, but others are not. Psychologists are no less prone than other professionals to coin new terms or to put new emphases on old terms in their communication of insight and theoretical construction. For instance,

Frank Barron uses "soundness," Erich Fromm coins "productive orientation," Marie Jahoda prefers "positive mental health," and Robert W. White chooses "competence" to mean similar things. What they say has something to do with maturity, although they do not use the word "maturity" straightforwardly as do Douglas H. Heath and others.[6] This is only natural in human perception, but sometimes creates perplexity and confusion.

Another caution in our attempt to obtain a psychological perspective is the possibility that since maturity involves ethical judgments, psychologists' concepts of maturity tend to reflect partially, if not totally, their moral values and personalities. An often-quoted example of this is Abraham H. Maslow's study of "self-actualized" persons.[7] It is observed that those whom Maslow considered to be "self-actualized" were in fact very much like him. Perhaps no one is exempt from this charge in forming concepts of maturity and social perception because no one is totally free from perceptual distortion.

Psychological findings are always determined by the choice of samples from which psychologists draw their data, and their samples are frequently drawn from college students. So we know how relative psychological findings are.

Although psychological maturity is defined differently by psychologists, Marie Jahoda in her study of the "current concepts of positive mental health" groups all factors that characterize mental health into six categories, namely, (1) "the attitudes of an individual toward one's own self," (2) "the individual's manner and degree of growth, development, or self-actualization," (3) "integration," (4) "autonomy," (5) "the adequacy of an individual's perception of reality," and (6) "environmental mastery."[8] By conceptual analysis, these qualities can be further summarized according to two mutually related, interwoven, underlying principles: (1) internal integration and harmony and (2) external integration and harmony. "Integration" seems to be the key word. The mature person is *internally* integrated and integrating. At the same time, he or she is *externally* integrated and integrating. The two are conceptually separate, but in reality they are inseparable.

The internal and external integration is a never-ending process that presupposes two opposing polarities, subjectivity and objectivity, which constitute a dualistic dynamism in which the dialogical, internal-external, integrative process is one process rather than two processes and manifests itself in the six categories mentioned above. The category—"the attitudes of an individual toward one's own self"— has to do with one's self-acceptance, self-image, identity, and the like. Self-acceptance comes from internal integration, whereas its opposite, self-hatred, comes from internal disintegration. Likewise, "self-actualization," "autonomy," and "integration" are oriented to the internal integration and its manifestations.

6

In the growing process of a child, mental images are formed like small islands emerging on the ocean and become parts of the child's consciousness. These separate islands come together as a continent, "a continuous land-mass of consciousness" (Jung).[9] This process of coming together is no doubt the internal integration because the psychic elements constantly seek to get together in forming a coherent whole. By integrating internally, one finds meaning and comes to make sense of life. Eventually, individual personhood emerges, "style of life" develops, and identity forms itself. On the other hand, the disruption of internal integration leads to self-alienation and self-doubt as well as self-assertiveness, pride, and arrogance. From the Freudian point of view, the healthy mature person is the one who integrates the three psychic forces, namely, the id, the ego, and the superego, in good harmony. Just as Freud's dictum, "Where the id was, there shall ego be," shows, so too "Where the superego was, there shall ego be."[10] This dictum well expresses a mature person's internal integration.

A person who is internally integrated is also externally integrated. A mature person's external integration is manifested in one's multiple involvements and participation in external affairs; in one's respect, trust, and love of others; and in one's concern and care for the well-being of the community. Perceptually, it is manifested in one's accurate perception of the external and realistic assessment of other people in interpersonal relationships and in one's objectivity and respect for the integrity of facts. Furthermore, it is manifested in one's creativity, productivity, entrepreneurship, and dedication to worthy causes.

When someone asked Freud what a normal person can do well, Freud did not give a sophisticated answer. He simply said, "*Lieben und arbeiten*" (to love and to work).[11] This simple formula expresses a mature person's external integration. One may suspect that Abraham Maslow advocates egocentricity by his "self-actualization." This is not so. Neither Carl Jung's "individuation" nor Maslow's "self-actualization" is self-centered. Certainly, care for other people is implicit, if not explicit, in a person's individuation, and the "self-actualized" person is characterized by his or her "all embracing love for everybody and for everything."[12] Likewise, Jahoda's "environmental mastery" mentioned above is focused on a mature person's external integration.

However, defining maturity as internal and external integration and harmony has its limitations because it seems to imply that the process of maturation is conceptualized as if it were always on the same level. Likewise, "life cycle" is inaccurate and misleading in describing maturation because it seems to imply that the process of growth is on the same level. In fact, whenever one experiences growth, there is always a transition from the lower level to the higher level. Even though we may become like a child in old age, we do not return to the same state of childhood; childhood childishness is qualitatively different from mature childlikeness, although both look alike. It is significant that Erikson uses a diagonal movement rather than a cycle in describing human growth in his chart on Eight Stages of Man in *Childhood and Society*.[13] Therefore, it is imperative to include "transcendence" in conceptualizing maturity and maturation because the internal and external integration is inadequate in delineating the dynamics of human life sufficiently. For life is not a cycle—it yearns to move up and transcend. "Life cycle" is more a Hindu-Buddhist *samsara* (the eternal cycle of birth, suffering, death, and rebirth) than a scientific discovery of truth. There is something teleological in life. Human search for excellence is indicative of this.

Modern civilization has its strength in science and technology but its weakness in recognizing the importance of transcendence in life. That is why maturity is in short supply; heroes are difficult to find; when found, they are soon dead. Heroes symbolize transcendence, and modern society cannot stand its challenge. For the sensitive person, transcendence is not difficult to find, and its traces are everywhere—as the shining stars to the ancient psalmist or the moral imperative to the eighteenth-century German philosopher Immanuel Kant. The teleological element in life is part of transcendence and manifested in self-transcendence.

"Transcendence" is often used to signify the supernatural being, but it has its natural counterpart. One may detect transcendence in the hierarchy of human needs (Maslow)[14] or the hierarchy of adaptive mechanisms (Vaillant)[15] or the hierarchy of moral values and the like. They are natural expressions of the transcendent and scales of growth. The transcendent is immanent in the internal and external integration in human growth to enable it to reach dynamic homeostases and balances and grow from one level to another. Maturity is expressed in how one satisfies one's needs and what they are. The "mature mechanisms" are considered to be "sublimation, altruism, suppression, anticipation, and humor," whereas the higher levels of human needs include the need for love and belonging, self-esteem, and self-actualization. One cannot be just concerned about the basic needs for food, shelter, sex, security, and so on, although they are essential, because once these needs are met, one has to move on to satisfy the higher needs. This indicates that even in the natural realm one finds transcendence that alludes to the vertical dimension of life.

Furthermore, it seems to me that "transcendence" as a basic principle in human growth is interwoven with dichotomous principles of "differentiation" and "integration" in constituting what I propose to call the Triune Dynamism in facilitating the internal and external integration of life. This is so, especially when one sees maturity as a process of becoming. Maturity then can be interpreted in terms of its full functioning, and immaturity, its functional disruption or fixation to one of them. The full functioning of the Triune Dynamism may be what psychoanalysis wants to achieve. As affirmed by Erikson, "the goal of psychoanalytic treatment has been defined as a simultaneous increase in the mobility of the id, in the tolerance of the superego, and in the synthesizing power of the ego."[16] This is reflected in the functional affinities between the id and differentiation, between the ego and integration, and between the superego and transcendence. Furthermore, this is reflected in Freud's dictum: "Where id was, there shall ego be."[17] It is what the interweaving of the three basic principles (which constitute the one-in-three, three-in-one dynamism) signifies. Maturity is the goal, and it is the full functioning of the Triune Dynamism in life.

Although we need all three principles to be operative in every stage of life, "differentiation" seems to take the leading role in childhood: birth is the child's physical differentiation from the mother, and the major developmental task of childhood is to become an individual person (the child's psychological differentiation from the family). Likewise, beginning from adolescence and in young adulthood, "integration" seems to take the leading role: identity formation is an internal integration of self-images, and the developmental tasks of young adulthood are to establish a family and career (an external personal integration with members of the society and its institutions). In midlife, one takes stock of one's life and reintegrates one's philosophy of life internally and takes care of the younger generation in and outside the family (an external integration). Later in life, "transcendence" begins to take the leading role: having integrated oneself with members of the society and its institutions and having encountered not only human limitations but also frustrations and pains and failures, one becomes more self-transcendent in reality perception and in interpersonal relationships, and more transcendent from this world in search of the spiritual and the eternal in preparation for the inevitable end of this earthly pilgrimage. Integrity, the crown of life in Erikson's Eight Stages of Man, is a product of the full functioning of the Triune Dynamism, not just internal integration and transcendence from oneself and the world as well as imminence of the transcendent in oneself. Integrity is a sign of maturity.

This conceptualization has its limitations as any human endeavors. Yet it tries to convey something that is ignored by many in modern culture—that is, the teleological element in life and its vertical dimension, especially when one sees maturity as a process of becoming.

3. Christian Maturity

What is Christian maturity? One may be tempted to answer this question with a list of moral virtues such as the fruit of the Spirit: "love, joy, peace, patience, kindness, goodness, faithfulness, gentleness, self-control" (Gal. 5:22). Perhaps this is a reflection of puritan moralism of the past. But this is an inadequate answer because it lacks the dynamic aspect. Such a list of virtues may be misunderstood—as if Christian maturity were a new set of moral codes to be obeyed as the Torah. Christian maturity is related to Christian living, and Christian living is a dynamic process, a growing process. Christian maturity does not point to the life of slavery but to the life of freedom in Christ; it always refers to God's perfection (Matt. 5:48), "the measure of the stature of the fullness of Christ" (Eph. 4:13), the Holy Spirit, the triune God. The biblical equivalent to "maturity" in Greek is *teleios* ("having attained the end or purpose," "perfect," "complete"), which comes from *telos* ("end," "goal"). God is the prototype of Christian maturity. The *telos* of Christian living is the living God. But God's perfection as an ideal state is something to which we can only aspire but never reach by our own effort although we may have been touched by it or have a glimpse of it here on earth.

In our understanding of God's perfection, it may be helpful to make use of the Triune Dynamism of differentiation, integration, and transcendence discussed above as a point of reference in affirming that the Holy Trinity is by far the most mature interpretation of the divine-human relationships experienced by Christians. The belief in the Holy Trinity, one God in three persons, Father, Son, and Holy Spirit, is something that can only be understood experientially in one's relationships with God in worship: it involves not only human imagination and intellectual speculation but our encounter with the divine. The Triune Dynamism in the Holy Trinity cannot be grasped by mathematical reasoning. One who limits his approach to God intellectually will inevitably find the the Holy Trinity a stumbling block and end up rejecting it because the dynamics of unity-in-diversity is beyond his grasp. Christian maturity is more than moral uprightness; it is a life in Christ by the grace of God through the Holy Spirit. Moltmann rightly affirms that the Holy Trinity is a basis for Christian community,[18] and I might add that the Holy Trinity is a basis for the maturity and maturation of its individual believer. It seems that the Holy Trinity provides a paradigm for the full functioning of the Triune Dynamism in human life.

Christian maturity, as a process of becoming, is traditionally known as "sanctification." It is divided into three stages: (1) the Purgative Stage, turning from sin and overcoming of evil; (2) the Illuminative Stage, a growth in understanding and commitment; (3) the Unitive Stage, the goal of perfect union with God in Christ.[19] John Bunyan calls it Pilgrim's Progress, implying that sanctification is an ongoing process departing from sin and evil, the City of Destruction, for the City of God. Sanctification for Barth is "the claiming of all human life and being and activity by the will of God," and for Brunner

10

it is to follow the steps of Jesus Christ in his self-surrender on the cross.[20] However, for Tillich sanctification is characterized by increasing awareness, increasing freedom, increasing relatedness, and increasing self-transcendence.[21] In other words, it is characterized by the "courage to be oneself" and the "courage to be a part."[22] For others, sanctification may be simply to become "the person we are and were created to be."[23] Since sanctification is a maturation of our relationships with the triune God, with ourselves, and with the external reality, the Triune Dynamism may help us see it in a new perspective. From this point of view, sanctification is characterized by increasing differentiation, increasing integration, and increasing transcendence.

Christian maturity has its psychological dimension, which Christian believers share with nonbelievers, atheists, agnostics, and others because Christians are human—they are neither the angel nor the devil. In his *Individual and His Religion*, published decades ago, psychologist Gordon W. Allport points out that the mature religious sentiment is "well differentiated," "dynamic in character in spite of its derivative nature," "productive of a consistent morality," "comprehensive," "integral," and "fundamentally heuristic."[24] Very recently, in his study *Stages of Faith*, James W. Fowler identifies six stages in faith development: (1) Intuitive-Projective Faith, (2) Mythic-Literal Faith, (3) Synthetic-Conventional Faith, (4) Individuative-Reflective Faith, (5) Conjunctive Faith, and (6) Universalizing Faith.[25] This is based on Erikson's psychosocial, Piaget's cognitive, and Kohlberg's moral developmental theories in meaning-making which Fowler calls "faith." Does life have meaning or purpose?" "What gives *your* life meaning?" are important questions in his study. Faith in this context as Fowler defines it is not particularly Christian: "Faith is recognizably the same phenomenon in Christians, Marxists, Hindus and Dinka."[26] Yet it helps our understanding of the psychological dimension of Christian maturity.

From the point of view of the Triune Dynamism, I find both Allport's description of mature religious sentiment and Fowler's faith development very relevant. Although their ideas, terminologies, and expressions are not exactly the same, one can find a number of correlations with the Triune Dynamism; some are easily found while others may need careful analyses of and sensitivities to the similarities behind them. Mature faith is dynamic, well differentiated, integrated, heuristic, comprehensive, and consistently moral. Morality requires self-transcendence, and without self-transcendence, morality is merely a rationalization. So, transcendence is inherently operative in mature religious sentiment along with differentiation and integration, and this is also true with faith development.

Faith in its primal form is basic trust. Trust in someone, be it divine or human, is a form of integration from the point of view of the

Triune Dynamism. Faith begins with integration, and then differentiation takes the leading role in its development in the first two stages, Intuitive-Projective Faith and Mythic-Literal Faith, which are characterized by wholeness and undifferentiation in one's perception and cognition in meaning-making, although both integration and transcendence are inherently operative in each stage. The transition is the increase of differentiation of one's own perspective from and with others as well as coordination in logical operations. In the third stage, Synthetic-Conventional Faith, integration again takes the leading role in the form of mutual perspective-taking in interpersonal relationships and hunger for approval and affirmation of others and in the centering of values and commitments in forming a tacit, largely unexamined conventional faith. However, in the fourth stage, Individuative-Reflective Faith, differentiation returns to take the leading role in the form of critical examination of the tacit system of beliefs, values, and commitments of the last stage in forming one's own faith through reflection. The increasing differentiation leads to a more explicit meaning system and expressive identity, a new power of conscious control, and even to the attempt to demythologize religious symbols in one's relation to them. In the fifth stage, Conjunctive Faith, integration takes its leading role in dealing with the new awareness of polar tensions within oneself and paradox in the nature of truth, trying to bring together the opposites in mind and experience. Furthermore, this increasing integration makes one humble, receptive, and permeable in encountering with the mystery and eager to be part of the larger movement of the Spirit. Finally, in the sixth stage, Universalizing Faith, transcendence takes the leading role in the form of "detachment" or *kenosis* (emptying of self), self-transcendence reaching its climax in viewing the world and identifying with and participating in the Ultimate in bringing about the transformation of the world. However, transcendence has been operative in previous stages. Those who reach this stage are indeed rare—only one person in Fowler's sample of nearly four hundred people (3.1 percent).[27] They are highly differentiated, integrated, and self-transcended simultaneously in their lives.

Faith development is not particularly Christian, as Fowler points out. Structurally it is neutral. Neil Hamilton's *Maturing in the Christian Life* is an attempt to fill this gap; so also is Fowler's subsequent book, *Becoming Adult, Becoming Christian*. Mature Christian faith needs to be Christian in its theological content, not just faith in the Ultimate but in the triune God, the Holy Trinity—Father, Son, and Holy Spirit—who is the prototype of Christian maturity and whose Triune Dynamism is the center of Christian living and growth. Christian faith is grounded in Jesus Christ, and Christian maturity is to "attain to the unity of the faith and of the knowledge of the Son of God, to mature manhood, to the measure of the stature of the fullness of

Christ" (Eph. 4:13). In Christ Jesus one finds the full functioning of the Triune Dynamism: "Christ Jesus, who, though he was in the form of God (transcendence), did not count equality with God a thing to be grasped (differentiation), but emptied himself (*kenosis*, self-transcendence), taking the form of a servant (integration), being born in the likeness of men (integration)" (Phil. 2:6–11). Christian maturity is life in Christ Jesus, becoming increasingly differentiated like Him with distinctive consciousness of being the Son of God with unique identity and sense of mission in the world; integrated like him with humanity reaching out to the fishermen, the sick and the hungry, tax collectors, men and women of his time; and transcended like Him from Himself in identifying with the will of God the Father even death on the cross. Life in Christ is to live in the transforming love of God by the Spirit through faith; it is God's grace and not human works. God's love is the motivating power for the Triune Dynamism in Christian life; God's love is love with justice; God's justice is justice with love.

In response to my survey a few years ago, a minister from Illinois wrote:

> I think that maturity and "wholeness" are very much the same. As I watch people in the maturing process, I discover that those individuals who have a close and personal relationship with Jesus Christ as their Savior and Lord in their life, exhibit maturity in a way which others do not. This is particularly true of young people who often mature "overnight" as they come into a new relationship with Jesus Christ and as they find a purpose and a center to their thought process and their entire being. I watched a whole group of thirty-two young people go through a remarkable spiritual awakening when I was a pastor of—Church, Indiana.

Christian maturity has a corporate sense that refers to the maturity of the church as community. It signifies the growth of the church toward its unity and participation in the fullness of Christ who is the head of the church in common trust and obedience. Ideally the church is the community of God's redeemed people in which one can speak truth in love, but in reality disunity and strife in the church is a more common phenomenon than unity because every person is by nature a small god to his or herself and is to be liberated continually by God's redeeming power. It is through the indwelling Spirit in the church to inspire and to bind together that true fellowship and unity is attained. This may be understood in terms of the full functioning of the Triune Dynamism in the church.

In any community, the leader is oriented to integration, whereas its members are oriented to differentiation. When integration dominates the life of the community, it becomes totalitarian and oppressive, whereas when differentiation dominates the life of the community, it becomes anarchy. Transcendence is needed to bring them together into full functioning as Triune Dynamism. From this point of view, it is significant that the Apostolic Church affirms the presence of the indwelling Spirit in its midst to give gifts to its members for the ministry in building up the Body of Christ. But conflicts exist. What is needed is transcendence from one's childish egocentricity in search of a common commitment and shared vision of the fullness of Christ who is the Head of the church.

Individuality is important in the life of the church, but childish egocentric individualism is not; sectarianism becomes questionable if it is dominated by self-righteous differentiation, namely, the tendency of playing God. Likewise, orthodoxy becomes oppressive if it is not accompanied by love and compassion for the unorthodox. Although orthodoxy is important to the unity of the church, individual freedom must be preserved. Modern ecumenism is meant to be a remedy for the divisive denominationalism manifested in the expansive missionary movement of the previous centuries. However, the pendulum may swing to the other extreme in emphasizing church union so that the proper role of differentiation in the life of the church is neglected and church union becomes a strategy for retreat and survival rather than for mission.

Christian maturity is a process of becoming. Sanctification is an ongoing process. As recalled by Tillich, when Martin Kähler was in his seventies and lecturing on the principle of justification by grace through faith, he told the class: "Do not think that at my age one becomes a fully serene, mature, believing, and regenerated human being. The inner struggle is going on to the last day no matter how old one becomes."[28] This process of becoming involves a vision of one's self-image in the larger context of the vision of the fullness of Christ in history and the understanding of the full realization of the teleological element in life that gives birth to the "Evolving Self" (Kagan), namely, the seed of the Triune Dynamism, whose origin is found in the Holy Trinity. It is an ever-renewing process by which one finds meaning and purpose of life.

14

Notes

1. Lewis J. Sherrill, *The Struggle of the Soul* (New York: Macmillan Co., 1951), p. 1.

2. Harvey Brooks et al., "Some Issues of Technology," *Daedalus* (Winter 1980), p. 17.

3. Ibid., p. 3.

4. Ibid., pp. 3–4.

5. Gordon W. Allport, *The Individual and His Religion* (New York: Macmillan Co., 1950), p. 52.

6. Frank Barron, *Personality Soundness in University Graduate Students* (Publications of Personnel Assessment Research no. 1), quoted in Gordon W. Allport, "Personality: Normal and Abnormal" in Hung-ming Chiang and Abraham H. Maslow (eds.), *The Healthy Personality* (New York: Basic Books, 1958); Erich Fromm, *Man for Himself* (New York: Rinehart and Co., 1947); Robert W. White, "Motivation Reconsidered: The Concept of Competence," *Psychological Review* 66 (1959), pp. 297–333; Douglas H. Heath, *Explorations of Maturity* (New York: Appleton-Century-Crofts, 1965); Marie Jahoda, *Current Concepts of Positive Mental Health* (New York: Basic Books, 1985).

7. Abraham H. Maslow, *Motivation and Personality* (New York: Harper, 1954); *Toward a Psychology of Being* (New York: Van Nostrand, 1962).

8. Jahoda, *Current Concepts of Positive Mental Health,* p. 23.

9. Carl G. Jung, *The Development of Personality,* in Sir Herbert Read et al., eds., *Collected Works,* vol. 17, tr. by R. F. C. Hull (New York: Pantheon Books, 1953), p. 190.

10. J. A. Arlow and Charles Brenner, *Psychoanalytic Concepts and the Structural Theory* (New York: International Universities Press, 1964), p. 81.

11. Erik H. Erikson, *Childhood and Society* (New York: Norton, 1950), p. 229.

12. Maslow, *Motivation and Personality,* p. 342.

13. Erikson, *Identity and the Life Cycle* (New York: International Universities Press, 1954); *Childhood and Society,* p. 273.

14. Maslow, "A Theory of Human Motivation," *Psychological Review* 50 (1943), pp. 370–390.

15. George E. Vaillant, *Adaptation to Life* (Boston: Little, Brown and Co., 1977), p. 80.

16. Erikson, *Identity and the Life Cycle,* p. 40.

17. Arlow and Brenner, *Psychoanalytic Concepts and the Structural Theory,* p. 81.

18. Jürgen Moltmann, *The Trinity and the Kingdom* (New York: Harper & Row, 1981), pp. 95–98.

19. John Macquarrie, *Paths in Spirituality* (New York: Harper & Row, 1972), p. 115.

20. Emil Brunner, *Dogmatics* vol. III (Philadelphia: Westminster Press, 1962), p. 229; Karl Barth, *Church Dogmatics* vol. IV, part 1 (Edinburgh: T. & T. Clark, 1961), p. 101.

21. Paul Tillich, *Systematic Theology* vol. III (Chicago: The University of Chicago Press, 1963), pp. 232-239.

22. Tillich, *The Courage to Be* (New Haven: Yale University Press, 1952), passim.

23. John Eudsden and John Westerhoff III, *The Spiritual Life: Learning East and West* (New York: Seabury Press, 1982), pp. 74–75.

24. Allport, *The Individual and His Religion* (New York: Macmillan Co., 1950), pp. 52–74.

25. James W. Fowler, *Stages of Faith* (New York: Harper & Row, 1981), pp. 117–211; also, see the synopsis on stages of faith in his article "Pluralism, Particularity, and Paideia," *The Journal of Law and Religion* (Spring 1985).

26. Fowler, *Stages of Faith,* p. xiii.

27. Ibid., p. 322.

28. Tillich, *Perspective on Nineteenth and Twentieth Century Protestant Theology* (New York: Harper & Row, 1967), p. 154.

II. Faith Development and Spirituality

James W. Fowler

1. Stages of Faith and Varieties of Congregational Presence*

Any time a pastor or priest greets a congregation of any real size gathered for worship, he/she addresses persons whose range of stages of faith includes at least three or four stages. The congregation is an ecology of multiple stages of faith. In a typical service of worship, the clergy leads the congregation in one liturgy, with one sequence of prayers, one creedal affirmation, one set of Scripture readings, one offering of the Eucharist, and one sermon or homily. But because the congregation represents a pluralism of stages of faith and selfhood, that experience is subject to constructive interpretation in at least four or five distinctly different models. From young to old, from the Intuitive-Projective to the Conjunctive stage or beyond, participants literally make sense of what is going on in that service in a variety of systematically different ways. Preachers know this from the comments people make after their sermons. The listener constructs the meanings in accordance with the particular set of experiences, needs, hopes, and beliefs that he/she brings to the service, to be sure. But the listener also constructs meanings from and within the service in accordance with the structuring patterns characteristic of his/her stage of selfhood and faith. These structuring patterns constitute basic elements in the person's *hermeneutics*—the patterns of knowing, valuing, experiencing, and reasoning, by which personal meanings are constructed and appropriated. Let us consider some of the typical patterns of interest and interpretation we can anticipate in congregations—and in those who seek the special help of spiritual guidance or care.

---

*The present writing includes in modified form parts of chapter 4 from *Faith Development and Pastoral Care* by James W. Fowler, Copyright © 1987 by Fortress Press. By permission.

19

1. Intuitive-Projective Presence. The *Intuitive-Projective* presence in congregations is most obvious among children of preschool age. They bring to the community their curiosity, their energy, their imaginations, and their special quality of living *liminally*. By living liminally I mean that children in this stage move freely back and forth across boundaries that they only later will sort out as conscious and unconscious, or as fantasy and reality. They also bring their impulsiveness and their need for a relational environment with a set of stories and symbols that can provide experiences and templates for the ordering of their souls.

In terms of spiritual development, this is the first stage in which we can explicitly begin to plant the seeds of vocation and partnership with God. By sharing biblical stories such as the callings of Moses and Samuel, of Joshua and the apostles, of Judith and Esther, and of Mary the mother of Christ, we can awaken a sense that our God is one who has special tasks in God's purposes for all who are willing to listen and respond. By praying with and listening to the prayers of children, we can deepen their sense of the actuality and presence of God. By providing relationships with older members of the community who have shaped vocation in accordance with offering their lives and work to God, we can begin to awaken them to membership in a *local* ethos of calling and response.

Spiritual formation with persons of this stage needs to provide for our children's forming faith and selfhood what Horace Bushnell called "gifts to the imagination." We must share biblical narratives with our children in ways that are open-ended and that avoid tying the intriguing suggestiveness of story and parable too quickly to a moral or moralistic meanings. As Jerome Berryman once put it, both we and they will be refreshed and informed by sharing biblical narratives in a way in which we "wonder together" about their meanings and implications.

We are in the very early stages of understanding what the long-term impacts will be of the exposure of very young children to heavy doses of commercial television. We know that an important part of the spiritual work of the Intuitive-Projective stage is the forming of deep-going images that can hold together, in a rudimentary coherence, the child's experiences of everyday life. The symbols and stories of faith, mediated by personal relations of trustworthy affection, can enable him/her to incorporate into the early coherence of faith the threatening mysteries of death, evil impulses, power, and the uncanny. All of these are vividly alive to the child. In the absence of an environment that mediates this kind of coherence with trustworthy affection, children are exposed extensively to a scrambled hodgepodge of narrative and vivid sensation that exploits, without ordering, children's fascination with violence, action, impulsive destructiveness, and death.

Intuitive-Projective children are fascinated by the metaphysics of a God introduced to them as invisible and living in an inaccessible realm, who is at the same time everywhere as a loving God. Their fascination increases as they come to see this same God as one who entered our world as a helpless baby in a stable, taught, healed, loved, and preached the Kingdom of God, and then died and was raised from the dead. Telling, enacting, and participating in these stories provide the opportunity for identification and attachments to develop, and for the Christian master story to begin to structure their perspectives and values.

2. *Mythic-Literal Presence.* The presence in congregations of the *Mythic-Literal* stage of faith has some unique features. When the congregational context is one of middle- and upper-class parishes, in the mainline Protestant or Catholic stream, this presence consists mainly of children of elementary- and middle-school age. Some adolescents in these settings will also be best described in this stage, as well as a limited number of adults. In other theological and/or social class settings, however, Mythic-Literal faith and Imperial selfhood can constitute the modal developmental level for the community (the average expectable level of adult development in it). Here again I have in mind certain fundamentalist and some Pentecostal communities. Though the structural features of faith and selfhood at this stage are similar in these two different kinds of settings, it makes a considerable difference whether this stage is experienced in a community as a way station on a longer journey or as having the characteristics of a final destination.

In both its childhood and adult forms this stage enables persons to construct a stable, linear, and predictable experience of the world. Cause and effect relations are understood; systems of classification and sorting have been created; simple perspective taking is a reliable acquisition. Narrative emerges as the powerful and favored way of forming and conserving meanings and experience. This stage, however, is largely limited to the world of concrete experience and of literal interpretations of symbols and events. It does not yet rise to the level of reflective consideration of its stories and experiences in order to formulate meanings at a more generalized level.

From the standpoint of spiritual nurture, one of the most valuable insights developmental theories offer us about this stage is its relatively undeveloped understanding of the *interiority of persons*. Almost in the manner of behaviorist psychology, persons of this stage regard others—and themselves (though without ever raising the question)—as being rather like B. F. Skinner's characterization of the psyche as a "black box." By this term he suggested that the structure of persons' interpretations, motivations, internal evaluations, and shaping of actions is largely inaccessible to scientific investigation and

21

understanding. Moreover, he was also suggesting that there may be little or no reliable relation among what people say they are going to do, the motives they claim, and what they actually do. Like Skinner, though without developing a theory of their position, persons best described by this stage are largely inattentive to and unaware of the internal patterns that constitute their own and others' "personality."

In the absence of an ability to understand interiority, persons of this stage must construct some basis for discerning predictability and pattern in the behavior of God and of other persons. Consistently we find that lawfulness and order are imposed on the universe in this stage by recourse to the idea of *moral reciprocity*. In simple fairness, the cosmos is construed as rewarding good actions and as punishing bad actions. God is seen from the analogy of a stern but just and fair parent or ruler. In effect, this is a strong and clear narrative imposition of meaning based on a concrete understanding of cause-effect relations.

In young people this construction frequently gives way during a phase we have come to call "eleven-year-old atheism." This phase comes when thoughtful children, whose religious and social environments have given them sufficient emotional space to question and reckon for themselves, begin to come to terms with the fact that ours is not a "quick payoff universe." The good do *not* always get reward; the wicked are *not* always punished.

For other youths, however, where religious norms and beliefs have been enforced with rigidity and forms of emotional coercion, this construct of moral reciprocity becomes a more permanent fixture in their souls. Though they too may reject the God of the quick payoff universe at the level of cognitive self-understanding, *emotionally* they get stuck in the structures of the Mythic-Literal stage. They move on into adolescent and eventually adult roles and relationships without the emotional freedom and capacity for intimacy that are required for mutual interpersonal perspective taking. Often they operate in the areas of relations and religion with the kind of naive manipulation that first arose as a result of the embeddedness of the Mythic-Literal stage in the structure of its own interests, needs, and wishes. In fact, we see a fair number of persons—usually men—who may exhibit considerable cognitive sophistication in their occupation worlds (as physicians or engineers, for example) but who, in their emotional and faith lives, are rather rigidly embedded in the structures of Mythic-Literal faith and Imperial selfhood. To their marriages and family life they bring a rigidity, often coupled with authoritarian patterns, that inflicts psychic, and sometimes physical, violence on their partners and children. It often leads them to a kind of baffled bereftness in their forties and fifties where, in the shambles of their shattered families, for the first time they may begin the painful task of learning about the interior lives of selves—starting with their own.

Spiritual nurture, at this stage, centers in sharing the stories of the community of faith and in helping young persons comprehend the ways in which these stories are enacted in sacrament and liturgy. The faith of this stage is an *affiliative* faith—a faith of belonging, of identifying, of initiating and participating. Prayer will be concrete, in keeping with the structuring of this stage. But compassion, fairness, and love for God and the neighbor can both be taught and caught as young people come to find their places in the living and teaching of the church.

3. Synthetic-Conventional Presence. A large number of persons in the congregation, if it is typical, will be best described by the *Synthetic-Conventional* stage of faith. With varying degrees of intensity, these folk bring to the service the desire to be in a personal relationship with God, and with the important persons of their lives. They want to feel that they are living up to the expectations that these important others have for them. Prayers of confession and penance will be approached as occasions for asking forgiveness for failures of attitude and action, and for restoration in the love and acceptance of God. Persons best described by this stage feel that their very selfhood is constituted by their roles and their relationships. It is likely, therefore, that any sense of alienation from God they experience will be derived from, or closely related to, feelings of estrangement or tension with persons from their circle of family, lovers, friends, work associates, and acquaintances. When the sermon or prayers of petition include concern for the welfare of persons from other social classes or other nations, this group will likely envision both needs and solutions in interpersonal terms.

In the spirituality of this stage, then, is the hope for a sense of emotional confirmation of their personhood and a sense of warmth and connectedness with the priest or pastor. There is a hunger for a sense of confirmation in the meanings they invest in the roles and relationships that constitute their selfhood. They may feel a special gladness in thinking of the congregation as an intergenerational community bound together in friendship and shared experiences. Such persons long for harmony and conflict-free interliving in the community of faith. Conflict and controversy are disturbing to them because they seem to threaten the basis of community. The maintenance of peace and the restoration of good feelings and unity within the community frequently loom as far more important to them than dealing with issues that might cause conflict.

The underlying metaphor for church most commonly held by persons described here is that of the ideal or romanticized extended family. The community of faith is seen as a network of persons related through their common values and beliefs in God and/or their common love for Jesus Christ. These values and beliefs do not need to be made too explicit or clear; they sense that such an effort might lead to

23

disagreements and breaches of relationships. The important thing is to provide mutual support in times of trouble or difficulty and to maintain a supportive web of interpersonal connectedness through the community of faith.

The kind of person we have been describing often constitutes the most consistent corps of committed workers and servers in the church. Though they typically are not innovative leaders, they have a special sensitivity and fidelity to those parts of the Gospel that call for bearing one another's burdens and for building up the body of Christ. They bring gifts of inclusion and care for each person in the community, and often their loyalty to the church, viewed as an extended family, can sustain them in a kind of acceptance of and loyalty to others whose faith outlook may be somewhat threatening to their own. They have limited ability to take account of the *systems* that shape, constrain, and sometimes oppress persons. They have difficulty in relating their faith to social, economic, and political *structures*. Analytic approaches to religious experience and to the central symbols of the faith may be uninteresting or threatening to such persons. In confrontation with pastoral leadership or groups who insist upon critical and analytic approaches to matters of faith, persons of the Synthetic-Conventional and Interpersonal stage may take a stance that seems anti-intellectual, oriented to emotions and experience, and defensively conventional.

In pastoral counseling and spiritual guidance with persons of this stage, there are a number of predictable sources of struggle and dis-ease that derive from the structuring of Synthetic-Conventional faith and selfhood. Due to the absence of third-person perspective taking, persons in this stage are overdependent upon significant others and the community for confirmation in selfhood and faith. Adults in this stage have internalized significant others from previous years who help to play a balancing and guiding role in their internal life. And there is a collection of present face-to-face relations that are significant. It is likely for church-oriented adults in this stage that the pastor and some other persons who have institutionally important roles in their lives, such as bosses, respected associates, and community leaders, are invested with a kind of double significance or weight as regards the maintenance of a sense of selfhood and self-esteem. Crises or times of distress can arise when a person feels dissonance between him/herself and one or more of these significant others. Dissonance can also occur when two or more of the important authorities in one's life are in conflict or serious disagreement. Similarly, experiences of conflicting role expectations can be upsetting and disorienting.

In all these cases, the person feels distress that he/she cannot resolve because there is no transcending standpoint from which the issues leading to tensions, struggles, or conflicts can be seen, evaluated, and adjudicated. Developmentally helpful counseling calls for a kind of

24

teaching and modeling that can help persons in this stage to recognize the possibility of a third-person perspective—its liberation and responsibility—and to provide support in beginning to rely upon it and to exercise the new quality of self-authorization it brings. In this pastoral alliance, several kinds of resistance can be expected. Throughout there will likely be a dynamic arising from the person's recognition of dependence upon the pastor and other authorities that gives rise both to feelings of gratitude and affection, on the one hand, but also to often unrecognized feelings of resentment on the other. This resentment, coupled with anxieties about change, anxieties about one's ability to cope with new responsibilities, and anxieties about the effects of new self-authorization on one's network of relations, can all make the person ambivalent about the course of pastoral counseling.

Persons in this stage are likely to experience a special kind of crisis from a different source at times of loss or threat to their central relationship and roles. Since identity and faith are inextricably tied up with these central roles and relationships, events such as the death of a spouse or close friend, divorce, retirement, or sudden unemployment can have devastating effects. The grief or loss takes on a special power because the role or relation (or both) that has been lost constituted one of the fundamental elements of one's sense of self. The loss drastically diminishes the sense of selfhood and threatens its very existence. At such times, the person, deeply at risk, needs a consistent and continuing outpouring of community assurance about the worth, the value, the identity, and special selfhood that the person continues to have in the eyes of those who care for him/her. Developmentally, it becomes a time to face the question, "Who am I when I am not defined by this key relationship/role that has been taken from me?" It can be a time of deepening one's reliance and relation for selfhood and faith upon God and the community. It can also be a time for claiming a different kind of basis for one's faith and sense of self. In either case, one needs consistent affirmation and support in reconstructing the basis of one's selfhood and outlook.

4. *Individuative-Reflective Presence.* In many congregations another substantial presence is constituted by that group of persons who may best be described by the *Individuative-Reflective* stage of faith. What characteristics mark the spirituality of this stage? Such persons approach faith and an experience of selfhood that contrasts in some important ways with those described in our previous section. In the fully developed forms of this stage, persons are aware of an "I" or a sense of selfhood that has emerged to control and manage the various roles and relations that make up their life structures. This "I" has had to struggle, to some significant degree, with those external authorities—both personal and institutional—that guide, constrain, and support one in growth toward adulthood. It has also dealt in some clear ways with the internalized voices of parents and other authorities from the past. From the service of worship, the preaching, and the spiritual direction, the person of this stage wants an acknowledgment of and support in his/her self-authorization. Worship needs to recognize and celebrate the hard-won assumption of responsibility for choices regarding life-style and beliefs. Persons at this stage want what they perceive to be a fully adult form of worship and faith.

At the same time, these persons seem to ask the church to provide, in worship and community, spaces and relationships in which the stress of consciously orchestrating and managing the self-responsible self can periodically be relaxed. Persons who perceive themselves to be rowing their own boats in competitive and multiply demanding circumstances respond to communities of others like themselves where it is safe to let down a bit. They find release in acknowledging their need for relationship and solidarity with like-minded others. Worship and other settings will make this possible if they combine a certain measure of intellectual stimulation and challenge with a quality of community fellowship that does not try to reimpose external and conventional religious expectations and authority.

The underlying metaphor for church correlated with this stage is likely to be a kind of unspoken pragmatic, contractual individualism. One *has* roles, relationships, commitments, and intentions. One *has* now a more explicit and clear set of beliefs and values. Church is valued, and Christian faith is interpreted, in accordance with the contribution they make to supporting and extending the perspectives and commitments that express and support one's selfhood. Depending on the depth and intensity of one's commitments, Christian faith can also constitute a source of accountability and normative direction for one's selfhood and goals. The Christian tradition can be selectively appropriated and interpreted to shape and support one's Individuative orientation. In this process, demythologization and conceptual restatements of central elements and symbols of the tradition are welcomed and relied upon.

Persons best described by the stage of Individuative-Reflective faith have an often unrecognized need for both a confessional and a wailing wall. The structuring patterns of this stage and the pressures of our particular culture place heavy burdens on persons of Individuative faith to be "tubs that sit on their own bottoms." They are called on to be self-sufficient, self-starting, self-managing, and self-repairing units. In the absence of a trusted community of others with whom one shares central meanings and values, and with whom one can afford to disclose the self in depth, this set of expectations can lead to privatized and sick self-dialogues. When things are going well, persons caught in this privatization are vulnerable to forms of inflation and inflated self-deception. They may identify with self-aggrandizing personal images that result from the continual pressures to overadvertise the self and to identify with the advertisements. In that state of overinflation, they can fall into the trap of allowing themselves privileges and moral leeway that later prove to be terribly destructive of work patterns, of relationships and values that they temporarily took for granted. On the other hand, the person who is too dependent upon private self-dialogue for the maintenance of a sense of self and direction is also subject to deflation and excessive despair about the self, when things go badly. The pervasive individualism that characterizes this society—and too often our churches as well—makes the provision of a context of spiritual direction to persons caught in these dangerous orientations difficult. It is imperative that we develop groups where persons who are susceptible to the pressures I have described can find trustworthy community with peers and the help of competent spiritual direction. We need to provide circles where the armor of their defenses can be ventilated and where they can learn approaches to prayer in which they submit their images of self to each other—and to the Gospel—for correction.

5. *Conjunctive Presence.* Generally persons best described by the *Conjunctive* stage have begun to form a spirituality that embraces the paradox that God's self-revelation is always a matter of both disclosure and concealment. They have come to know in their bone marrow that the mystery we name God can only partially be represented in our best symbols and parables. They bring to church a tensive conviction that "it is meet, right, and our bounden duty" to pray, praise, and proclaim the reality and love of God. At the same time, they instinctively avoid the kind of symbolic domestication that makes of favored formulations and doctrines idolatrous and shoddy graven images of an exceedingly elusive transcendent reality. I am trying to describe a dialectical form of faith and selfhood in which persons find it necessary to affirm perspectives that maintain polar tensions in faith. God is both transcendent and immanent; God cannot be contained in anthropocentric categories, yet there is that which is personal in our experience and testimony to God.

Most of the persons who can be identified with this stage are at midlife or beyond. Occasionally, by virtue of early experiences of suffering and loss or due to a kind of precocious spiritual or religious seriousness, a younger person may move into the Conjunctive stage. But usually, as the brokerage that advertises that it "makes money the old-fashioned way," such persons *earn* it. They ear it by taking on irrevocable responsibilities for others or for some sector of our shared life. They earn it by having their noses rubbed in our finitude, through the sacrament of failure and through the death or loss of loved ones. They earn it by recognizing that our feelings of autonomy and self-control as a species, and our vaunted capacities for technical management of our vastly interdependent systems, are maintained at the cost of a considerable degree of self-deception and illusion. Put positively, they have come to the spiritual insight that the principal acting units in human and divine history are the great social and economic systems of which we are a part. Individual human beings, while responsible and gifted with a measure of genuine freedom, must learn to exert that freedom effectively in the interdependence of systems.

Selfhood, at this stage, no longer focuses its concern so heavily on control and self-management, and on maintaining the boundaries of a consciously chosen set of affiliations and commitments. In this stage concern with selfhood becomes a matter of attending to deeper movements of the spirit within and working at disciplines by which to discern and integrate elements from the unconscious structuring and wisdom of the self into consciousness. The self continues to be a responsible actor and agent in his/her world. In that action and agency, however, the agenda is set less by socially determined aspirations and more by attention to the subtle but insistent impulsions of the spirit.

In this attending to the impulsions of spirit, the person of the Conjunctive faith should not be understood primarily in Jungian terms. There the guiding truths and insights for one's individuation are seen as coming from one's psyche with its archetypes and symbols and its balancing responsiveness to the ordering and integrative power of the collective unconscious. In contrast, the Christian of this stage is learning to trust Christian tradition and spirituality in new ways and at new depth. Its symbols, doctrines, narratives, and rituals are acknowledged as structuring means of grace. Prayer and discernment become modes of opening oneself and attending radically—that is, with both conscious attention and with a responsiveness of the deeper self—to the truth that takes form and comes to expression in the Scriptures and tradition, and in the living interpretations of the community of faith.

In Conjunctive faith, and in communities influenced by it, there is a taste for the stranger. Persons have begun to learn to acknowledge and live with their strangers within—their own spirit and unconscious life. Having an experience of the disclosure and concealment of God in revelatory traditions, they begin to encounter the religious traditions of others as strangers that may be sources of new depth of insight and of correction in our appropriation of our own traditions. Further, for Christians there seems to be in this stage a coming to terms, at stirring new depths, both with Jesus Christ as the liberating and redeeming stranger and with the Christ's radical sense of solidarity with the despised or oppressed stranger.

But there are spiritual pitfalls for Conjunctive Christians, as well. In ways that are perhaps distinctive to this stage, people can feel a deep sense of cosmic aloneness or homelessness. The dark side of their awareness of God's revelation, both as disclosure and concealment, lies in a deepened appreciation of the otherness and the nonavailability of God. The dark side of their receptiveness to the witness and truth of other traditions can be a subdued sense of the imperative to share and commend the Christian story in evangelization. The dark side of their awareness of our being enmeshed in vast and complex systems can be a sense of paralysis and retreat into a private world of spirituality. Having had their eyes burned by all that they see and have seen, Conjunctive Christians can fall into a kind of immobilization that—if prolonged—cuts the nerve of the call to partnership with God. In these respects, Christians best described by the Conjunctive stage—as Christians of other stages—need the gifts and the structuring orientations of persons of other stages to encounter them with correcting emphases and energies.

6. Universalizing Presence. We now come to the last stage we are aware of in this process. I call it the *Universalizing* stage of faith and the stage of the God-grounded selfhood. In this stage, we see persons moving beyond the paradoxical awareness and the embrace of polar tensions characteristic of the spirituality of the Conjunctive stage. The structuring of the Universalizing stage derives from the radical completion of a process of "decentration" from self that we have been tracing throughout the sequence of stages. We have seen a steady widening in social perspective taking as we have considered each subsequent stage. Gradually the circle of "those who count" in the meanings of faith and selfhood expands, until at the Conjunctive stage it extends well beyond the bounds of social class, nation, race, ideological compatriots, and religious traditions. In Universalizing faith, this process comes to a kind of completion. In the previous stage, despite an openness to the stranger and despite a commitment to a commonwealth of love and justice beyond any of our present communities, persons continue to live in the tension between the inclusiveness and transformation of their visions toward a new, ultimate order and their rootedness in and loyalties to their segment of the existing order. The Conjunctive self is a tensional self.

With those persons who are drawn beyond the Conjunctive into the Universalizing stage of faith, we seem to see a movement in which the self is drawn beyond itself into a new quality of participation and grounding in God, or the principle of Being. In the completion of the process of decentration from self at this stage, the self is no longer the prime reference point from which the knowing and valuing of faith are carried out. Figure and ground are reversed: where previously the self has been apprehended as a figure interposed upon the (back)ground of Being, now self is relinquished as epistemological and axiological center. To say it more simply, with the Universalizing stage, persons are drawn toward an identification with God in which the bases of

29

identity, knowing, and valuing are transformed. There is a relinquishing of self into the ground of being, a kind of reversal of figure and ground, in which the person of faith now participates, albeit as a finite creature, in a kind of identification with God's way of knowing and valuing other creatures. In this sort of perspective, those whom one has experienced as enemies come to be seen transformingly as God's children who must be loved radically and redemptively. This kind of transvaluation of valuing gives rise to strategies of nonviolent opposition to entrenched evil in hearts and societies. It gives rise to activist efforts, through the pouring out of the self, to transform present social conditions in the direction of God's commonwealth of love and justice.

Such persons manifest the fruits of a powerful kind of *kenosis,* or emptying of self, which is the fruit of having one's affections, one's love, powerfully drawn beyond the finite centers of value and power that bid to offer us meaning and security.

From the standpoint of a Christian understanding of the future God intends in creation, governance, and liberation/redemption, we may describe such persons as "colonists of the Kingdom of God." Because of hearts and wills that have become vitally connected with the divine spirit, they live as though God's commonwealth of love and justice were already a decisive reality among us. As such, they constitute both transforming and critically challenging presences among us. In them, we see the human being in some approximation of its fullness and completion and are drawn to it. At the same time, in relation to them we see the compromises, numbness, and enmity toward God's future that mark the social and personal patterns of our lives and are repelled.

What kind of self is this? I believe that the self in this stage is, in a radical sense, reground beyond itself in God. I am not talking about moral perfection here; nor am I speaking of perfect psychic balance or integration. Persons of Universalizing faith continue to be finite creatures with blind spots, inconsistencies, and distorted capacities for relatedness to others. But this is a selfhood and spirituality that transfers the burden of self-integration and self-justification radically into God and therefore has a new quality of freedom with the self and with others. She/he moves beyond the structuring of the world and others from the self's perspective, taken as a meeting place of systems, of ideologies and relations. She/he moves beyond usual forms of defensiveness and exhibits an openness based on groundedness in the being, love, and regard of God. I think that the yearning of this stage, insofar as I have any sense of it, is that all creation should be complete and that all God's creatures should be one. The vision, in New Testament terms, is of the messianic banquet, where all will be seated together in the glory of God's presence, where wound will be healed and enmities resolved, and where there will be food enough for everyone. What is arresting about these persons of Universalizing faith and God-grounded selfhood is that in quiet or in public ways, they live as though the Kingdom of God were already a realized fact among us. They thereby create zones of liberation and redemption in the world that are both threatening and freeing to the rest of us.

2. Stages of Faith and Spirituality:
Toward a Mutual Critique and Clarification

In my first lecture I offered an overview of stages of faith, with hints about the character of spirituality at each stage. Now I would like to offer some preliminary observations regarding some parallels, and some distinctions, between the last three stages of faith and the three traditional movements in Western Christian spirituality. From the early Desert Fathers to Teresa of Avila, from John of the Cross to Baron Von Hügel and Evelyn Underhill, a broad consensus on the description of three major movements (and transitions) in the Christian spiritual pilgrimage have taken on classic status. These movements have come to be called the *purgative,* the *illuminative,* and the *unitive* ways. With the help of contemporary spiritual directors Gerald May[1] and Benedict Groeschel,[3] and with some of the great cloud of spiritual witnesses who have contributed to this tradition, I want to bring the last three stages of faith into comparison and dynamic interchange with the great classical Christian accounts of the mystical path to partnership with God—the threefold path of the *purgative, illuminative,* and *unitive* ways. In this exercise we may find that in interplay with the sketch of the great movements identified in the spiritual classics of Christianity, a hidden, latent, but important core of spiritual insight captured in faith development theory and research can be brought to light. In turn, we may also find that the largely phenomenological descriptions of the experiences and dynamics of spiritual development given in the classical tradition can be given additional precision and clarity through the structural characterizations of faith stages.

Prior to undergoing the opening of the purgative way, the tradition has identified a prerequisite moment or event. This is the moment, the *parataxis* in time and experience, which the classical writers call "awakening." This event or series of experiences might well come in the transition between the Synthetic-Conventional and Individuative-Reflective stages. It marks a moment when the self becomes radically conscious of self before God. It is a time when one's pursuits and patterns of life are glimpsed against the backdrop of Infinity. It is a moment when the quality of one's goals and self-investments are made sharply visible by the lightning flash of God's perspective and judgment. The experience may be consoling, or threatening, or both. Let me illustrate:

A man of twenty-seven has been called to comfort his uncle, who is the brother of his dead father, at the time of the death of an aunt. This

31

aunt had mothered him at various times in his childhood due to the protracted illness of his tubercular mother. From twenty to twenty-seven he had put the religious influences of his troubled childhood and youth out of his life. Marriage, divorce, and a troubled second marriage caught up his struggle for intimacy, meaning, and home in his young adult years. Alcohol, drugs, and the carryover of athletics from high school provided the main sources of meaning and diversion in his life.

The funeral home stood across the street from the church he had attended as a child and youth. He went into the funeral parlor to pay respects to the dead and console the living. Then he emerged; he stepped into the street. The form and the presence of the church arrested him. As he paused and gazed, he felt coming over him a powerful sense of the reality, the presence, and the love of Christ. Returning to his home, he wrestled for two weeks with the strong urge to accompany his wife and children back to church and to make a public confession of his faith. He finally determined to do just that. He publicly confessed his sins to the community of faith, and he testified to his experience of the forgiveness of Christ. And then he set about the business of changing and straightening out his life. Like the Prodigal Son, he "came to himself"—he took stock. "How many hired servants of my father have plenty to eat?" And then he acted to initiate a new chapter in his life. This is the experience of "awakening."

To the degree that a person responds to the awakening, for response is always necessary, the awakening inaugurates change in the life. One person may turn away, and the experience of grace will pursue him; another may turn away, and the invitation will not be extended again. Yet another will be haunted by it—never being quite able to stifle the call, yet never fully answering it. Still others may respond totally, as St. Paul, St. Francis, Martin Luther, and Mother Teresa. When the awakening occurs in a person of real depth and dimension, and it is accepted or rejected, that person will never be the same again. The awakening inaugurates, when it is taken seriously, as was the case in the example I gave you, the first stage of the mystical journey, the stage called purgation—the purgative way. It may require years for an awakening to take hold, or it may reoccur frequently. When at last it is accepted, the individual must begin to put his or her life into some relationship with that call. In the case of the man I described a moment ago, the awakening initiated and gave energy for the struggle to bring his life into coherence and congruity with his response in love, faith, and desire for obedience to the Lordship of Christ.

The steps of the purgative way are basically integrating, bringing coherence, congruity, clearness of being. The individual brings his or her external behavior, activities, attitudes, and desires into increasing agreement with what he or she believes and accepts as reality. Integration requires the remembering and repentance of serious sin, then of all deliberate sin, and finally the confrontation of unseen omissions and responsibilities. The striving for perfection this sets in motion is neither more compulsivity, nor is it moral nitpicking. Rather, it is an effort to confront and change the whole value system constructed from childhood and internalized from one's society and culture that keeps a person from living the Gospel fully.

In this struggle one experiences conscious and unconscious conflict. One must look for ways to minimize the control of certain egocentric aspects of the personality and to liberate the more generous altruistic and intuitive impulses of our being. The individual is faced with two selves: the first self is the true child of God, gradually emerging in a person's life, under the influences of grace and the participation in the virtues of Christ. The second self is the egocentric image, which can be apparently very devout, but ultimately relates everything, even the divine will, to his or her own preferences. The first strategy Gerald May calls the "willing" self, the second he calls the "willful" self.[4] Groeschel points to an insight that faith development theory helps us grasp more fully: if the realization of the two selves comes in one's twenties, it may precipitate a conflict temporarily incapable of resolution. This is because the personality in the twenties is still developing an initial self-conscious unity, and the life dream has yet to be resolved. Or in the more picturesque language of Sam Keen, you can't burn your karma until you have some! One is required, in the purgative stage, to grow and decline simultaneously and seemingly in the same areas of development.[5]

The end of the purgative way, with its gradual victory of the willing over the willful self, is a time of generosity and generativity, often bound up with powerful experiences. Daily prayer and frequent contact with the living Christ in the Eucharist can begin to transform the individual. A response of generosity and zeal can overcome the conflict generated when family and friends no longer understand what one is about. A person is growing in the life of virtue. New moral virtues and values begin to take hold and to shape his or her life under the influence of the Holy Spirit.

It is then that the person meets rejection, misunderstanding, dissonance, among friends, associates and family. Others experience a threat to their life balance, and their equations, due to the transformation working in the one who is completing the purgative way. This brings what Groeschel calls "the first darkness." This is a time of doubt and resistance born of the response of others, to be sure, but it is also born, it seems to me, of a response to the glimpses of the divine light of illumination promised by the next stage. Chastened and struggling toward faithful virtue and willing obedience, one sees in the light of God's grace how far one has yet to go, and how much still one has to change, how much risk of alienation and loss of primary relationships

33

and roles one must become vulnerable to, and one simply feels there is not enough power to go on. This first darkness is less profound than the later dark night of the soul, but it is similar and it is powerful. One must endure it, one must persist and remain faithful to the call, even though one feels exiled and bereft; one might even say one feels dead to his or her former self. One must yet go on, and then in God's time this darkness ends. Groeschel describes it this way: "In an hour or a day or a week, a new world dawns sharp, clear, free; the basic anxiety of life has been silenced because all is lost. All is quiet because the individual is resting at the bottom of the sea. A strange light breaks; strange, because it has always been there, but it had been hidden behind the hill. It is as if great doors opened in the eastern sky. In the silence music is heard; there is a presence at once familiar and strangely new, soft, gentle, but commanding."[5]

This brings us to the second phase or stage, which is called the *illuminative way*. For those who choose not to go back, the illuminative way has begun. Some refuse to pass through the gates, afraid of the possibility that they might find real happiness and fulfillment and therefore suffer an identity crisis in the loss of their miserable self. Some avoid it, fearful of the life no longer marked and filled with self-seeking. St. Augustine's vices called out to him, "You will never have us again! Can you live without us?" The relative freedom of the illuminative way is often more frightening because one may become aware of more deeply rooted conflicts. Repressed pathologies, disguised doubts, recesses of egotism in the soul, deprived of their virtuous masks, become visible before our eyes. One has a bit more strength so the challenges become greater. As one moves on, guilt is replaced by sorrow and worry by tears. Not only the past with its failures must be acknowledged, but also the present with its imperfections are mercilessly enlightened in this illumination. The description of purgatory, given by Catherine of Genoa, takes on added significance for someone in the illuminative way, according to Groeschel. He or she may be drawn to live with the poorest and most rejected out of the need to share and give. This need is there also to assuage guilt, and to begin to take on some of the things that Christ suffered and still suffers in the poor. One is frustrated by the inability to do more. Good works, then, become the hallmark of the illuminative way. Little do most people in the illuminative way realize that in the very experience of seeing their lack of love, they are beginning to prepare for the searching trial of the dark night of the soul. As the illuminative way proceeds, a silence and calm envelops the individual. This is reflected mostly in prayer, the prayer of quiet, wherein listening brings more answers than speaking; a gentleness becomes the individuals' salient emotion. If he or she is going through later midlife, this person may be working at the integration of major polar tensions in his or her life, polar tensions of being both a creative person on the one hand and recognizing that one is, despite one's best intentions, also a destructive or harmful person. One has to deal with the polar tension of attachment and being part of a group, and, at the same time, of separateness and being apart. One has to deal with the polarities of masculinity and femininity in one's life, and one has to come to terms with one's finitude on the one hand, and one's possibility of oneness with the eternal. Here we're talking about the coincidence of opposites, which is a characteristic of the later stages of the illuminative way. The resolution takes place in the presence of the infinite, simple being of God. God appears to have become the all of the individual. One has given away all and seems to have all, and it has been worth it.[6]

But then there comes the moment called the "dark night of the soul." Here I would like to quote Benedict Groeschel's brilliant description of the dark night of the soul:

> Suddenly it all disappears; darkness fills the inner temple. Beauty, honor, love, hope—even the divine presence, are disconnected, like a power line that has come down. There is no great storm as there was in the earlier experiences of darkness. There is only a hot, stuffy night without wind or air, and in the midst of this a frightened soul feeling totally alone, a complete failure and altogether bereft. . . .[7]

Groeschel likens this experience of bereftness to the biblical parable of the man who had cleansed his house only to return and find it filled with seven devils (Matt. 12:44–45). During this time of desolation (which according to Groeschel actually involves both a "dark night of the Spirit" and a "dark night of the Senses") it is important that persons maintain the structure of work, relationships and duty in their lives. Paradoxically, among those who teach, preach, or provide counsel and spiritual direction, persons find that others may be helped by their services and care, often finding their words and insights beneficial, while those who offer them gain no consolation at all from what they commend. As Groeschel puts it:

> Those who have experienced the dark night say that they become almost dissociated from their work, so that the Holy Spirit puts into their mouths words and wisdom which help others but which never touch their own hearts.[8]

During the dark night the comforting affection, the sweet penitence and healing tears of the illuminative way have dried up. In their place there grows a terrifying sense that one is lost, is perishing, and will never task the union with God for which the soul longs. One feels a profound sense of kinship with Christ on the cross: 'My God, my God, why has Thou forsaken me?" (Matt. 27:46).

In time the dark night comes to an end. Groeschel, drawing on the tradition and experience, says there is no dramatic ending to the dark night. Descriptions about it have an anticlimactic tome. Henry Suso's words are representative:

> And later when God judged that it was time, He rewarded the poor martyr for all his suffering. And he enjoyed peace of heart and received in tranquility and quietness many precious graces. And he praised the Lord from the very depths of his soul and thanked Him for these same sufferings which for all the world he would not now have been spared.[9]

The result of the terrors and bereftness of the dark night seems to be a transformation of the self in which all elements of selfgroundedness, pride, and confidence in one's own ability to adhere to God have been stripped away. Groeschel says,

> What has happened is that everything is lost and gone. All that is let is the stripped human will, unsupported, unadorned, without reinforcement or reward. One preserves the *desire* to remain loyal to God. T.S. Eliot in the *Four Quartets* suggests that this experience is unlike any other experience of faith, hope, and love in the past. It is a simple "yes" to the simple presence of God; the simple acceptance of the grace to love. The inner icon is gone. God speaks to the individual not by "tongue of flesh nor voice of angel nor darkness of parable nor sound of thunder but in silence. He speaks His word, which neither begins nor ends" (St. Augustine). Union with God has begun.[10]

This brings us to the last stage—the unitive way. Here words really fail to capture with precision the experience to which the testimonies of the mystics point. Groeschel takes the tack of first describing what the experience is *not*.

> It is not spectacular in any sense; rather, it is like the sun at high noon in a cloudless sky. One suspects that if we were able to experience it without being

first purified of all egotism and imperfection, we
would be bored as little children are bored with great
music.[11]

Without being spectacular the unitive way is also totally absorbing,
like love's quiet joy. Perhaps human love, beyond its initial powerful
impulses, is a good analogy. Many saints have used the analogy of the
love of husband and wife as a symbol of the unitive way. But human
love is finite and timebound, and the only way for lovers to make it
everlasting is to link it with the reality of divine love from which it
flows and which it symbolizes. The unitive way completes a process of
decentration from self and finding a center beyond self and inclusive in
its love of all being in unity with the One who is being's source and
ground.[12]

Final question: how do these two perspectives on human growth
and development relate to each other, and what does each add to the
other in mutually critical correlation? I'll have to telegraph my
conclusions very quickly to you.

My conclusion in the main is this: rightly understood, there is a
kind of parallelism between the last three stages of the faith
development theory and, on the other hand, the movements of the
purgative, illuminative, and *unitive* ways. And if we look at this
parallelism, we will see that a hidden kind of spirituality in the stages
of faith is brought to clarity. On the other hand, we may see that the
structurally describable stages of faith give us the possibility of a more
precise understanding of something of the movements in the spiritual
way. Let me say, though, by way of necessary preface to these
concluding remarks, it is certainly possible that a person who develops
to the fourth stage, the Individuative-Reflective stage, might well
preserve his or her way of being in that stage by honoring the willful
self rather than the willing self. He or she might respond to the
awakening or the call of God to the spiritual path by saying, 'Not
today, thank you," or "Hell, no, I won't go," or affirming another way
of life. What I'm trying to clarify here are the parallels between these
last three stages of faith and the classical spiritual path if one does
respond to that awakening and enters into the spiritual path of ongoing
communion we have tried to describe in these latest remarks. We'll have
to leave aside for the moment the question of whether it's possible for a
person to move beyond the fourth stage in stages of faith without some
sort of relinquishing of the willful self.

It seems to me that there is an interesting parallelism between the
Individuative-Reflective stage and the *purgative* way. I think the
structuring that makes possible the fourth stage helps us understand
some of the things going on in the purgative way. The structuring
makes possible the distinction between self, the executive ego, and the

roles one plays. In Jungian terms we could say that the Individuative-Reflective stage represents the possibility of separating the ego from the *personae,* the masks that the ego wears, and a new quality then of responsibility for the ego. This gives rise to a concern with authenticity, with congruence, with fit between life-style and belief. All of those, it seems to me, are necessary for a real engagement with the challenges of the purgative way. These structural capabilities seem to be required for a thorough and radical entering into and carrying through of the purgative way. At the same time, however, the purgative way really takes hold only as the ego, which claims control of the self in the Individuative-Reflective stage, acknowledges its need for a savior, a guide, or its willingness to be obedient. Only when it acknowledges its need to relinquish its efforts at willful control of its own destiny is it open to the work of the purgative way. The struggle of the purgative stage is made clear by the recognition that the hard-fought, developmental gain of the Individuative-Reflective stage and the quality of self-consciousness and self-conscious control that it brings, is a hard-earned pearl of great price. We really prize this autonomy, this capacity for self-responsibility, this capacity for inner control that the fourth stage brings. This means, then, that one resists seeming to give this up. Having claimed the self, to relinquish this illusion of willful control feels like the very danger of the loss, the total loss, of the self. But the paradoxical processes of the purgative stage, in which we say, "The good I would do I do not, and the evil I would not do, I find myself doing," bring one to the point of recognizing the futility and the self-deception of willful self-control, hence the first darkness that we talked about above.

Now note the parallelism between the *Conjunctive stage* and *illuminative* way: The Conjunctive stage is a time when the sharp, clear boundaries of the previous stage become more porous and permeable. It's a time when unconscious elements of the psyche must be acknowledged and a process of integration into consciousness and responsibility for the unconscious must be undertaken. It is a time for relinquishing the illusions of control. It is a time for the confrontation with major polar tensions, the coincidence of opposites about which we have spoken. It is an awakening to paradox and the ironic imagination. The Conjunctive stage involves the recognition of the relativity of all of our images of God, relativity not to one another but to the reality that they mediate. Now, these qualities of the Conjunctive stage parallel the illuminative way in some very striking respects. Here we see self and striving in the light of the divine radiance and wholeness. We see the gap between our efforts, on the one hand, and the perfection of God, on the other. As a result, we have a more profound awareness of the grace and the illumination of God. And in that paradoxical awareness the tension of seeing the divine light and of yet dwelling in darkness, we are pressed to do all we can to transform the world and at the same time to feel with great poignance and despair our finitude and our limits to transform or redeem that world. Here we see the structural qualities of the Conjunctive stage giving precision to the operations of faith that constitute the illuminative way.

From this standpoint, the "dark night of the soul" would appear to be the emotional and subjective experience of struggle through which one relinquishes the self as the reference point for knowing, valuing, and acting. This is the subjective experience of the reversal of figure and ground that occurs in the movement to the Universalizing stage. Gandhi said, "There comes a time when an individual becomes irresistible and his action becomes all-pervasive in its effort. This comes when he reduces himself to zero." The "dark night" seems to represent that interval of the death or radical relativization of the egotistic self. Caught up in it are the resistance (conscious and unconscious) of the egotistic self to its demise and the corresponding doubts and ambiguities one feels toward the Ground of Being that is exerting such a powerful and seemingly engulfing pull. In the span between the trapezes, suspended and risking all, one feels a leaden numbness in the bowels of the soul. Until the grasp of the Other becomes firm, and until one discovers that the self is not negated, but deeply regrounded, the turmoil and dread the soul experiences can be pervasive.

As the *unitive* way takes form in a person, there seems to be an experience of a deeper seeing and experience of the social, political, and economic worlds. Injustices and oppressions are more sharply etched and felt. But something has happened to the hatred for perpetrators and oppressors. Both they and their victims are seen in the light of an available redemption, liberation, and healing. Such persons, it seems, experience a freedom from self-regarding reactions to conditions and persons of threat and can become, thereby, vicars or deputies for God's love and transforming power. In the blare of publicity and media pressures or in the hidden struggles of smaller communities, they bring oblique and transforming angles of vision and action, arising from the transvaluation of valuing being worked by the Spirit in their souls. They see, taste, participate in, and invite us to respond to a Kingdom of God.

1. For fuller accounts of the stages of faith, including a discussion of origins of faith in infancy not dealt with here, see the author's *Stages of Faith: The Psychology of Human Development and the Quest for Meaning* (New York: Harper & Row, 1981) and *Becoming Adult, Becoming Christian* (New York: Harper & Row, 1984). For critical discussion and assessment of this research and theory, see Craig Dykstra and Sharon Parks, eds., *Faith Development and Fowler* (Birmingham, AL: Religious Education Press, 1986).

2. Gerald G. May, MD, *Care of Mind, Care of Spirit* (New York: Harper & Row, 1982); idem, *Will and Spirit* (New York: Harper & Row, 1982).

3. Benedict J. Groeschel, *Spiritual Passages: The Psychology of Spiritual Development* (New York: Crossroad, 1984).

4. May, *Will and Spirit*, ch. 1.

5. Jim Fowler and Sam Keen, *Life Maps: Conversations on the Journey of Faith* rev. ed. (Word Books, 1985), pp. 130–155.

6. Groeschel, p. 81.

7. Ibid., p. 84.

8. Ibid., p. 85.

9. Quoted in Evelyn Underhill, *Mysticism* (New York: Dutton, 1961), p. 412.

10. Groeschel, pp. 85–86.

11. Ibid., p. 86.

12. Ibid., pp. 86–87.

III. Maturity, Spirituality, and Theological Reconstruction

Charles C. L. Kao

The theme of this chapter is significant because it deals with faith, one of the most fundamental aspects of life—namely, our search for meaning and identity; it deals with spirituality and theological reconstruction, the affective and the cognitive aspects of faith. It is not only significant but timely since, in this postmodern era, many of those who decades ago had high hopes and unflinching optimism for the coming of a new age are becoming increasingly disillusioned. The mood is doom in this nuclear age. "Science and reason have fallen from their previous positions of esteem. The growing distrust of technology has eaten away at unquestioning trust in science and technology," observed Harvey Cox in his *Religion in the Secular City*.[1] The spiritual climate has changed. Religion, which was once considered to be dying, just refuses to die, because spirituality is an integral part of human nature and to destroy it is to destroy life altogether. Although organized religious, like all human institutions, have their problems, human spirituality reasserts its power and vitality and reclaims its proper place in life again and again in the course of human history. Every human being yearns for fulfillment of life.

Shortly after World War II, David E. Lilienthal, chairman of the Atomic Energy Commission of the United States, spoke to a group of university students and faculty and said, "The foundation of our strength and amazing vitality is not in material things at all but. . . . in the faith we cherish."[2] Indeed, faith is the foundation of our strength and vitality. And yet the faith that should be the foundation of our life is often on a shaky ground. The critique of religion that was begun in ancient times and later developed by Feuerbach, Marx, Nietzsche, Freud, and others is still a powerful challenge to many believers whose faith is built on their immaturity, ignorance and superstition, dependency, and egocentricity—no matter how strongly they uphold it.

On the other hand, there are those who earnestly seek for authentic spirituality and relevant theology to help them make sense out of life.

But they often do not find what they look for in the religious tradition and institution of their upbringing and so seek it in others that again turn them out. It seems that people often withdraw from active engagement in the church because they have grown beyond the religiosity they encounter there.[3] We live in an era in which the old world seems dead but not yet buried and the new world is struggling to emerge despite a tendency to return to the old.

Our growing pain is not only spiritual but also theological. As long ago as 1857 Archbishop Frederick Temple said, "Our theology has been cast in a scholastic mould, i.e., all based on Logic. We are in need of and we are being gradually forced into a theology based on psychology."[4] Perhaps this is the direction toward which we are moving. The accuracy of this observation is for the historian to determine, but one thing is clear: increasingly, humanity is becoming the focal point in theological reflection and discussion among theologians and church leaders in their attempts to make traditional Christian faith meaningful to modern men and women.[5] Therefore, it is appropriate to focus our attention on the concept of maturity and draw its implications for our understanding of mature spirituality and theological reconstruction in guiding us through the critical years, particularly the concept of maturity as the full functioning of what I call the Triune Dynamism, discussed in chapter 1.

1. Maturity and Spirituality

Like maturity, spirituality can be defined in various ways. Paul Tillich defines it in terms of "the actualization of power and meaning in unity," and for Martin Buber, "spirit in its human manifestation is man's (woman's) response to his (her) thou. . . . spirit is not in the I but between I and thou. It is not like the blood that circulates in you but like the air in which you breathe."[6] In his *Will and Spirit,* Gerald May points out that "spirit is the energy that impels our beings."[7] It is the aspect of human existence that gives power, energy, and vitality to life.

In this scientific and technological age the word "spirituality" is something one wants to avoid in ordinary conversations with others because it carries the connotations of being "unscientific," "superstitious," "irrational." Understandably, some ministers try not to deal with topics related to spirituality except on occasions such as Pentecost because the word "spirituality" signifies otherworldliness, individualistic piety, and indifference to social justice. Furthermore, spirituality is sometimes considered to be merely "a spooky allusion" or a psychic phenomenon or simply a term some pastors use to intimidate their parishioners or to cover up something they cannot fully articulate. However, in Christian experience, spirituality is essential to human nature, and it is the core of human identity; it is what differentiates human beings from other creatures; it is rooted in the belief that human beings are created in the image of God and is manifested in the divine-human relationship that Christians claim to have through the Holy Spirit. Despite faddish spirituality, I believe there is a spirituality that is basically profound and mature. If so, what constitutes, such a spirituality?

First, mature spirituality is *dynamic*. Spirit is "the energy that impels our beings"; the Spirit of God was described as something "moving over the face of the waters" in the creation story; it is symbolized by "dove," "wind," and "fire" in the New Testament. Mature spirituality is powerful and dynamic because it is rooted in the Spirit, a power (*dunamis*); but it is not ordinary power: it is the power that turns the world upside down, the power that has moral quality and authority in defense of truth, justice, and peace, the power that liberates human beings from the bondage of sin and evil. This power is clearly manifested in the life of Jesus Christ and his faithful disciples; it is the source of courage, commitment, and dedication that we find in the stories of those unusual individuals whose love and sacrifice make our hearts burn and fill our eyes with tears. The power of their witness to the true meaning of life is manifested more in their being and action than in their words, for their deeds speak louder than words. However, when they advise, their words, though little, carry power and authority of the wisdom that springs out of the very foundation of their inner being and the wisdom of the Spirit. As one examines these individuals, a significant feature stands out—their love of life does not fade away as the flower of the field, nor does their enthusiasm to serve others wither quickly, because they are in touch with themselves, with others, and with God at the deepest level of their being. When they encounter difficulties in life and suffer, their faith endures, their courage persists, their integrity remains. The power that is manifested in their lives has its own life; it is the life that comes from the Spirit of God. This power has the healing power; it makes us whole and helps us put together our bits and pieces as it heals our broken spirits.

Second, mature spirituality is integrated and yet differentiated. There is a variety of developmental theories, but in general, the process of maturation seems to go through transitions from an undifferentiated stage to a differentiated stage, and then to an integrated and yet differentiated stage. This can be seen from Alfred North Whitehead's *Religion in the Making*, in which he summarizes three stages in the experience of God and probably more specifically his own experience of God: the first stage, God the Void; the second stage, God the Enemy; the third stage, God the Companion.[8] God the Void symbolizes an undifferentiated stage in which there is no boundary, whereas God the Enemy symbolizes human rebellion against God in an effort to become differentiated as an adolescent turns against the parent in the process of growing up. God the Companion symbolizes an integrated and yet differentiated stage in which the rebellious child has grown to become a friend of the parent and vice versa, with mutual respect, an adult-to-adult relationship.

A similar transition can also be seen from the French philosopher Paul Ricoeur's analysis of the three stages in human experience: the first is the stage of primitive naivete, a stage in which one is immersed in one's symbols so that the distinction between self and symbols becomes blurred, an undifferentiated stage. The second is the stage of critical distancing in which questioning supplants commitment. By questioning one differentiates from the symbols and creates a critical mode of existence comparable to Whitehead's second stage—God the Enemy. The third stage, which he calls "second naivete," is a stage in which one returns to the immediacy of one's symbols without discarding the critical mode.[9] In this way one becomes reconciled with the symbols with one's heart but does not lose one's mind. In this process, the nature of relationship with one's symbols is changed; it is differentiated and yet integrated.

Similar transitions can also be found in the process of identity formation in groups, according to the study of psychologist Arnold R. Beisser.[10] He has identified three phases in the process: (1) the "dedifferentiated phase," (2) the "differentiated phase," and (3) the "phase of true identity." Terminologies are different, but the basic nature of the transitions is the same. The process begins with the effort to do away with differences (dedifferentiated phase) among members of the group for the sake of group unity; but their differences become recognized and cannot be ignored (differentiated phase) as they get to know each other and their relationships become more authentic. And, finally, they accept one another's true self without ignoring their differences (phase of true identity)—they are integrated and yet differentiated.

Spirituality is no exception in this regard although it involves the dimension of transcendence. Mature spirituality is integrated and yet differentiated. This is well pointed out by Dietrich Bonhoeffer in his *Life Together*: "Let him who cannot be alone beware of community" and "Let him who is not in community beware of being alone."[11] Life together is in a state of paradox in unity in which the paradox is dialogical and the unity dynamic.

Such dialogical paradox and dynamic unity can be discerned from St. Bernard of Clairvaux's understanding of spiritual transformation. He sees four stages of love as the milestones of spiritual growth: (1) loving self for self's sake, (2) loving God for self's sake, (3) loving God for God's sake, (4) loving self for God's sake.[12] A great leap occurs between stages two and three in that one is no longer self-centered but God-centered. The growing process does not stop at stage three, loving God for God's sake. In response to God's love, a transformation of will and selfhood takes place within the person so that one loves self unselfishly. God's love is self-giving and enables a person to love oneself affirmatively because it is unpossessive: God's love heals the broken self and nurtures it. If stage three were the ultimate stage of spiritual growth, there would be no dialogical paradox between God and self. The transition from stage three to four is from obedience to a relationship, an I-Thou relationship, in which I and Thou are integrated and yet differentiated.

The primal dialogical paradox and dynamic unity is symbolized by the doctrine of Holy Trinity, which epitomizes individuality and community and whose dynamics provide a metaphysical paradigm for interpersonal relationships as well as divine-human encounters. This paradox is inherently present in the inner experiences of the Prophets, Jesus, and Paul in that the Prophets said, "I, not I, but Yahweh"; Jesus said, "I, not I, but the Father"; and Paul said, "I, not I, but Christ," in their declaration of God's Word. Their expressions are different in words, but the same in essence. The I is integrated with, and yet differentiated from, God. This is the basic nature of Christian spirituality, whose aim is to be united with God after the steps of what is classically called "Purgation" and "Illumination."

In response to my survey a few years ago, a minister serving a church in Illinois wrote me, saying, "I think that maturity and wholeness are very much the same." The function of religion is to restore wholeness of life through the restoration of the "bond between man and the gods" (*religio* or *religare*).[13] But one must be aware that mature wholeness is differentiated and yet integrated, and that is is dynamic. Undifferentiated wholeness is totalitarian, static, and immature: it has no individual personhood, freedom, and autonomy. Any paternalism, be it religious or secular, if it perpetuates infantile symbiosis in human relationships, tends to be totalitarian and oppressive. Undifferentiated wholeness in religion can be immature and suffocating spiritually if religion is used merely as a political means to fulfill human ambition to control and manipulate. Spiritual slavery can be more subtle and insidious than physical slavery. Therefore, Purgation and Illumination are important before one reaches mature wholeness. Another dimension of this paradox is in the process of human encounter with God and knowing God: it is the experience that St. John of the Cross calls the "Dark Night" in which one encounters God. It is in this paradox that the Cross of Jesus becomes the revelation of God. In this Darkness one also finds Light. After "My God, my God, why has thou forsaken me" one also says, "Father, into thy hands I commit my spirit" (Luke 23:46). This darkness is caused by the presence of God, as the shadow is caused by the Light. The alienation one experiences in the Dark Night is a form of differentiation in which one also finds integration and transcendence as the three basic principles

45

are interwoven and constitute a Triune Dynamism in human life reflecting the image of the Triune God. In death one finds life and resurrection. In sorrow and suffering one finds strength and peace that passes human understanding. This paradox makes mature spirituality dynamic even in the experience of God's absence.

Third, mature spirituality is transcendent and yet this worldly. This is what the Incarnation is all about. "The true light that enlightens every man (and woman) was coming into the world. He was in the world, and the world was made through him, yet the world knew him not" (John 1:19–10). "The Word became flesh and dwelt among us, full of grace and truth" (John 1:14). He was born in the likeness of man, died on the Cross, and was raised from the dead, being exalted into Heaven, and yet immanent in the world in the form of the Holy Spirit for the reconciliation of humanity unto God, as it is believed in the Christian tradition. Mature spirituality is to be in the world, and yet not of the world, although it encompasses the whole person in the totality of human existence in the world, not just a small segment of a person's private sphere. It has something to do with the integration and coherence of ourselves as experiencing and acting persons influenced by historical, cultural, and social circumstances, not merely inner feelings, in relation to God, who is the ultimate source of power and meaning in life. It has something to do with the discovery of a sense of vocation infused with religious passion, a consciousness of the living God in the midst of daily living here on earth, and a sense of purpose and the direction for the future. If human existence were only a maze, a jungle in which only the fittest could survive, devoid of meaning, life would become intolerable. Furthermore, it has something to do with the discovery of meaningful relationships between oneself and the universe in which one moves, a frame of reference by which one grasps intuitively a sense of meaning to life, a calling to serve the purpose of God in the world. What marks mature spirituality is the "synergy" in which, as Thayer has expressed it, "our experience in prayer and our actions in the world reflect and influence each other."[14] It leads to the restructuring of personality and reorganizing of the information so that new solutions to life problems may emerge, for it is believed that the living God is at work both historically and existentially, acting incessantly to renew the integrity of human life in this world.

The experience of God's presence is the most characteristic feature commonly found among a number of cases in the study of religious experience by the late Oxford biologist Alister Hardy.[15] It is the feeling that there is a spiritual reality that appears to be beyond the conscious self with which the individual can have communion in one way or another. The experience often becomes a transforming moment in one's life in a time of personal crisis—in the dead of night. In reflecting on his personal experience, Edward E. Thornton said, "God came uninvited, unexpected, and unwelcomed. The Presence was totally absorbing. A focal problem was illuminated, and in that instant my ambition was transformed from career goals to a desire to be at one with God."[16] It is a moment of praying with the mind in the heart, a way of being with one's true self, with others, and with God. God's presence transcends human understanding and expectation, and its impact is beyond human control.

In my personal interviews, I came across three ministers who recalled their mystical experiences. For the first, it was while visiting a college chapel in California; for another, while driving a car and the euphoria lingered on; for the third, while having counseling with a psychotherapist who happened to be an atheist. Spiritual growth is not a bag of religious tricks one can turn on and off. It is the transformation of the inner being through the Presence of God. "The wind blows where it wills, . . . so it is with every one who is born of the Spirit" (John 3:8). It has a transcendent dimension. Each person experiences spiritual growth differently, but the person who is spiritually mature shares two orders of being simultaneously, the infinite and unconditional in its root and the finite and conditional in its phenomenal expression.

Another dimension of mature spirituality is self-transcendence; that is, to transcend one's own egocentricity, which is a characteristic of early childhood. Egocentricity makes the child think of God anthropomorphically and distorts one's reality perception. Self-transcendence makes one humble without false humility, authentic and affirmative without pride, self-critical without cynicism, and objective in perceiving others. In the process of self-transcendence, the omnipotent fantasy of early childhood is forced to come down to the real world and be reconciled with reality as the child experiences frustration, pain, disappointment, and restrictions. Dialogically, in coming down to the real world, one becomes more self-transcended and transcends from the concrete world in cognitive development capable of handling concrete reality with abstract images, symbols, and languages. Increasingly, one becomes more rationally reflective and even theological, trying to break the small shell of oneself in search of the Common Good and the Ultimate Reality. But this search does not remain on the cognitive and the philosophical level for it too will be transcended in search for the spiritual and the religious, namely, the living God who is the ultimate reference for the whole person as one becomes more self-transcended and yet this worldly.

"The God we seek is always an idol: the God who leads us is our redeemer," said James E. Griffs in his book *A Silent Path to God*.[17] This is another way of describing the paradox of self-transcendence in spiritual maturation. The God we seek is merely our own creation and the God who lead us, though immanent, is transcendent. The path to God calls for repentance, a change of attitude from willfulness to willingness, which is a form of self-transcendence: it requires the willingness to be led by the Word of God. We must give up self-justification and confess our total helplessness in the face of the power of death and be willing to receive God's saving grace. The true meaning of self-denial is not self-destruction, but self-transcendence, whose paradoxical nature is the key to unlock the mystery of Jesus' death symbolized by his parable of a grain of wheat (that "falls into the earth and dies"). The same paradox is in his premise that "he who loves his life loses it, and he who hates his life in this world will keep it for eternal life" (John 12:24–26). Self-denial leads to self-discovery and true selfhood in God.

As we become more self-transcendent and in touch with God through experiencing the Presence of the Spirit and in touch with our past and present reality, we become more in possession of a distinct self-knowledge and a clear sense of purpose in life. The query "Who am I?" merges with the question "Where is God?" at this point. To be spiritually mature is to be able to say as Jesus did in answer to Pontius Pilate who asked him, "So you are a king?" "You say that I am a king. For this I was born, and for this I have come into the world, to bear witness to the truth. Everyone who is of the truth hears my voice" (John 18:17). Self-transcendence is accompanied by self-individuation and self-actualization. The power of prayer enhances self-transcendence. This is the heart of spirituality. It is contrary to the use of spiritual practice, experience, and insight to increase self-importance, which is spiritual narcissism and not a fruit of the Spirit.

Mature spirituality is dynamic, differentiated, and yet integrated; transcendent and yet this worldly; it is paradox-in-unity and unity-in-paradox, in which the paradox is dialogical and the unity dynamic. This is also true for theology.

2. Maturity and Theology

Theology is the work of the church; it is the product of the community of faith. Faith seeks understanding, and theology is the product of this effort. Theology is needed for self-understanding as well as for making one's faith known to the world. It is part and parcel of cognitive development in the life of the believer. The perennial question in spiritual maturation is: how can we best reconcile the theology that we have learned with the theology which we have experienced personally and with which made sense out of life? The discrepancy between the two requires theological reconstruction. This has been going on throughout history, for example, in the Reformation of the sixteenth century, and in Vatican II of the twentieth century.

The need for theological reconstruction is particularly acute in midlife when the theology one has learned in the past becomes inadequate to make sense out of life. The story of Job is a classical example (in which the traditional theology is challenged by undeserved suffering that leads to a deeper understanding of God and of himself). If one finds the "truth" of the first half of life becoming false during the second half of life, theological reconstruction is in order.

St. Thomas Aquinas' life provides another often-quoted example. The great theologian died at the early age of forty-nine in northern Italy on his way to the Council of Lyons. Shortly before he died in the Cistercian Monastery of Fossa Nova, he knelt before the crucified Lord. He later said to his secretary that "he had learned more theology on his knees in those fifteen minutes than from all the theology that he had ever studied and written about in many tomes." A "logion" says that St. Thomas asked his secretary, Brother Reginald, to throw into the fire everything that he had written about God, saying, "All that is valueless and as worthless as straw. It is nothing but mockery."[18] For some reason, he did not live longer to reconstruct his theology and left the unfinished task to others.

Since theology is the product of the community of faith, the process of theological reconstruction involves the paradox-in-unity that exists between the individual and the community in that one wants to be integrated into the community and yet wants to be differentiated as an individual person. This takes place on the intellectual level in theological reflection, and yet it involves the whole person. Furthermore, it involves the emergence of authentic spirituality in the individual and the discovery of one's true identity and meaning of life. The existential quest for authentic spirituality and theology is part of human nature, and it is clear even in the words of an ancient master to his disciple in a different context: "Unless it grows out of yourself, no knowledge is really of value to you: a borrowed plumage never grows."[19] When this dimension is lost, theology becomes an ideology for oppression and political rationalization. Religious freedom and human right ensure the development of this dimension. It is essential to preserve the paradox (in-unity) between individual and community in theological reconstruction. Mature theology preserves this paradox in dynamic dialogical unity.

Spirituality and theology cannot be divorced because intuition and reasoning are integral parts of knowing and experiencing the reality of God. Spirituality is largely affective, intuitive, and experiential, whereas theology is cognitive, intellectual, and imaginative. Both are essential paths by which one reaches out beyond the self in search of Ultimate Reality: spirituality is by way of prayer, whereas theology is by way of intellectual inquiry, as pointed out by John Mcquarrie.[20] The theology that is dynamic, meaningful, and authentic is often shaped by the living knowledge of God in prayer, worship, and daily affairs. Theological reflection requires both "tacit knowledge" and "explicit knowledge" (Polany). If theology is to be mature and have meaning, it will be the result of more than just a claim of logical thinking; it needs to be accompanied by profound spirituality that is rooted in the Christian tradition of the past, the experience of the present, and the vision for the future; it is dynamic and always renews itself; it is holistic, yet particularistic and contextual.

The fact that we have gone through a cycle of what Dr. James I. McCord calls "pop theology" almost every other year after the forceful Neoorthodoxy of Karl Barth indicates that we are in an age of theological uncertainty. This calls for the examination of what mature theology really is in the midst of theological mutation. It is interesting that in his discussion on religious experience in relation to biology, Alister Hardy refers to C. H. Waddington's comparison of social transmission of tradition with the mechanism of heredity. In the mechanism of heredity as well as in social transmission of tradition, erroneous information may be passed on to the individual who at first may accept but later reject it after attempts to verify if what has been taught can be made fit with the facts as one finds them.[21] This shows how natural it is for the individual to verify whether the theology learned since childhood can be made to fit with the facts of life personally experienced later on. This attempt at verification involves theological reflection, reinterpretation, and reintegration, in short, theological reconstruction.

It seems there are three things to be kept in mind in the process: (1) to be faithful to the tradition from the past, (2) to be truthful to the experience of the present, and (3) to formulate a vision for the future.

Notes

1. Harvey G. Cox, Jr., *Religion in the Secular City* (New York: Simon and Schuster, 1984), p. 44.

2. *New York Times,* January 16, 1948.

3. Nelson S. T. Thayer, *Spirituality and Pastoral Care* (Philadelphia: Fortress Press, 1985), p. 102.

4. Quoted by H. D. A. Major, *Basic Christianity* (Oxford: Blackwell, 1945), p.54.

5. Wolfgang Pannenberg's *Anthropology in Theological Perspective* (Philadelphia: The Westminster Press, 1985) is an indication of the trend.

6. John J. Heaney, ed., *Psyche and Spirit* (New York: Paulist Press, 1973), p. 156; Thayer, *Spirituality and Pastoral Care,* p. 54.

7. Gerald May, *Will and Spirit: A Contemplative Psychology* (New York: Harper & Row, 1982), p. 34.

8. Alfred North Whitehead, *Religion in the Making* (New York: Macmillan Co., 1927), pp. 16–17.

9. Heaney, ed., *Psyche and Spirit,* p. 19.

10. Arnold R. Beisser, "Identity Formation with Groups," *The Journal of Humanistic Psychology* 9(2), 1971, pp.133–146.

11. D. Bonhoeffer, *Life Together* (New York: Harper & Row, 1954), p. 77.

12. For Bernard's contribution to mystical theology, see Etienne Gilson, *Theologie mystique de saint Bernard* (Paris, 1934), translated by A. H. C. Downes as *The Mystical Theology of Saint Bernard* (London, 1940).

13. *The American Heritage Dictionary of the English Language* (Boston: Houghton Mifflin Co., 1969). S.V. "religion."

14. Thayer, *Spirituality and Pastoral Care,* p. 54.

15. Alister Hardy, *The Spiritual Nature of Man* (Oxford: Claredon Press, 1979), p. 132; idem, *The Biology of God: A Scientist's Study of Man the Religious Animal* (London: Jonathan Cape, Ltd., 1975), p. 67.

16. Edward E. Thornton, *Being Transformed: An Inner Way of Spiritual Growth* (Philadelphia: The Westminster Press, 1984).

17. James E. Griffs, *A Silent Path to God* (Philadelphia: Fortress Press, 1980).

18. James E. Loder, *The Transforming Moment* (New York: Harper & Row, 1981), pp. 185–186; Morton Kelsey, *Encountering with God* (Minneapolis: Bethany Fellowship, Inc., 1972).

19. D. T. Suzuki, *Zen Buddhism* (New York: Doubleday Co., 1956), p. 97.

20. John Mcquarrie, *Path in Spirituality* (New York: Harper & Row, 1972).

21. Hardy, *The Biology of God,* p. 67.

IV. Maturity, Spirituality, and the Bible: Job's Search for Integrity

Harrell F. Beck

The general lecture heading, "Maturity, Spirituality, and the Bible," could be used as opportunity for a random compendium of observations about biblical characters, episodes, and qualities. It is difficult to speculate whether such a lecture would be more abusive of ancient materials or contemporary listeners.

Rather, I invite your consideration of several parts of the poem of Job, his lament, the arguments with the three friends, the speeches of God from the whirlwind, and especially Job's solemn oath of self-vindication (Job 31), a mature and noble statement of ethical ideals unexcelled in the Old Testament, the literature of the ancient Near East, or in the New Testament, not excluding the Sermon on the Mount.

The ancient folktale of Job forms the prologue and epilogue of the poem. It may not even have been Israelite in origin. The historic impetus for the appropriation of the ancient folktale as for the writing of the poem was the Babylonian exile. Surely the tragic debasing of the faith of an uncommonly wealthy and faithful person is hardly occasion for a major biblical book. Job is Israel in exile, covenanted Israel for whom the Lord has had such distinctive expectations. It is Israel who has lost its sons and daughters, its property, health, and reputation among the peoples. It is Israel who mourns in sackcloth and ashes; Israel languishes in exile.

Clearly the Job of the ancient folktale subscribes to the Deuteronomic doctrine of divine earthly retribution (you get what you deserve, and you deserve what you get), a formulaic understanding of the ways of God with humans that is expounded by the three friends in the poem of Job. Human sinfulness evokes divine punishment in the form of human suffering; for the Job of the folktale, as for the three friends, a glib corollary follows: human suffering may be taken as evidence that the ones who suffer have sinned. It is a simplistic view that had been applied with some tacit popular acceptance to corporate Israel for centuries, but it raised harsh questions, probably in every century, but especially when applied to individual Israelites in Diaspora.

We may note in passing that the Satan passages in the prologue are probably a late insertion, that Satan is more the advocate than the adversary of God, and that neither these passages nor Satan is ever mentioned again by Job, the three friends nor in the prose epilogue.

The response of the Job of the folktale to his plight is familiar: "The Lord has given; the Lord has taken away; blessed be the name of the Lord." Despite further testing, the Job of the folktale did not sin or charge God with wrong; he did not sin with his lips. As a consequence, Job was handsomely rewarded for patient faithfulness. Whatever virtue may be seen in such acquiescence, it is not a theologically promising response.

If the author of the poem of Job (chs. 3f.) had acquiesced to the dictum of the Job of the folktale, we should have been deprived of one of the classics of world literature, a poem that has probably influenced thoughtful persons, especially in the secular world, as much as any book of Hebrew scriptures. The author of the poem reflects considerable maturity in accepting the task of a human being to become a responsible self in community.

The unknown poet cuts the folktale in two and inserts a panel discussion among Job and three friends who come to console and correct him (3–31; 38:1–42:6). We must commend them for coming. In deference to Job's terrible suffering, they sat with him in silence for seven days and seven nights (which may have been their signal contribution). There follow three rounds of discussion; the subject is the causes and purposes of Job's suffering and loss, an attempt to understand any meaning in such events, and especially to understand the ways of God with men and women.

Job leads off with a lamenting protest (3:1f.). He curses the day of his birth (but never curses God). At the very beginning, we sense the poet's belief that strong, honest faith encourages questioning and does not disallow protest.

Why is light given to a person whose way is hidden? whom God has hedged in? (3:23). The explanations of the three friends (who might as well have been one) are essentially restatements of the doctrine of divine earthly retribution, half-truths that are more theologically orthodox than imaginatively pastoral and redemptive. "You have sinned." "Your children died because they sinned against God." "Through suffering God tests and instructs." "We are born to trouble as sparks fly upward." The three friends discourage honest inquiry, rehearse the tradition that sin leads to evil and suffering, and belabor the point that Job's suffering is patent evidence that he has sinned, that he is guilty before God. Indeed, the sin of the three friends is an eagerness to reduce the ways of God to a formula. They will simply not confront the possibility that the cause and purpose of the suffering of an individual may be indeterminable.

Job's sin during the course of the argument is that he comes dangerously close to letting his insistence on a knowledge of good and evil become more important than his knowledge of God. His self-imprecating oath of innocence (ch. 31) comes at the end of his final defense against charges that Job deserved the sufferings that overtook him and that the justice of God is above questioning. After recalling a happy past (ch. 29) and reviewing his recent sorrow and humiliation (ch. 30), Job vigorously affirms that his faith in God has removed all lust from his heart, and he calls down a curse on himself if he has been guilty of deceit, adultery, casualness toward human suffering and need, if he has been guilty of secret idolatry or of rejoicing over the ruin of others. He rests his case with a plea that the charges against him be written on a bill of indictment to which response directly before God would be possible. In response to Job's oath of self-imprecation, the climatic theophany takes place. God comes to Job out of the whirlwind.

The Job of this poem is a reflection of the maturity of an unknown poet, a remarkably religious poet, whom we shall, for want of a historic name, call Job. The maturity of the poet is evident in his contribution as theologian, ethicist, pastor, and artist. I invite your consideration of each of these aspects of his maturity.

1. The Poet as Theologian

By any informed criterion, 586 B.C. and the fall of Jerusalem to Babylon was a significant period in the literary history of Israel. On the battlefield Marduk and the Babylonian pantheon had eclipsed the God of Israel. The inviolable Jerusalem temple had been desecrated and razed. The Ark of the Covenant disappeared, never to be recovered. The holy priesthood was scattered; holy rites could not be celebrated; leaders were carried into exile. More than one believer, perhaps in Jerusalem as well as Babylon, must have asked grievously, "How shall we sing the songs of the Lord in a foreign land?" (Ps. 137). That is, of course, the place where such songs are most desperately needed.

It is difficult to imagine what the fall of Jerusalem and the exile did to the self-esteem of a faithful Judean. In this same historic context, Jeremiah hailed exile as a just punishment from which repentance, regeneration, and a new covenant written upon the human heart could result. Ezekiel envisioned a restored and faithful Israel whose Temple and ceremonies would be at least as magnificent as the Temple of Solomon had been. Priestly writers worked at the codification of Torah, perhaps envisioning Judaism as the religion of a book, a guide for the faithful and the perplexed, whether in Jerusalem or in Diaspora. Nearer the end of the exilic period, when Cyrus issued the edict freeing Jews to return to Jerusalem, the unknown author of Isaiah, chapters 40–55,

55

concluded that the exiles had suffered double for their sins, that Jerusalem would be restored, and the returned exiles would find salvation by becoming a light to the nations, by bringing forth and establishing justice across the earth. God has blotted out the sins of Israel for his own sake and will remember those sins no more. New things are being declared.

Also in this same historic context, the ancient Wisdom genre took on striking new vitality. New occasions teach new possibilities. A variety of subjects is addressed in the canonical wisdom documents, some mundane, some disturbing, all of them prompted by a concern for understanding the recent history of the covenant people in relationship with a God of *hesedh, mishpat, tsedhaka* (steadfast love, justice, and righteousness).

For the sage who wrote Genesis 1:1–2:4a (a commentary perhaps on the older creation story), it is an affirmation that the God who created long ago will now recreate meaningful life for the people. The anthology we know as Proverbs is primarily a collection of counsels for middle-class success in vocation, social relationships, and traditional religious practices. For Ecclesiastes, it is an anxious question as to whether life, taken altogether, has any real purpose or meaning, especially in the face of a sometimes shrill orthodoxy. The author of the Song of Songs provides a brief and memorable collection of erotic poems, encouraging persons hardened by historic tragedy to remain open to enriching, nurturing, life-giving relationships with God and humans alike.

But the majestic poem of Job has even greater pastoral and theological promise. In the face of suffering, death, and exile, Job poses the searching questions, What are the ways of God with human beings? Why do the beautiful weep? Why do the innocent suffer? Is the God with whom Israel is covenanted really just? The author of the poem of Job began to live out that insightful dictum: the questions of God may ultimately be more satisfying than the answers of men and women. In asking such questions, the poet calls into sharp question the Deuteronomic doctrine of divine earthly retribution. History and biography did not seem to conform to the theological drama. The poet's faith in God and his concern for the people were strong and fluid enough that he dared call out the grand theological word: *aggiornamento.* I submit the poet we call Job would have applauded the notion that theology is not simply a repetition of traditional teachings. It is a creative activity in which thoughtful persons, often poets, encourage creative responses to new human experiences.

In his search for a more adequate orientation for human life Job combines the honest question, an unforgettable expression of his own emotions (we shall say more of Job's lamentation shortly), and an asseveration of his own moral standards, the last as evidence that he has

56

at least tried to live an appropriate, Torah- and prophet-informed response to the divine human relationship.

Job admits the universality of sinfulness and believes in the almighty power of God. He denies that human conduct is justly rewarded or punished on this earth by a just and merciful God. Job does not contend that he is sinless, but he has certain virtues. And the punishment he has received simply does not seem to fit the crime. God has been unjust and heartless. Since God is responsible for all that exists, God is responsible for evil. Unless evil can be shown to have rational purpose or explanation, God cannot be regarded as just or benevolent. True, human suffering is often the direct result of human actions. But not always. Even in the argument Job is at odds with himself. Profoundly believing in one God, Job cannot simply attribute evil to lesser deities or demonic spirits.

The vastness of God's power, God's wisdom, God's transcendent holiness, is universal and incomprehensible. For Job such a God is not bound by even the highest standards of human justice and mercy. "As for power, he is strong; but as for justice, who will summon him?" Beset by the problem of evil, the poet could only have cleared God of responsibility for evil by admitting that God was good but not sufficiently powerful to eliminate evil. Such a notion seemed absurd. Job realized that in view of God's inscrutable transcendence and of limited human understanding a solution of the problem of theodicy was impossible. He acknowledged that the only solution acceptable to him—God is almighty but not just—could not be final. In a world that manifests God's power and wisdom perhaps Job's own miseries have some incomprehensible purpose. They can hardly mar the character of the Creator.

Beset with pain and perplexity in which he saw no purpose, Job seems to have responded in ways that elicited a divine response, ways that proved theologically creative. God appeared out of the whirlwind and encouraged Job to stand up to his humanity: "Gird up your loins like a man; I will question, and you declare to me" (40:7). Out of the encounter Job comes to a new level of relationship with the Divine: "I had heard of thee by the hearing of the ear, but now my eye sees thee" (42:5). The theophany recalls Job to a promising humility: "I know that thou canst do all things, and that no purpose of thine can be thwarted. . . . I have uttered what I did not understand, things too wonderful for me, which I did not know" (42:2, 3bc). This newly affirmed relationship does not terminate but rather encourages continuing inquiry and response. Even now Job dares to put to God in hope the very words God had put to Job in warning: "Hear, and I will speak; I will question you, and you declare to me" (42:4).

Thus the poet reminds us that faith and affirmative agnosticism, affirmative skepticism, are not inimical but corollaries for the mature believer. In a final confession, Job celebrates the concern of God, repents any arrogant spirit in the earlier questions, and, by implication, affirms a promising and continuing relationship: "I humble myself and repent in dust and ashes" (42:6). Perhaps Maimonides caught this promise by translating: "I recant and change my mind concerning dust and ashes."

The poet's conclusion is a statement of promising submission, not of dull, uncreative resignation. One senses the possibility of a new response: "The Lord has given; the Lord receives; blessed be the name of the Lord." The ending implies a new beginning, a newness in Job's relationship with God. I for one am thankful for the theological impatience of Job.

2. The Poet as Ethicist

Secondly, I believe the statement of ethical ideals of Job, especially as summarized in his oath of self-clearance, reflects a remarkable ethical maturity (Job 31). In this declaration, Job discerns the spirit and thought that lie behind the act and goes beneath conduct to the motives of the heart. A refined social thoughtfulness and generosity, itself a landmark in the history of ethics, is based on Job's central conviction that all men and women—master, maidservant, manservant, and neighbor—are the work and concern of God, the only Creator. (I remind you this belief was held in the sixth century B.C.!) Thus, the Job of this ancient poem emerges as a noble human, loyal to the covenants he has made, a considerate master, a benevolent civic leader, a devout monotheist. Many a scholar has observed that the picture of Job is extraordinarily like that of the citizen of God's kingdom as etched by Jesus in the Sermon on the Mount.

Some interpreters have charged that Job, in reciting his virtues, has lost his sense of creatureliness, that he is arrogant in pleading for an indictment or a writ of acquittal—"As a prince I shall approach God!" (31:37). It is argued that the religious claims based in Job's statement of morality threaten his religion just as earlier Job's questions about the knowledge of good and evil threatened his knowledge of God. Possibly that is true; at this point Job has certainly not been freed from the notion of divine retribution simply because he has raised serious questions about it. Nor have the orthodox arguments of his three friends convinced him of the validity of such a view.

Yet Job's earnest plea does not reflect so much a *hubris* about his own righteousness—the perennial threat of religious moralism—as agonizing perplexity about the way of God with humans and the possibility of harmony with God. Whatever these objections there is faith at the center of Job's perplexity; Job trusts God enough to plead for and risk a hearing with God.

58

May we not also infer that this amazing summary of the ethics of the Bible, a dramatic portrayal of the requirements for the good life as taught in the Torah and by the prophets of Israel, had been attempted by at least a remnant in Israel. In light of that possibility, how is God to account for their suffering at the hands of idolatrous nations that have defied such moral standards?

Perhaps Job has overshot the mark so that the celebration of integrity becomes a barrier between himself and God. But the hapless, daring Job is not abandoned, and God does respond. Job is chided for uttering "words without knowledge," but he is offered a new relationship that is tantamount to acquittal of charges brought against Job by the three friends or by modern commentators.

In this new relationship Job is asked by God to pray for the three friends whose words God does not regard as right (42:7f.). Job's obedient response suggests that there, as earlier, his righteousness rested on more than self-interest.

3. The Poet as Pastor

Thirdly, it would be quite inadequate to treat the poem of Job simply as a theological excursus on the problem of theodicy or as a memorable summary of biblical ethics, striking as those contributions are. If the Job of the poem is indeed a personification of exilic Israel, then the poem, as with much of the Wisdom genre, is profoundly pastoral. In some ways, the author's pastoral insight and creativity are epitomized in the simple fact that the dialogue among Job and the three friends begins with a woeful lament, a grievous cry, a description and expression of pain (3:1f.). In the lament, Job curses the day of his birth and declares that he would rather not have lived—ever. It is true that Job stops short of cursing God; but his bewilderment about the agony of the existence God has given is unbridled.

Here is a contribution that form criticism helps us appreciate. Lament is to be distinguished from the confession of the penitent. Repentance involves acceptance of responsibility for sin and ways in which it has alienated the sinner from God and other humans. Lamentation is a bemoaning of adverse circumstances for which taking responsibility would spell arrogance. Lament is a common biblical response to suffering for which neither cause nor purpose is discerned. More than a third of the Psalms in the Hebrew Psalter are laments. With rare exceptions those Psalms move from cleansing lament to renewed and vigorous affirmations of faith and sometimes to a newly discovered theological meaning or vocation. Such elements of lamentation are often discernible in the great psalms of praise.

This progression from lament to affirmation is suggested in Psalm 22:1–2, which begins:

> My God, my God, why hast thou forsaken me?
> Why art thou so far from helping me, from the words
>   of my groaning?
> O my God, I cry by day, but thou dost not answer;
>   and by night, but find no rest.

Characteristically such psalms of lament move suddenly to a memorable new affirmation. Again from Psalm 22:25f.:

> I will tell of thy name to my brethren; in the midst of
>   the congregations I will praise thee;
> You who fear the Lord, praise him;
>   . . . .
> For he has not despised or abhorred the affliction of
>   the afflicted;
> and he has not hid his face from him,
> but has heard, when he cried to him.

It is this bond between lament and affirmation in the Psalms of lament that led Frederick C. Grant to warn us that when someone like Jesus cried out the first line of Psalm 22 at the crucifixion he was really citing the entire psalm.

The lament of Job with which the poem begins (and strands of which can be found throughout the dialogue with the friends) is to be seen as a cleansing essential to the resolution that comes near the end of the poem. The pastoral wisdom of the poet as seen in the lament is important in at least two respects.

1. The faith of Job is sufficiently strong that he dares register serious complaint. In that complaint his initial questions are rhetorical: "Why did I not die at birth, come forth from the womb and expire? Why did the knees receive me? . . . . why was I not as a hidden untimely birth, as infants that never see the light?" (ch. 3). But they lead to a third question (3:20) that expresses Job's fundamental inquiry concerning God's way with men and women:

> Why is light given to him that is in misery, and life
>   to the bitter in soul,
> who long for death, but it comes not . . . .
>
> Why is light given to a man whose way is hid,
>   whom God has hedged in?

(I hardly need dwell here on the tragic fact that many believers see lament as an act of religious disloyalty.)

2.   Without owning one's anguish and anger, the process of discovery and healing has little opportunity of success. In Job we see, as often in biblical history, that great discoverers and affirmers have been the great questioners. The expectation of discovery and healing carries with it the need to put the honest question.

The poet of Job would have appreciated the ancient *midrash*: "I met a man who knew all the answers and didn't ask any questions. I wondered whether he was religious."

4. The Poet as Artist

The poet who was theologian, ethicist, and counselor was also a great literary artist. Significant literature is an expression of engrossing thoughts in memorable diction, significant content matched by beauty of style. Tennyson called Job "the greatest poem of ancient or modern times." One of my teachers, Robert H. Pfeiffer, whose profound literary interest in the Old Testament may still be his most distinctive scholarly contribution, ranked Job with the Greek tragedies, Lucretius' *On Nature,* Dante's *Divine Comedy,* Milton's *Paradise Lost,* and Goethe's *Faust.* This debate in Job contains numerous poetic pieces that bear reading as independent compositions—descriptions of the attributes and works of the deity, hymns in praise of divine wisdom, the incomparable speeches of God out of the whirlwind. The poet not only raises the question of theodicy but puts it in a form that encourages further discussion.

In this memorable poem, poetic skill and remarkable learning, centering on a question of universal concern, are delineated through the greatest vocabulary of any Hebrew writer. Our poet thought profoundly and with originality on ultimate problems of religion and theology. His concerns and his conclusions are put in storylike biographical form with an intensity of moods and emotions that account for the continuing influence of the book.

As a person of faith, the artist who wrote the poem believed in a deity before whom the expression of any human emotion was in order. The poet took seriously the immediate actuality of his words, whether of affirmation or question. As a consequence, the poet's admiration for the magnificence of the natural world and his disappointment with the human situation are memorable (chs. 38f).

The poet dared call a popular dogma into question, to raise questions for which there were no easy answers. Through the centuries, thoughtful persons have read this poem gladly, sensing in it the work of a provocative artist who cared enough about human survival to press significant questions. One would like to have read the committee notes from Jamnia when the Book of Job was proposed for canonization. In questioning the Deuteronomistic philosophy of history and of retribution, the poem flies in the face of cherished biblical doctrine. But the poem was canonized, and we are richer because of it.

With students across the generations, we are indebted to the mature author of the poem of Job, who was an adherent to the view that biblical faith is not primarily propositional but fundamentally relational. When history and biography provide new data for faith, many persons are tempted to repeat traditional theological cliches with increasing zeal, even vehemence. Fear of change and a strange lust for certitude reduce faith to a set of propositions. The author of the poem of Job reminds us that change is inevitable, but growth is an option.

When history and biography provide new data, some persons, usually a minority, moved by a sense of caring and of justice, feel impelled to seek more adequate theological orientation for human life. Such seeking is a creative and mature activity of human thought and imagination. As Kazantzakis might have put it, such persons are "saviours of God." They remind us that the story of a civilization may be told in terms of its images of the future. For Job the poet an appropriate image of the future is a continuing substantive relationship with the Creator to whom honest questions may be addressed and before whom affirmative skepticism is a corollary of faith.

In Willa Cather's somewhat great novel, *Death Comes to the Archbishop,* the leading character is a French aristocrat become missionary bishop of Santa Fe. He was indeed a historical figure, and the more Cather wrote of him the greater her admiration for him. In the novel she says of the archbishop that he was at one and the same time a connoisseur and a pioneer. A connoisseur, one who understands the principles of an art and is competent to act as a critical judge, one who enjoys with discrimination and appreciation. A pioneer, a person who helps open up a new line of thought or activity, a new way of thinking, a new possibility. Taken together the two terms suggest the kind of maturity that is appropriate to spiritual and theological growth and leadership. The maturity and competency of the author of the poem of Job are evident in the fact that he did not shrink from the promising and awful demand of a continuing dialogue with the divine. In that dialogue the poet proved profoundly religious as that quality is defined by Ralph Halverson, a contemporary poet and divine:

> To be religious is to be proud without being arrogant;
> It is to be humble without being subservient;
> It is to believe without being superstitious;
> And it is to be committed while remaining open.[1]

Notes

1. Used by permission of the author.

V. Maturity in Ministry in Biblical Perspective

Krister Stendahl

It is always difficult to deal with a topic such as this when one approaches it head-on, although it seems obvious that a mature minister is better than an immature minister and that maturity is a good thing. How do we approach this topic?

Being a biblical scholar, I habitually go first to the concordance for a clue, and I am often struck by the fact that one cannot find everything in it and that the words that are absolutely indispensable and natural for us today did not exist in the ancient languages or ways of thinking. The word "maturity" is a case in point. The closest equivalent is the Greek word *teleios*.

1. *Teleios:* Mature or Perfect?

In the third chapter of the Letter of Paul to the Philippians, the same Greek word *teleios* is sometimes translated as "mature" and at other times as "perfect." This is significant because it shows how the translator is a participant in the development of the meaning of *teleios* and that it is natural for the translator to do so. It says, "Not that I have already obtained this or am already *perfect;* but I press on to make it my own, . . ." (Phil. 3:12). Then a little further down in verse fifteen, it says, "Those of us who are *mature* be thus minded; and if anything . . . ." Here the word "mature" is used in its translation. Perhaps the translator thinks that good Christians do not say that they are already perfect when it has already been said that they are not perfect. Thus, the word "mature" is chosen so as to soften the contradiction and to make them feel humble. And yet, it is true that the word *teleios* does not really mean "mature."

Since the word "mature" has process-oriented connotation and is very much a biological word, there is not much difference between "ripe" and "mature" in meaning, although "ripe" is Anglo-Saxon and "mature" Latin in origin. What makes the difference is that the more developmental view of personality, which is one of the strong features

65

of contemporary psychological thinkers, has been introduced in this translation. I am not saying, however, that, hence, on biblical ground, we should not speak about maturity.

If you press the biological imagery of maturity, the question of decay comes in. Everything in the realm of nature starts to decay when it is mature. For example, when you have a peach just ripe in your hand, it is hardly possible to keep it even for another day. For those who have been involved in developmental studies, the question is: is it Pollyanna optimism that prevents one from thinking about the fact that when one reaches maturity, decay comes in? In saying this, I am asking myself, "Am I playing the word, or am I saying something profound?" I am not so sure about it myself. But I find it an interesting reflection.

Furthermore, when we speak about fruits being overripe, the meaning is clear. But when we speak of people being "over mature," what do we mean? Does it mean a certain kind of sophistication that becomes self-defeating? Or is there a way in which we have seen too much and learned too much? Or does being wise make it different for us to really get to the energy and express our valid anger? This is something I have not thought about.

Sanctification is a classical term for growing in maturity. The Calvinists and the Methodists are very much interested in it, but for the Lutherans, to be mature is not to worry about your maturity, because if you worry too much about your maturity, you become too self-centered and that is certainly not very mature. As Luther said, the only thing we can do is to return every morning to our baptism as the newly born.

2. Decisiveness, Risk Taking, and Wisdom

In the Old Testament in general, there are a couple of images for the mature person. When I think of Abraham, Isaac, and Jacob, or when I think of Moses and the early prophets Elijah and Elisha, I think of them as *decisive* and *risk-taking* people. However, they are not pictured as John Waynes. In fact, they are often described as persons who wonder about what God might be doing and how they are put in a great quandary and downcast. So often when you put too great a value on decisiveness, you get a frozen personality. But these people are not. They are decisive people who suddenly speak of their fears, and in that sense, they are people honest to themselves, even though these are folk stories.

Then, there is another side of maturity that is not totally different. And that is the whole dimension of wisdom and the wisdom literature. If one reads Ecclesiasticus, an Apocrypha, which is called "Wisdom of Jesus, the Son of Sirach," one finds that it retells the stories of the greats in the old Testament and how they are not only decisive and risk taking but also *wise*. This "wise," this wisdom, is very much a kind of common sense wisdom, which comes from observation and life experience. Wisdom is another term for maturity.

In the Gospel of John and the First Letter of John, there is very little interest in wisdom because there everything is centered around the acceptance of Jesus as Messiah. That is wisdom! In the Pauline Letters, wisdom is identified with Christ through whom redemption comes into the world as against the worldly wisdom of the philosophers. "Christ the power of God and the wisdom of God" (I Cor. 1:23). The wisdom that is imperfectly manifested in the Old Testament is now perfectly manifested in Jesus Christ who embodies the wisdom of God.

However, if somebody is called perfect (*teleios*), it certainly includes a great deal of wisdom. I do not think that you can be *teleios* in the biblical sense by just being morally upright. That is not enough! It must include faith in Jesus Christ.

3. Maturity in Biblical Preaching

As a biblical scholar, I am interested in linking biblical exegesis with preaching and the arts of ministry. It seems to me that maturity in preaching depends in part on the grasp of specificities. If the text is chosen from one of the Pauline Letters, the basic question is: how can the Letter, which is written to a particular church or churches with specific problems, speak to us? The important thing is to grasp the specificities of the *then,* the text, and the specificities of the *now,* us. However, in this effort, the preacher needs to preserve the historical objectivity of the text and should not try to *make* the text relevant but dig deeply into the text to *discover* its relevance. (This requires that the preacher be self-transcendent enough to be objective and humble enough to let the text speak for itself without perceptual distortion and transcendent enough to be in touch with the power of God and the wisdom of God.) The mature preaching is what I call "Incarnational Preaching."[1]

History repeats itself but never completely. As Luther once said about a passage, "It is God's Word all right, but not for me." The Bible is for the whole church through time and place. But who says that everything in it is "for me"? Specificity is important in preaching. It is said that once you have homogenized the milk, you can never make whipped cream out of it. Likewise, in biblical preaching, once you have homogenized texts by ignoring the specificities, you can never preach a powerful sermon. On the other hand, the good preacher does not make the pulpit a place for biblical exegesis. One needs to be aware that the hungry souls would cry out, "Don't read the cookbook, serve the food!" Preaching without specificities has no teeth in it. No doubt you will read more about maturity in preaching later. So, I move on to other things.

4. Maturity, Humility, and Love

Now I like to talk a little about Paul's maturity in ministry. His profound grasp of the Gospel, his deep understanding of human nature, and his skillful dealing with the specific problems of individual churches are good examples; but, above all, his honest dealing with himself is the most illuminating sign of his maturity. In his Letter to the Romans (Rom. 7), we find his profound understanding of the inner struggle of the divided self and its restoration of wholeness through Jesus Christ. His deep analysis of human nature makes us see more clearly how on occasions even the moral commandments can be misused as deadly weapons of oppression in the hands of the moral people, how the real evil in the world is often done by those who claim to do good, and how our true self yearns to be on God's side even though we fall into the temptation to do evil many a time.

Furthermore, his humble and agonizing dealing with his own weakness is also an obvious sign of maturity. It has something to do with his ill health, "a thorn in the flesh" (II Cor. 12:1–10). After all, he was the apostle to the Gentiles and wanted to be fully fit for the task as an itinerant preacher; one could expect God to keep him healthy and well. Three times he had gone on retreat praying to God to do just that. But God did not. So, he had come to learn that God could use him better when the power of Christ was shining through his weakness. This sick apostle was certainly not a good witness for the healing power of the Gospel as he might be ridiculed by his enemies, but he could use the argument about his sickness against such people. This painful experience is the root of his understanding of the meaning of weakness. We do not know exactly why his physical problem was. Epilepsy is a good guess.

There is so much teaching about love in Paul's First Letter to the Corinthians (I Cor. 13) by which he dealt with tensions among various factions within the congregation. On the whole, it is his most ironic and "ecumenical" letter. The reason he spoke so much about love was that he needed love because the people at Corinth were running him out of town. He was not high up on the totem pole. So he came up with the idea that love is the capacity of accepting and handling tensions. The Letter is about the conflicts within the congregation, and he tried hard to find ways by which the tensions among various teachers and life-styles could coexist. For him, the church is a garden and a body, not a battle ground (I Cor. 3). Love is not a way of overcoming tensions; love is the capacity of dealing with tensions, and love is a sign of maturity.

In dealing with adversaries, Paul was humble enough to await God's final judgment as to what is the good teaching. Perhaps he was opting for pluralism to settle the matters. In his advice he was anxious not to claim more authority than he had. Here we see a Paul of strong conviction; he was sure that he was right, nevertheless willing to accept the pluralism of the Corinthian Church. Without love, pluralism cannot exist safely. "Knowledge puffs up, but love builds up" (I Cor. 8:1). The acceptance of pluralism is a sign of humility and love.

One of the issues in the Corinthian Church is that of charismata—gifts of healing, glossalia, secret knowledge, which were thought of and sought as signs of spirituality. Paul claimed to be more in glossaria than anyone, but he was against it. His overarching criterion is what builds up the church, and he showed the superior way—love, a style of action along with, and above, faith and hope. Without love, even the greatest gifts of the Spirit cause divisiveness. For him love is not measured by the degree of warmth; rather, it is measured by how much tension one can take. In my opinion. Nygren's view of love is questionable; so also is the contemporary notion of romanticized love.[2] Love makes diversity, even conflict, possible without rupturing the church. Love is part of Paul's theology of weakness. We understand love when we need it, not when we give it out of our sense of superiority and affluence.

Jesus' death on the cross is believed to be the supreme expression of God's love which surpasses human understanding. But in ministry we may encounter unbelievers who insist that Jesus was crucified because of his immature idealism of youth such as today's radicals who are eager to die for their causes, almost committing suicide. Likewise, there are radical ministers who get into trouble with authorities in the society or the church because of their immature idealism and eagerness to become martyrs. Such things can happen as we all know; and it could be argued that that is not a mature attitude. There is one point about which we have to be very careful, however, because true maturity may lie in the fact that one does understand the argument why this would not be mature, but one estimates that "for this or that reason I would act against the rational reasoning on this one" and that can be done in a very mature way. I do not think that all martyrs have been death seekers. Otherwise we trivialize maturity. As we know, in the Jewish tradition the first duty is to stay alive, and the Jews are very strong on this point. Maturity does not advocate the Jonestown syndrome at all. In looking into the historical materials, I do not believe that Jesus was a way-out radical; and I do not think that Jesus sought martyrdom.

5. Maturity, Ministry, and Issues

Finally, I want to deal briefly with some of the issues related to maturity in ministry. If you are interested in the developmental approach to the study of the Bible, there is an article by C. H. Dodd in his collection of essays, *New Testament Studies*.[3] It suggests that one can formulate a chronological order of the maturation of Paul's thoughts. Now these are shaky things because Paul speaks about many things in his Epistles. There seems to be a crude developmental scheme as one looks at Israel's religion as primitive, and then in time a little more mature, and finally the mature fruit, Jesus Christ, in the New Testament. But scholars in general are doubtful about such things because one usually achieves these patterns by very selective references. The other day I read something psychologically very moving that I had never thought about. In Exodus, it says that God reveals to Moses and Moses goes to his people with God's revelation, but they do not listen to him "because of their broken spirit and their cruel bondage" (Exod. 6:2–9). This is very moving. The Israelites were hungry for such words, but their spirits were so broken that they had no mental energy to hope and listen. Such an understanding of human nature is very mature. Most of the folk stories run like this: people are depressed, the liberator comes, and the people embrace the message of liberation joyfully. But this is not the case with the Israelites. We have this profound psychological observation early in the biblical materials. There are developments of thought in the Bible, but I would not put too much emphasis on the developmental scheme. Rather, I would put emphasis on the importance of understanding the oppressed people whose spirits are so broken and whose bondage so cruel that they cannot even listen to the message of the Gospel in our ministering to them.

The minister has many temptations, and one has to be careful. There is the danger of hiding behind God's authority and God's will; there is the danger of doing so much of our ministry just by talking, even in the official way of preaching on Sunday in the church where the people cannot speak against us. I often sound more prophetic on Sunday than other days and feel embarrassed when somebody comes and says something such as, "Would you like to come with me to the board meeting of my corporation?" This reminds me of the story about a preacher who poured into the congregation prophetically from the pulpit one Sunday. When the people shook hands with him afterward, an old lady said to him, "It must be nice to get it off your chest!" There is a great deal of opportunity for the minister to grow into maturity in seeing oneself from the perspective of being human. A large part of maturity is the capacity of seeing oneself accurately.

The minister is a person of God. No one can make himself or herself a minister. It is the community of faith that calls the minister, and the minister's role is a representative role. For some people, this can be hard and humiliating. When they come out of the seminary, they want to be their own persons. To be treated like somebody who performs the representative role is not easy for the ego. To be mature is to accept this role.

Notes

1. Krister Stendahl, "Biblical Preaching from the Pauline Epistles," in James W. Cox, ed., *Biblical Preaching* (Philadelphia: Westminster Press, 1983), pp. 306–325.

2. Anders Nygren, *Agape and Eros* (London: S.P.C.K., 1953).

3. C. H. Dodd, *New Testament Studies* (Manchester, England: Manchester University Press, 1953).

VI. Maturity, Spirituality, and Theology: A Historical Perspective

Richard F. Lovelace

1. The Interrelationship of These Elements

Season of mists and mellow fruitfulness,
    Close bosom-friend of the maturing sun;
Conspiring with him how to load and bless
    With fruit the vines that round the thatch-eves run;
To bend with apples the moss'd cottage-trees,
    And fill all fruit with ripeness to the core. . . .
            — John Keats, "To Autumn"

Keats offers us a romantic symbol of maturity which is idyllic. Our own era is more likely to prefer the ironic echoes of Wallace Stevens:

This luscious and impeccable fruit of life
Falls, it appears, of its own weight to earth. . . .

It comes, it blooms, it bears its fruit and dies. . . .
Our bloom is gone. We are the fruit thereof.
Two golden gourds distended on our vines
Into the autumn weather, splashed with frost,
Distorted by hale fatness, turned grotesque,
We hang like warty squashes, streaked and rayed,
The laughing sky will see the two of us
Washed into rinds by rotting winter rains
            — Wallace Stevens, "Le Monocle de Mon Oncle"[1]

This is how religiously uncommitted psychologists must view human maturity. They have no grounds to believe in any maturity which is more meaningful, balanced, beautiful or enduring than this brief period of ripeness on its way to dissolution.

73

That is one reason why this conference is an encouraging sign. There is a clear recognition here that "life. . . . in all its fullness" (John 10:10 NEB) is available only through Jesus Christ.

True Christianity, to extend the implications of Johann Arndt's title, is inevitably the source of true humanity. Christians long ago learned to say with Irenaeus that "the glory of God is man fully alive." But it is exciting to see a group of scholars attempting to bring human maturity into close connection with so many aspects of Christian faith and life.

Pastors, if they are fulfilling their calling, are used to doing this. They may not always recognize that as they are "admonishing and teaching everyone with all wisdom" (Col. 1:28a NIV), they are really working to "present everyone mature (*teleios*) in Christ" (Col. 1:28b NIV amended, cf. RSV, NEB). In the letter which focuses on the maturing of all things under the headship of Christ, Paul commends Epaphras for "always wrestling in prayer. . . ." so that the Colossians "may stand firm in all the will of God, mature (*teleios*) and fully assured" (Col. 4:12 NIV). The fact that we do not see many congregations or even individual parishioners measuring up to this picture does not mean that pastors are failing to aim for spiritual and theological maturity, as ultimate goals of their service to the rest of Christ's body.

My question is rather how much academicians are helping equip them to do this. Much of what is taught in our seminaries aims only to move students and their future parishioners toward intellectual maturity in the various disciplines. It does not seek to transmute knowledge into wisdom as the Holy Spirit focuses learning and applies it to life and pastoral responsibilities. It is not looking for what I call "live orthodoxy" (or even "live heterodoxy," for that matter). Instead, to adapt Kierkegaard's metaphor, it simply hands students endless maps of Massachusetts without including a single road map of Boston.

Part of this may come from our personal limitations as theologians. As E. H. Harbison points out in *The Christian Scholar in the Age of the Reformation*, Luther had high standards for maturity in teachers. In his view the theologian is an instrument to be tuned by time and experience. "One becomes a theologian," he says, "by living, nay rather by dying and being damned, not by understanding, reading, or speculating." "I did not learn my theology all at once, but I had to search deeper for it, where my temptations (*Anfechtungen,* buffetings) carried me." Again, "No one can understand Virgil's *Bucolics* unless he has been a shepherd for five years, nor Virgil's *Georgics* unless he has been a farmer for five years. . . . and no one can think he has sufficiently exhausted the Holy Scriptures unless he has governed congregations with the prophets. . . . for a hundred years."[2]

But another part of the problem is that we try to confine the three elements in the title in water-tight categories, when in fact they cannot help influencing one another at the deepest levels. In fact, there may be schools which build airlocks to keep one or another of these outside. Protestant seminaries have too often mislaid their own spiritual tradition. Thomas Merton says somewhere that he tried to locate and evaluate Protestant spirituality but the only example he could find seemed to him about as supernatural as a Sears Roebuck catalog.

This is, of course, a great mistake. Protestantism, like every branch of Christendom, is full of indigenous spiritualities. Each tradition needs to recover its spiritual *tropoi paideia,* to quote Zinzendorf, and share these distinctive gifts with its new generations and with the rest of Christ's church. But academic competition, and the fact that we are building Greek academies instead of nurturing communities of Christian humanism, can force spirituality into cracks and corners, or threaten to expel it entirely.

(This is true of virtually all our schools today. I work in a conservative Evangelical seminary. Evangelicals sometimes imagine they own the patent on Protestant spirituality; but when spiritual growth happens at Gordon-Conwell it often seems to come upward from the students rather than downward from professors.)

At any rate, in more than one kind of seminary students have been known to tell theologians that they are having trouble finding any pastoral use for what they are learning, any way to use it for the nurture and maturing of the flock. Curriculum structures, in the meantime, guide students in every direction except toward the disciplines which might be practically useful: pastoral theology; spiritual theology; soteriology taught with a view to pastoral applications; and counseling taught from a perspective which integrates Scripture and theology and psychotherapy.

Theology as it is taught is often weighted toward difficult theoretical questions without also considering loci which are central for Christian living, thinking and ethical decision. Even Lutherans repeatedly find it easy to collapse away from *theologia crucis,* theology of the cross, into *theologia gloriae,* a theology of glory which imagines that it can psychoanalyze God and read between the lines of biblical revelation to find its basic axioms.

Philip Spener put it well in *Pia Desideria,* attempting in 1675 to promote spiritual renewal in German Lutheranism:

> Although by God's grace we still have pure doctrine derived from the Word of God, we cannot deny that much that is alien, useless, and reminiscent of the world's wisdom has here and there been introduced gradually into theology. . . . The illuminating words which Luther addressed to the people in Erfurt ought to be borne in our minds. . . .: "Beware! Satan has

the intention of detaining you with unnecessary things and thus keeping you from those which are necessary. Once he has gained an opening in you of a hand-breadth, he will force in his whole body together with sacks full of useless questions, as he formerly did in the universities by means of philosophy." Here we hear that no little damage is done when one tries to be smart and clever without the Scriptures or beyond them. . . .

Compare the writings of our dear Luther. . . . with a majority of the books being published today. To speak candidly, in (Luther) one will assuredly encounter and experience great spiritual power, together with wisdom presented with the utmost simplicity. . . . In the newer books one will find more materials of showy human erudition, of artificial posturing, and of presumptuous subtleties in matters in which we should not be wise beyond the Scriptures. . . .[3]

I hasten to add that an unbalanced concentration on spirituality, divorced from philosophical reflection and theological interaction with current developments in science, culture, and society, will lead to an insular and encultured faith. Such an approach will lose both the truth and the next generation, just as surely as will theologies which marry the *Zeitgeist* in order to remain up to date. And a piety which concentrates on Christian experience while neglecting theology will soon collapse into a mere epiphenomenon of culture.

And so other things besides reason can charm us away from a spirituality which is truly Christian. Today we encounter some movements in the church which are attempting to combine fairly traditional doctrine, and some allegiance to accepted forms of spirituality, with life-styles which ignore or directly contravene biblical norms. This is unsettling whether it occurs in a "Conservative" context (racist and sectarian Fundamentalism) or a "Liberal" one (sexually antinomian Christianity, whether straight, gay, or lesbian).

These may be flawed forms of genuine Christian commitment. Every subculture which is reached by the Gospel attempts to bring its distinctive sins into the church, as we learn from Paul's first letter to the Corinthians. But these mixtures will not lead to mature Christian lives. Paul says to the Corinthians, "We. . . . speak a message of wisdom among the mature (*teleiosis*). . . . But I could not address you as spiritual but as carnal, as infants in Christ" (I Cor. 2:6, 3:1).

76

That variety of new feminist spirituality which is promoting goddess worship, the occult, and even witchcraft seems to me to be even more radically flawed. Here we seem to have non-Christian theology *and* spirituality invading the church, although this may be understandable in view of the way the church has usually treated women.

August Herrmann Francke, who built the University of Halle according to Spener's blueprints, for the most part avoided these pitfalls. Reacting against orthodox Lutheran scholastics, he nevertheless stayed close to the core of historic orthodoxy. He did not neglect the cultivation of student minds. And he gave careful attention to maturing their social outlook in order to avoid egocentric piety.

The local government in Halle today, which is Marxist, is paying for church people to maintain and catalog Francke's large library. The librarian comments that when they probed to find out why Francke's name was connected with so many structures in Halle, they found that he had planned and achieved more social reform than anyone in the history of the Leipzig area. As Erich Beyreuther comments, Francke supported and remained open to the humanist concerns of the early Enlightenment. He was aiming at the same goals of personal and social maturity as Enlightenment humanists: the utopia sketched in the works of Erasmus, Thomas More, J. V. Andreae's *Christianopolis,* and other writings of Christian humanists.[4]

At the core of Halle, however, was a concern for nurturing spiritual maturity among students and a program of spiritual formation which aimed to achieve this. I recommend that any who are interested in academic models of Protestant spirituality look at H. E. F. Guerike's life of Francke, along with Archibald Alexander's *The Log College,* which describes the birth of American Presbyterianism in a spiritual awakening generated by a seminary.[5]

(Sometimes I feel that today we are generating more sleep than awakening. I worry that Charles Finney may have been right and that our graduates may have to thaw out for three years before they are capable of leading a prayer meeting.)

So far I have concentrated mainly on clarifying the relationships between theology and spirituality. The rest of this paper will focus on how these two relate to maturity, understood in terms of biblical norms of wholeness and completeness. I want to examine the interaction of these three elements in some historical models of Christian spirituality. I have chosen to offer a variety of brief case studies to stir up our thinking, rather than to select a few cases to argue a thesis. I hope this will be edifying and not bewildering.

2. Models of Maturity in Spiritual Theology

The discipline which Roman Catholics call Spiritual Theology combines the history and theology of Christian spirituality. Among its principal concerns are the definition of goals of spiritual maturity and the prescription of means to reach those goals. Thus it combines all three of the terms we have been considering, although of course through most of its course it has not employed psychological criteria of maturity. (German Protestantism has developed an analogous discipline called *Frommigkeitsgeschiechte,* history of piety. Both Catholic and Protestant seminaries routinely ignore these disciplines.)

This second section of the paper will examine the interaction of theology, spirituality, and maturity in the history of Christian spirituality. We shall look at maturity both in terms of individual growth and corporate health and community within the body of Christ, since these are often closely interrelated. It is my assumption that all of these models, while not equally viable, are complementary and instructive, in the sense that each is seeking to preserve values in biblical spirituality and human maturity.

If we select from the apostolic era a single picture of the goal of Christian maturity, the most useful is probably Paul's image of individual believers and redeemed humanity restored and renewed through mystical union with Christ.

> We died to sin; how can we live in it any longer?. . . . Or don't you know that all of us who were baptized into Christ Jesus were baptized into his death? We were therefore buried with him through baptism into death in order that, just as Christ was raised from the dead through the glory of the Father, we too may live in (Spirit-empowered) newness of life (Rom. 6: 2–4, cf. Kittell on *kainotes* and *kainos*: "Newness, with a secondary suggestion of the unusual. . . . New creation by the Spirit releases from bondage to sin and law and gives a new quality to life and service." "As distinct from *neos*, "new in time," *kainos* means "new in nature" (with an implication of "better." Both words suggest "unfamiliar, "unexpected," "wonderful". . . .).

Christian maturity in the present age is thus to live increasingly as those who "have become partakers of the Holy Spirit, and have tested the goodness of the word of God and the power of the age to come" (Heb. 6:4–5 RSV). The process of spiritual maturation is our continuing experience of the life of Christ progressively invading and transforming our own lives:

78

Do not conform any longer to the pattern of this world, but be transformed by the renewing of your mind. Then you will be able to test and approve what God's will is—his good, pleasing, and perfect (*teleios*) will (Rom. 12:2 NIV).

Christian wholeness involves increasing proximity to the fullness of God's will. This may be expressed in terms of maturation in virtue:

.....Make every effort to add to your faith goodness; and to goodness, knowledge; and to knowledge, self-control; and to self-control, perseverance; and to perseverance, godliness; and to godliness, brotherly kindness; and to brotherly kindness, love (II Peter 1:5–7 NIV).

Or maturity may be defined as expressing the character of Christ through the fruits of the Spirit appearing in our lives: "....love, joy, peace, patience, kindness, goodness, faithfulness, gentleness, and self-control" (Gal. 5:22–23 NIV). Primarily, however, Christian maturing is being increasingly "conformed to the likeness of (God's) Son" (Rom. 8:29), "being transformed into his likeness with ever-increasing glory, which comes from the Lord, who is the Spirit" (II Cor. 3:18 NIV).

1. Western Spirituality Through the Late Middle Ages

In the immediate post-apostolic era Christian adherence to this goal is diluted by the influence of Jewish legalism and Stoic moralism, in many of the Apostolic Fathers, Hermas, and Clement of Alexandria.[6] As the goal is obscured, the means of achieving it is even more severely distorted in the theology, if not the experience, of the early church. In *I Clement* there is still the clear Pauline ring of salvation by grace through faith in Christ. But in many of the theologians of the second century, the concept of the Gospel as *lex nova* motivates a reversion to a Levitical theology of culture, along with an ascetic approach to sanctification.

Thus Tertullian and later patristic authors advocate a view of Christian perfection or maturity which involves amputation rather than redemption of whole areas of human experience (the theater, the dance, and so forth). The ascetic impulse which moves from Anthony through Athanasius to penetrate the whole movement of Trinitarian theological renewal through Augustine, despite its vital incorporation of many aspects of biblical spirituality at a depth beyond most later expressions of the Gospel, has an extreme solution for handling sin. If one is having trouble handling sex, money, or power, the prescription is to eliminate the problem area through subjection to the monastic regimen. The monastery, in fact, is a kind of sanctification machine.

God has been pleased to use this form of Christian community very wonderfully in spiritual nurture, cultural creativity, and evangelistic outreach. And monastic communities today, somewhat distanced from the doubtful theological bases attached to their origins, are still fruitful in bringing Christians to full growth. The ascetic path, however, often seems designed to frustrate maturity unless it is managed by very wise spiritual directors, as Teresa comments and as Thomas Merton later discovered with some pain.

A movement which offers spiritual perfection at the cost of giving up marriage, freedom, and control of one's property would be called a cult if it arose today (and of course it *does* arise repeatedly even among Protestants). Even so, the double standard of Catholic Puritanism at least made room for the sloppy lives of ordinary believers; and this has made it better able to harbor and nurture forms of human creativity rejected by more rigoristic Protestant expressions of the same impulse in the seventeenth century.

In the West, much of the soteriological legalism of the earlier fathers was corrected by the time of Augustine. The great theologian's fusion of Neoplatonic mysticism with a Pauline understanding of sin and grace formed the main channel of Western spirituality through the Protestant era and beyond, a strong undercurrent in the piety of Benedict, Bernard, the Rhineland mystics, Teresa and John of the Cross, Luther, Calvin, John Owen, and Jonathan Edwards. Augustine recoils from the works-salvation motifs or mixture of grace and works of earlier theologians.

In writings like *On the Spirit and the Letter,* with which the Protestant Reformers found a deep affinity, he moves close to the border of a kind of solafideist piety. Salvation is by perseverance to the end, not in works but in faith, in humble dependence on Christ and his atoning work. Despite the importance of asceticism for Augustine—his "conversion" is really commitment to the monastic ideal and not initial faith in Christ—his reaction against Manicheanism makes him friendly to the material creation and the notion of a matured humanity ruling over it. Human nature is a ruined palace, but a palace still, and one which invites creative restoration. Non-Christian culture is spoils from the Egyptians, but it can still be made into furniture for the sanctuary. Later Augustinians, however, including Protestants like the Puritans, can adopt an over-harsh estimate of sinful humanity which really inhibits human maturation.

Neoplatonism in Augustine is fairly muted compared to the mystical stream descending from the Pseudo-Dionysius. The mystical goal of supraintellectual contemplation of God is attained by the *via negativa,* stripping away all positive predication with respect to divinity and all sensory and intellectual content from the mind. This experience, in Meister Eckhardt all its other exponents, strikes me as more like the Buddhist goal of *satori* (or even *Nirvana* itself!) than any pattern of biblical mysticism.

The *via triplex* of this mystical tradition, with its stages of purgation, illumination, and union, exactly reverses the Protestant understanding of Christian growth, in which union with Christ embraced by faith is followed by the illuminating and sanctifying operation of the Holy Spirit, comforting the believer and mortifying sin. (It may be, however, that Protestants enervated by Cheap Grace would be spiritually renewed if they traveled the triple way, especially the stage of purging sin, provided this were done with evangelical dependence on Christ.)

The various monastic orders, as H. B. Workman and later critics have admitted, could model an inspiring vision of Christian community when they were working well, akin to the apostolic church portrayed in Acts 2:42–47 and 4:32–35.[7] Unfortunately the motivation behind the ascetic way was all too often psychological and spiritual masochism, nipping the buds of human potential in order to achieve a flowering of the Christian life. Luther even suggests that the whole shape of Medieval Catholicism was distorted by the absence of a full theological understanding of justification: "Ah, if the article on justification hadn't fallen, the brotherhoods, pilgrimages, masses, invocation of saints, etc., would have found no place in the church. If it falls again (which may God prevent!) these idols will return."[8]

Following Augustine, the church had virtually reduced justification to sanctification. Believers were made acceptable to God by the inpouring of the life of Christ into their lives, bringing them into "a state of grace." Since this infusion of grace could never produce a state of perfection deep and stable enough to pacify the conscience, the ascetic way was liable to frustrate even its practitioners. Lacking any strong apprehension of the Gospel as authentic Good News, lay folk found both the ascetic model of Christian maturity and the ordinary way of involvement in the world spiritually intimidating.

2. The Spirituality of the Magisterial Reformation

During the late Medieval and early Renaissance periods, the Rhineland mystics, the Friends of God, and the Devotio Moderna began to alter subtly the pattern of ascetic spirituality, emphasizing mortification of sin rather than punishment of the body, and downplaying the fear of loss of salvation. Northern Christian humanists like Wyclif, Colet and Erasmus developed critiques of church life based on careful reading of the Scriptures in the original tongues. But it was Luther's theological innovation, justification by grace through faith on the imputed righteousness of Christ, which set the humanists of northern Christendom on fire spiritually and released a flood of cultural transformation, as Karl Holl has indicated.[9]

Lutheran piety at its best has a great wind of spiritual freedom blowing through it. P. T. Forsyth has a little book on *Christian Perfection* which shows how this theological framework promotes maturity in our relationship to God. A spirituality not based on faith collapses into self-centeredness:

> A Church of sanctified egoisms would be no Church. Its essence would not be faith but morals or spiritual achievement. . . . There are certain forms of self-edification which run out into self-absorption, and leave men. . . . working at goodness rather than at duty. . . . There is an absence of true humility. In its stead there may be either a laboured counterfeit, as painfully sincere as it is unsimple; or there is a precise self-righteousness which cannot veil a quiet air of superiority. . . .[10]

There is a great contrast between this piety of achievement and evangelical spirituality:

> *Perfection is not sanctity but faith.* . . . It is a perfection of attitude rather than of achievement, of relation more than of realization, of truth more than of behavior. . . . It is not a matter of our behavior before God the Judge, but of our relation to God the Saviour. . . . It is a fatal mistake to think of holiness as a possession which we have distinct from our faith. . . . Every Christian experience is an experience of faith; that is, it is an experience of what we have not. . . . Faith is always in opposition to seeing, possessing, experiencing. A faith wholly experimental has its perils. It varies too much with our subjectivity. It is not our experience of holiness that makes us believe in the Holy Ghost. It is a matter of faith that we are God's children; there is plenty of experience in us against it. . . . We are not saved by the love we exercise, but by the Love we trust.[11]

There is a little Lutheran hyperbole here, and this reminds us of how quickly Lutheran piety can decay into Cheap Grace. As Heinrich Heine said, "Things are admirably arranged: God likes forgiving sins, and I like committing them." Building on Luther's understanding of justification, Calvin's spirituality balances this with an extensive treatment of sanctification. The Swiss Reformer replaces the ascetic model with a careful analysis of the progressive mortification of sin in our lives, drawn from the teaching in the application sections of Paul's letters. Displacing sin leads to vivification or renewal of every aspect of our personalities, under the empowering control of the Holy Spirit.[12]

3. Evangelical Protestant Spirituality

Counter-Reformation spirituality, with its strong Augustinian base, began to put a certain competitive pressure on Protestants in the Seventeenth Century. Paralleling the sadness of the wars of religion, there was another, healthier contest unfolding: the struggle to see which side could perfect a spirituality strong enough to reform the church's life as well as its doctrines. This contest produced majestic achievements on the Catholic side, especially the deeply evangelical mysticism of Teresa and John of the Cross. It also produced two sibling movements of Protestant renewal, Calvinist Puritanism and Lutheran Pietism.

A central motif in both movements is conversion/regeneration as the cure for dead orthodoxy and merely "notional" faith. Today's "born-again" movements are ultimate derivatives of this kind of Protestantism. Both Pietism and Puritanism seek to adapt traditional spirituality to the Protestant base of justification by faith. Puritanism, especially, reintroduces much of Patristic piety. The efflorescence of devotional literature during this period makes it the Golden Age of Protestant spirituality, filled with manuals on sanctification, spiritual warfare, the person and work of the Holy Spirit, and the joys and comforts of communion with God. As with Luther, much of this is expressed with lyric power and crackling wit.

Puritans also reintroduced asceticism. Weber is surely right in calling Puritanism *innerweltliche Askese,* monastic asceticism translated into a pattern which could be followed by married laity active in the world. Both Puritanism and Pietism adopted ascetic attitudes toward many aspects of culture which we would consider *adiaphora*: the theater (in the Elizabethan era!), the dance, cosmetics, certain styles of clothing, blood sports (and all sports on Sunday), playing cards (and all games insulting Providence by employing "chance"), and so on.

Thomas Wood comments that Puritans did just as much casuistry as Jesuits, but did it to find and practice the most extreme conclusions rather than to evade them.[13] Counter-Reformation piety, which frequently saluted the same norms, still did not impose them on the whole church. But Puritans insisted on building congregations of provably regenerate "visible saints." If all Protestants had been Puritans or Pietists, we might lack many monuments of Christian art. As it was, Johann Sebastian Bach used Pietist librettos, but worked for orthodox Lutherans who were worldly enough to pay for music in the grand style.

During the Revolutionary period, Puritan ecclesiology shattered the unity of the English church, as Calvin had feared it might, into competing teams of doctrinal hi-fidelity experts: Presbyterians, Congregationalists, Baptists, Seekers, Quakers, Ranters, Muggletonians, Grindletonians, Diggers, and others. By the end of the seventeenth century Puritans and Pietists, like Richard Baxter, were developing an equal hatred of heresy and of schism, and were moving away from an essentially individualistic spirituality toward a concern for corporate renewal. Baxter's motto, "Unity without uniformity," was quietly affirmed even in places like Germany, where it could be considered treason to pray for the renewal of Calvinism, let alone for "Antichrist," the common term for Rome.

Spener and Francke had built a movement to renew German Lutheranism, centered in Halle. It remained for Count Zinzendorf, whom Barth has called the most original Protestant mind after Luther, to extend this vision to encompass the spiritual renewal and reunification of all Christendom including Rom. In his estate in southern Germany, Zinzendorf assembled a community which mirrored this vision, a microcosm of the reunited church. Herrnhut was made up of Moravian Hussite refugees, but there were also substantial contingents of Lutherans, Calvinists, Roman Catholics, and left-wing sectaries. It took three years, from 1724–1727, for this aggregation to stop fighting one another. Zinzendorf's remedies for division were essentially spiritual. He insisted that the contending parties get into small groups, confess their sins to one another after the pattern in James 5:13–16, and pray for one another.

On August 13, 1727, at an early morning communion service, Herrnhut experienced its "baptism in the Holy Spirit," a sense of the divine presence enveloping the community in an atmosphere of love and mutual forgiveness. After this juncture the all-night prayer-watch was established, an interesting variation on the monastic canonical hours which persisted for one hundred years. Teams of Herrnhuters began to travel outward from the community: some for evangelistic mission, in the most extensive movement of Protestant world mission yet appearing, others visiting the central leadership of many denominations including Rome, testifying to the need for the renewal of clergy and laity through conversion, experiencing "the death of Christ upon the heart." The theology undergirding this spirituality was radically Lutheran. Zinzendorf retained many Pietist insights, but Wesley found Herrnhut uncomfortable free from ascetic legalism.[14]

From 1727 onward, for several decades, the major Protestant traditions in Europe and America experienced renewed vitality and a recovery of their distinctive spiritualities and theological emphases. The

Great Awakening era also drew the various renewal movements into relationship with one another, at times close and at other times distant and uneasy. A new entity called "the evangelical movement" had appeared: a pandenominational movement of spiritual renewal, theological reformation, and active mission in evangelism and social and cultural reform.

Some of its leaders seem essentially conservative within their own traditions. Jonathan Edwards, for example, gives us the distilled essence of Puritan Calvinism in his treatment of the Holy Spirit, the sovereignty of God, and other matters—along with the most lucid and radiant accounts of mystical experience available anywhere. His postmillenial eschatology, on the other hand, provides a driving energy toward social transformation which is something new in Puritanism.

In the Wesleyan phase of the Awakening, the social dynamic is even more pronounced. Quakers, who did not know enough theology to confuse them, had brushed past Puritan casuistry to condemn slavery and war. Wesley had the good sense to listen to Quakers instead of discounting them as lunatics and to adopt parts of their social agenda. After the French Revolution the Wesleyan impulse re-entered Anglicanism through John Newton and others. Newton's Eclectic Society met regularly in a pub to plot spiritual revolution in England, formed the network of Protestant leaders which Charles Foster has called "the Evangelical United Front," and eventually secured the abolition of the slave trade and the freeing of all slaves in the British empire, without bloodshed, at a cost of twenty million pounds from the British treasury.[15]

Looking at the multitude of positive social changes emerging from the Second Evangelical Awakening, we can see that when the church in any region begins to approximate corporate maturity and attain the kind of unity which is connected with spiritual renewal and theological depth, all of culture can be changed into something which points more clearly toward the Kingdom of Christ. We must also acknowledge the role of non-Christian humanists in pushing the church closer to sanity in the area of religious tolerance and many social issues. Enlightenment humanists, "the party of humanity" as Peter Gay calls them, often rebelled against the church while advancing the divine agenda.

4. More Recent Forms of Spirituality

Enlightenment leaders sensed that there were too many straight-jackets for human nature still present in evangelical Protestantism, and they continued to seek a society which would be safe for mature creativity. This is our life store, here in New England. Conservative Unitarians like William Ellery Channing painted a kinder image of God than the Puritans had (D. L. Moody and Billy Graham would later follow this lead), and a perfectabilitarian view of man which was almost more evangelical than Charles Finney's perfectionism.

German Liberalism sought to reach and retain in the church the cultured despisers of religion. In a mixture of reactive heterodoxy and deep biblical insight, Albrecht Ritschl discovered the theological linchpin which can hold together and harmonize individual spirituality and social concern: the doctrine of the Kingdom of God. John Nelson Darby's Dispensationalism, on the other hand, promoted lay activism at the same time that it denied the relevance of the Kingdom and preached the ruin of the historic churches, causing the collapse of the evangelical movement into Fundamentalism.

American Christianity in this century has often tried to cultivate theology without spirituality. The result has seldom been growth in maturity. U.C.C. theologician Donald Bloesch, in a respectful book on Barth, comments that conservative evangelicals have outlasted and outreproduced Neo-Orthodoxy because with all their weaknesses they have inherited a strong pattern of spiritual nurture.[16] And the Pentecostal/Charismatic stream, which Henry Van Dusen called a Third Force in world Christianity beside the Catholic and Protestant forces, has a disorderly vitality which penetrates ecumenical barriers and builds monuments which are hardly believable, like Pastor Cho's congregation of five hundred thousand in Korea, neatly ordered in Wesleyan cell-groups and still growing because of these.

Neo-Evangelicalism, in the meantime, has worked hard to create theology which is biblical, traditional, and proof against the Enlightenment critique. Some Evangelicals are seeking also to respond to and incorporate the legitimate concerns of the Enlightenment. Few Evangelicals have much acquaintance with the wild and vital spirituality of the Awakening periods, although some, parched by their movement's fascination with reasonableness if not with rationalism, are drinking from the spiritual springs of Anglicanism, Roman Catholicism and Orthodoxy.

Are more recent theologies developing with careful attention to spiritual formation? James Cone, who began by reordering and italicizing white Liberal insights, has gone back to the spirituality of the black tradition for renewed strength. Feminists have attempted to develop both indigenous theology and spirituality (though much of what they have produced I find deeply unsettling). I am not sure whether liberation theologians have yet come up with anything as dynamic as nineteenth-century evangelicanism, which somehow managed to operate on the basic motif of liberating the enslaved and the weak without spelling this out.

Remarkably enough, the World Council of Churches is promoting a new emphasis on spirituality today. The WCC Statement on *Mission and Evangelism,* crafted by Emilio Castro and Orlando Costas, among others, combines liberationist motifs with a clear emphasis on proclaiming the Gospel and calling individuals to conversion. Even more interesting is the willingness of WCC leaders to interact with Charismatics (see the volume published by the WCC, *The Church is Charismatic,* ed. by Arnold Bitlinger). And in the unit on Renewal and Congregational Life, Gwen Cashmore, a veteran of the East Africa revival and disciple of Max Warren and John V. Taylor, is promoting a kind of Neo-Franciscan spirituality along with her friend Sr. Joan Puls (see Sr. Puls' book, *Every Bush is Burning*).[17]

Are there indications of a rebirth of Christian spirituality to match the fitful bursts of theological creativity at the end of this century? There seems to be an eagerness abroad for spiritual formation and spiritual theology. I have spelled out what I have been able to understand about individual and corporate spiritual renewal in two books, *Dynamics of Spiritual Life* and *Renewal as a Way of Life*.[18] The books of Henri Nouwen, Richard Foster, and other spiritual instructors are eagerly read in many diverse communities. Even republished Puritans are selling widely in some sectors of the church. These are good signs. It is unlikely that we can unify the body of Christ without a new movement of deep spiritual renewal, and only Christians who are spiritually and theologically renewed can lead mature lives and carry out effective mission for it.

Notes

1. Wallace Stevens, "Le Monocle de Mon Oncle," in *The Collected Poems of Wallace Stevens* (New York: Alfred A. Knopf, 1955), p. 16.

2. These passages are cited from E. H. Harbison, *The Christian Scholar in the Age of the Reformation* (New York: Scribner, 1956), pp. 131–132.

3. Philip Jacob Spener, *Pia Desideria* (Philadelphia: Fortress Press, 1964), pp. 51–53, 56.

4. See Desiderius Erasmus, *The Colloquies*, tr. Craig R. Thompson (Chicago: University of Chicago Press, 1965); Thomas More, *Utopia*, tr. Paul Turner (Baltimore: Penguin Classics, 1965); and Johann Valentin Andreae, *Christianopolis*, tr. F. E. Held (Oxford: Oxford University Press, 1916).

5. H. E. F. Guericke, *Memoirs of Augustus Hermann Francke* (Philadelphia: American Sunday School Union, 1831); Archibald Alexander, *The Log College* (London: Banner of Truth Trust, 1968).

6. See Thomas F. Torrance, *The Doctrine of Grace in the Apostolic Fathers* (Grand Rapids: Eerdmans, 1959).

7. H. B. Workman, *The Evolution of the Monastic Ideal* (Boston: Beacon Press, 1962).

8. Martin Luther, *Table Talk*, ed. and tr. by Theodore G. Tappert (Philadelphia: Fortress Press, 1967), p. 340.

9. Karl Holl, *The Cultural Significance of the Reformation*, tr. Karl and Barbara Hertz and John H. Lichtblau (New York: Meridian Books, 1959).

10. P. T. Forsyth, *Christian Perfection*, (London: n.p., 1899), p. 56.

11. Forsyth, op. cit., pp. 7–9, 73.

12. John Calvin, *Institutes of the Christian Religion*, tr. Ford Lewis Battles, ed. John T. McNeill (Philadelphia: Westminster Press, 1960), Book III: chs. 1–3.

13. Thomas Wood, *English Casuistical Divinity in the Seventeenth Century* (London: S. P. C. K., 1952), p. 64.

14. See A. J. Lewis, *Zinzendorf the Ecumenical Pioneer* (London: SCM Press, 1962).

15. See Charles I. Foster, *An Errand of Mercy* (Chapel Hill: University of North Carolina Press, 1960).

16. See Donald Bloesch, *Jesus is Victor!* (Nashville: Abingdon Press, 1976), ch. 7.

17. Joan Puls, *Every Bush is Burning* (Geneva: World Council of Churches, 1985).

18. Richard F. Lovelace, *Dynamics of Spiritual Life* (Downers Grove, IL: InterVarsity Press, 1978); and *Renewal as a Way of Life* (Downers Grove, IL: InterVarsity Press, 1985).

Part II

Life and Crises of Meaning-Making

VII. Maturity and the Minister's Family

Merle R. Jordan

The truest test of the maturity of the minister is the quality of interpersonal relationships with the family. The minister may be a superb preacher, a persuasive evangelist, an effective administrator, a dynamic social activist, the object of admiration by parishioners, community leaders, and colleagues, a ministerial success by almost any measure, and still be a failure as spouse and as parent; the minister may play many ministerial roles to Oscar perfection but still flunk the tests as marital partner and lover. The glittering public performances of ministry may be seriously tarnished in the private interactions in the home.

The minister's true self (revealing the quality of one's inner heart and being) tends to get lived out more authentically in the private intimate arena of the family than in the public context of ministry. "Street angel" and "house devil," which are terms usually applied to the public and private behavior of children, can also be relevant to the lives of some clergy. The maturity of the inward being of ministers can often be assessed most readily by the quality of their relationships with those who are closest to them. Therefore, it is important to examine the psychodynamics of minister's maturity and family.

This topic can be discussed in various ways. It is proposed to select four areas (as illustrative rather than exhaustive), in which the minister's maturity is manifested. These subheadings are: (1) Speaking the Truth in Love, (2) Leave Before You Cleave, (3) Transforming Idols, and (4) Coping with the Cacophony of the Church.

1. Speaking the Truth in Love

Sharing one's inner truth and authentic love with the family and listening to other family members with empathy, care, and understanding are fundamental to the minister in developing mature relationships in the home.

Generally a minister will be in deep connection with his or her spouse and children when the minister is able to be in touch with the inner depths of his or her own personhood and of the same depths of the family members; open to sharing with them from that central tender, vulnerable core of his or her being; and able to listen to and respond authentically to the same tender, vulnerable core of his or her spouse and children. Effective communication is central to building enduring relationships. Helpful communication generally emerges by the mutual sharing of our innermost feelings and thoughts from the vulnerable centers of our personalities. Such openness is risky, and so many clergy build defensive walls against intimate communication in their families in order to protect themselves from the possibility of repeated hurts and disappointments that they encountered in sharing their precious and often fragile inner thoughts, feelings, dreams, and fantasies to parents and significant others when they were still youngsters. These defensive patterns of communication often carry over into adulthood so that their mates and children get treated in the same manner, and the patterns that might have aided their survival in childhood now threaten healthy interpersonal communication and the development of mature family relationships.

Let us briefly look at three major ways in which clergy can protect themselves from the risk of being hurt in intimate communication: (1) fight, (2) flight, and (3) acting out. The defense by *fight* is the porcupine syndrome in which the minister protects his or her tender inner core by showing the "quills" to keep people at a distance. Those defensive quills may take the form of anger (or the threat of anger), criticism, blame, ego attack, character assassination, yelling, throwing things, hitting, and other myriad means of verbal and physical abuse. The Tyrant, Judge, Bully, and Dictator are masks used by the porcupine pastor to control intimate relationships.[2]

The second defensive style is *flight* through withdrawal, detachment, passivity, sulking, pouting, and the silent treatment. The minister might have learned early that people cannot get to you if you are "out to lunch," emotionally unavailable, a stone wall, an immovable object, an invisible person who does not disclose the inner self and is lost in work, television, books, etc. Furthermore, the sulking and pouting minister who pretends to be a victim tries to use the silence to induce guilt in others to get his or her own way. While the flight style is often considered to be the most powerful, the "martyr" who controls by distancing and looks like the helpless victim on the surface is in fact the most powerful person in controlling intimate relationships from the defensive side.

The third defensive style is *acting out*. Instead of communicating clearly and cleanly his or her own thoughts, needs, and feelings, the minister transposes an unspoken message to a member of the family into negative behavior outside the family. A case in point is a minister who could not deal with his own internal rage and preached a sermon on

Peter and the cock crowing while brandishing a hatchet from the pulpit over the heads of the congregation. Pastors sometimes need a safe, accepting environment in which they can get in touch with their vulnerable feelings of hurt, pain, sadness, and anger that usually lie beneath the surface of defenses.

Many clergy come from backgrounds in which there have been parental prohibitions linked with repressive religious injunctions that it is wrong, sinful, selfish, evil, and destructive to express one's emotions within the family. They sometimes grow up in families or institutions that quash feelings and repress emotions, particularly the aggressive, sexual, and grief feelings. With the negative attitude toward their feelings, they often have difficulty with intimate relationships that require the sharing of feelings and emotions. The following are some of the emotions and feelings:

1. *Hurt* is the first emotion to focus on. Hurt is a sense of disappointment, loss, and grief. These feelings are a natural part of any close interpersonal relationship. When we care about others, we are vulnerable to being hurt by them. Should this happen, we protect and defend ourselves against such feelings in various ways.

Reflect for a moment upon the ways in which you dealt with your hurt when a loved one disappointed you. Perhaps you masked your hurt by sulking and withdrawing, or you used the silent treatment to get revenge on the one who did hurt you. On occasion, you might directly retaliate and attack with anger, criticism, or blame in order to avoid the hurt feelings as well as to hurt the one who hurt you. How difficult it is to identify hurt for what it is and to express it cleanly and directly instead of converting it into some other expression or reaction. To communicate hurt as hurt, rather than concealing it, is a major step in growing mature.

During the last few decades, psychology has rediscovered the truth of Jesus' statement, "Blessed are they that mourn, for they shall be comforted" (Matt. 5:4). By expressing your hurt and grief, you may have more opportunity for constructive communication that leads to comfort, healing, and reconciliation in family relationships. However, such honest expression of hurt does not encourage the manipulative use of hurt feelings, whereby some people play on the guilt of others to get their way. I am supporting the authentic sharing of hurt feelings in family relationships as a constructive possibility for growth and not the immature game of "Poor, Rejected Me," a perversion of genuine encounter.[2]

2. *Fear* is the second emotion that clergy sometimes have difficulty dealing with in their families. Under the rubric of fear, I would include the experiences of fright, insecurity, inadequacy, and helplessness. Often one's past experiences and professional principles have informed clergy not to disclose fear. Male clergy may consider it unmasculine to reveal their insecurities and fears and act like the Rock of Gibraltar when they are really frightened inside; they are supposed to have all the answers, but they do not know what to do with their doubts and insecurities. They mask their fears and inadequacies behind criticism, blame, and anger in the family circle. They stake out the overcompensatory position of being right and strong in order to cover insecure parts of their lives. This defensive posture is reminiscent of the preacher who wrote himself a note in the margin of his sermon manuscript that read, "weak point, pound pulpit harder." In relating to his or her spouse, the minister needs to show courage and strength and acknowledge vulnerabilities and anxieties.

A case in point is the middle-aged pastor who found himself becoming more tired in his work as the years passed and came home at the end of the day with less energy for intimacy with his wife. Being exhausted during the day, he was unable to complete his love-making with his wife in the evening. Feeling humiliated by the experience and frightened of losing his virility, he contemplated various options. He could withdraw from sexual encounters with his wife as a way of avoiding his worry about his sexuality. He could test himself out by flirting with an attractive parishioner. But he decided to gather up his courage and talk to his wife about his fears and anxieties: "Dear, I'm afraid that I'm really slowing down as your lover, and I'm not the man I once was." He was pleasantly surprised by his wife's accepting attitude and affirmation: "I know, dear, that was difficult for you the other night. But it really was OK for me. You have been and are a wonderful lover. We are both slowing down in various ways as we age. But we can integrate that into our relationship and not have those changes threaten our life together."

Disclosing our fears and insecurities within intimate relationships and finding them accepted and not ridiculed is a profound experience that deepens the bonds of love. On the other hand, accepting the fears of one's spouse and children can also bring deep rewards in the relationships in the family.

3. *Anger* is often very difficult for the minister to deal with constructively with the marriage partner and with children. Anger may have been polluted with repressive injunctions masquerading as religious truths. "Be not angry" may be the distorted interpretation of the biblical directive, "Be angry and sin not," which has guided the pastor's belief system in dealing with anger. Sometimes, a minister has not felt the freedom to express anger in a constructive manner, particularly in the practice of the ministry, and the smoldering volcano inside tends to erupt on the loved ones in the home. The pastor needs to learn what are the most constructive ways of dealing with anger. Simply pushing anger down inside, which may fester into an emotional gunnysack of resentment, is potentially as destructive as the anger that

flails wildly in words and actions at the family members within reach. William Blake expresses the basic principle of the appropriate handling and discharge of anger in his poem "A Poison Tree": "I was angry with my friend; I told my wrath, my wrath did end. I was angry with my foe; I told it not, my wrath did grow." Finding appropriate outlets and creative discharge of one's anger in words, actions, and fantasies is an important step in developing constructive relationships in the parsonage.

However, dealing with anger by catharsis and ventilation is not sufficient. Cognitive therapists have suggested that much anger is caused by the absolutionist demands that we place upon others to behave exactly according to our prescribed expectations. The implicit theme of the self-righteous pastor angry with spouse or children may be "I am angry with you because you are not what I want you to be. You must be what I want, or I will remain justifiably angry with you." The arrogant shepherd badgering the flock in the home with anger until they become exactly what the pastor demands and expects can be compared to the haughty bishop in Bergman's movie *Fanny and Alexander* who, in the name of God, used his bullying anger so abusively and destructively with his stepchildren. Instead of focusing on the bad behavior and imperfections of the other family members with self-justifying anger, the pastor may need to look inward to challenge his or her own *shoulds* and *musts*. Challenging one's own assumptions about how other people should be may be a significant step in the transformation of the minister's anger-creating belief system.

4. *Love* is the final emotion to consider. While the essential "tools of the trade" of ministry are the preaching, teaching, and mediating of love, it is common to find clergy who, in the innermost depths of their being, are terrified of love in close relationships. How ironic it is to see the supposed proclaimers of love to be so fearful in the practice of what they are preaching. On the one hand, clergy are notorious for their inability to receive love. They have often grown up as the strong giving and mediating members of the family, and they find safety and security in avoiding the vulnerability of receiving by always needing to be in the strong defensive position of giving to others. It may be easier for them to provide a foot-washing ministry to others than it is for them to receive the foot washing of love and caring for themselves from others.

Psychodynamically, it is not uncommon for some male clergy to have smothering mothers and passive fathers; they learned early that to be close to mother's love meant that they needed to give up their assertive and independent side in order to maintain the approval of the most significant parent, since the father was emotionally absent and rarely, if ever, an advocate for the son's freedom. Thus, in adulthood, they may be frightened of being dominated and enveloped by their wife if they get too open to love. Likewise, they may be afraid of becoming intimate with God because God too was created in the image of the mother and would force them to do something against their nature.

On the other hand, it takes courage and faith to love others truly, intimately, and nondefensively. Love is sometimes defined as lowering one's defenses and becoming vulnerable to hurt. When clergy reach out in love, even in their own homes, there is no guarantee that love will be returned. Loving is a risk; loving is an inward cross.[3] If hurt too much in close relationships in the past, the minister may try to keep safe from the involvements of loving others with the inherent possibilities of being hurt again. Nevertheless, developing the courage to reach out in love from the center of one's being is essential for mature relationships in the home.

Furthermore, the minister needs to develop communication skills in dealing with his or her own feelings as well as with the ambivalent feelings of others. Being able to have the freedom for being oneself and the ability to affirm the freedom of the spouse and the children to express fear and anger simultaneously is a mark of healthy communication. "I'm afraid of hurting you and causing unhappiness in our relationships, but I also need to tell you that I was hurt and angry by your forgetting my birthday" is an illustrative statement of expressing two feelings at the same time.

The minister who needs to be "right" and "in control" may find difficulty in dealing with the problem solving and conflict resolution in the home, because it is difficult for such a minister to give respect to the feelings, ideas, suggestions, hopes, and dreams of others in the family. However, the research indicates that there is more opportunity for constructive problem solving in the family if the minister can affirm and understand the positions and feelings of others, even if minister does not agree. Agreeing to disagree agreeably is a mark of mature living in the home. All persons in the home need both a sense of affiliation and belonging as well as the experience of the validation of autonomy and independence. The poles of "roots" and "wings," namely, togetherness and freedom, are both important to affirm.

Speaking the truth in love is a difficult and complex task for most, but the mature patterns of such communication can be most rewarding and fulfilling.

2. Leave Before You Cleave

"Leave before you cleave" is a pithy way to state the idea that maturity in marriage and family is directly linked with the level and degree of individuation, liberating from harmful and obstructive patterns learned in childhood. In ministry, the pastor needs to become familiar with the way in which individual persons get programmed into roles, patterns, and "scripts" from childhood and how they need to have consciousness raising of that history so that they can have more freedom to choose other alternatives and options in their relationships. Howard Halpern has summarized this idea of the repetitive "script" from childhood that can continue to impact our adult lives: "Those stored transactions from our childhood can at times be 'switched on' and replayed in the present as current feelings and behavior without being modified by our more grown up experience," and they can be used creatively like "songs and dances" and lead to one's emotional and spiritual maturity.[4] The minister needs to reinforce those constructive messages in each individual's stored transactions from childhood, but we are particularly concerned here in dealing with the destructive "scripts," teachings, and beliefs that get passed from generation to generation and raise havoc with the maturity of the minister.

The history of the pastor's family (of origin with at least a three-generational perspective) can play a significant part in the pastor's maturity in marriage and family, usually unconsciously in three ways: (1) the unconscious selection of mate that leaves the pastor over the years in the same role in marriage as in the family of origin (if lonely and unaffirmed in childhood, then lonely and unaffirmed in marriage); (2) the unconscious restructuring of conflictive patterns with the spouse that are an exact replica of the unresolved intrapsychic hangups from the relationships with the family of origin (you're just like my father, or you're just like my mother); (3) childrearing practices that are parallel to or diametrically opposed to the childrearing practices of the pastor's parents (the pastor hears the echo of one of the parents when disciplining his or her own children, or the pastor subtly supports the rebellious side of the child to act out against parental authority in ways that the pastor was unable to do as a child).

The minister who did not receive enough nurturing, affirmation, and love from the family of childhood tries to be a marital partner, parent, and minister out of an emotional and spiritual bankruptcy. Having read over five hundred papers of seminarians regarding their experience in their childhood, I cannot overstate the case of how many, perhaps 95 percent, come from families that were filled with conflict, problems, and pain. Life is often an intense struggle for them.

Ministers are proclaimers of the good news to the people, but too often they lack the experience of the good news in their hearts. The joy of the Easter has not permeated the marrow of their bones, nor has it danced along the corridors of their parsonages. The acceptance, grace, and love that they preach have not been experienced in the depth of the heart and by the hearth of their homes. Too often, out of an inner emptiness and a nonnurturing theology, the clergy try to minister to the needs of persons and the institutions of society. Their psychodynamics can be traced as follows:

1. *Barriers to Grace Derived from Family History.* Too often the minister is blocked from experiencing being a beloved child of God because of the poor quality of interpersonal relationships that prevent enjoying the healthy dependency of childhood. Many ministers have grown up in a family in which they learned only to take care of others: in order to hold their parents and the whole family together emotionally, they had to "parent" their parents since the parents were unreliable authority figures. To be a child was to be too vulnerable to the vicissitudes of their family environments, and to survive in the family emotionally, they gave up the healthy dependency of childhood and lived by the text, "Unless you become like a strong parent, you will not enter the kingdom of heaven." This reaction formation of "messianic parenthood" to their childhood family leaves them in the position of repeating the same "script" and the same savior role throughout life. Their vocational choice of ministry is often a natural result from the formative years. Without corrective emotional experience or therapeutic interventions, they will unconsciously repeat in adulthood the overt role of the strong care-giver with the starving child within. They have been conditioned to be afraid of grace or being ministered unto because they found trust only in themselves and not in significant others. Such a pattern tends to block an openness to the experience of Jesus Christ as gracious Lord and Savior since they have learned to be the lord and to develop their own strategies for salvation through justification by works. Karen Horney speaks of this defensive pattern as the "neurotic glory."[5]

However, this view is not to be understood as supporting infantile dependency, unhealthy regression, or a cheap grace that allows the individual to cop out of responsibility. Carrying one's cross, coping with reality responsibly, and utilizing one's adult and parental ego states constructively are a significant part of the minister's life.

2. *Social Reinforcement of the Barriers.* The minister's internalized expectation to be a superman or superwoman is often socially reinforced. The spouse can reinforce it by playing the role of one or both of the pastor's parents, the unreliable figures. For example, the spouse may demand a lot of parenting from the pastor and be threatened by the child self of the pastor. Thus, the pastor is locked further into a defensive (parental ego) state. Furthermore, the local church can also reinforce such defensive parenting by expecting the pastor to be the only minister in the congregation in the sense that the laity abdicate their mutual ministry. Then, the pastor may experience the parish to be like the family in which the pastor used to perceive the role of being the central care-giver and peace maker while others in the family did not fulfill their responsibilities.

A typical example is Stan Brady. While Stan was not conscious of how closely his role as parish minister replicated his childhood role in his family, he was aware of the overwhelming pressure by the congregation and felt exhausted. He had grown up with an older brother in a New England town and learned at an early age that it was unsafe to be a vulnerable child in his home. He discovered before the age of six that he needed to take care of parents and that he could not rely upon them for love and affirmation. His mother was fragile, suffering from various illnesses, and so supersensitive that she would ready cry, get a headache, and so on, if anyone displeased her in the smallest way. Stan felt the need to protect her because his brother seemed unconcerned and his father tried to control the home by anger and threats. Moreover, he tried to be the peacemaker. Even as a preschooler, he acted as the care giver to his parents so that his parents would not separate. It appeared to him that the sickly, fragile mother and the critical, volatile father were in no way reliable authority figures. So he had to depend on himself for survival. In a sense, he was functioning as a minister in his own childhood family without having had the opportunity to be truly a child himself. He carried these basic patterns into adulthood and felt trapped by the never-ending demands placed on him as pastor. In addition, his nonnurturing wife pushed him to have more children. That meant more emotional and financial responsibilities for him, while he still had not had the experience of being loved as a child.

While Stan's particular dynamics may differ from other clergy, there are many internalized patterns of child roles replayed in adulthood and in ministry. This leaves the child self in the pastor unfulfilled and closed to receiving the good news.

3. *Unless You Become Like a Little Child.* Healing lies in such a pastor's risking to be like a little child. The pastor has to find the courage to place him or herself in anxiety-provoking situations in which the inner child may be open to experiencing new growth and life. Instead of avoiding life situations that could facilitate the expressiveness of the child self, the pastor needs to risk placing him or herself in those relationships and experiences that may nurture and free the child self. Growth experiences may be chosen from those that encourage the freeing of one's human potential. For instance, conjoint marital conversations in the presence of a counselor who does not need the minister to be a parent can be helpful. The use of parish consultants with expertise in organizational development can enable the laity to mobilize their resources for ministry and to lessen their superhuman demands on the pastor. This can help to evolve a sense of mutual ministry in the congregation. The pastor may choose to enter into the life of prayer and devotion not as another "should" or "ought" in strengthening the defensive parenting self but as an anxious and yearning child seeking to discover whether the Divine Parent is more dependable, trustworthy, and grace-full than the human parents.

Stan Brady, for example, could greatly benefit from a wide variety of growth experiences, whether it be counseling, spiritual devotion, growth group experience, or career evaluation, that could help him experience love and affirmation of his child self for the first time. In lowering one's defenses and risking revealing one's own inner child, needs, and feelings, the pastor may discover that the God revealed in Jesus Christ affirms the child self of the pastor and that the good news is for him or her also.

3. Transforming Idols

There is a dynamic interplay, often unconscious, between one's idolatrous images of God and the patterns of interaction with self, spouse, and children. The negative images of God generally are derived from one's perceptions of parents and other authority figures in childhood, and they are projected onto God. This idolatrous view, then, tends to dictate one's own self-image and worth. The experience of a loving God, for example, fosters a more positive self concept than the projection of a God who does not empower and affirm a person.

In order to survive in an imaginative world governed by idolatrous images of God, the pastor as a child had to construct a second idolatry around him or herself. This second idolatry is in reaction to the first idolatrous misperception of ultimate reality. It can be thought of as a defensive strategy of salvation or an attempt to provide one's own atonement to a negative God. The child may become involved in "good works" in order to guarantee survival in relationship to this perceived ultimate reality. Thus the youngster may become a "little Christ" in the sense of having to be one's own savior in the world as perceived. The crucifixion of some parts of one's personhood for the sake of making it in a world governed ultimately by someone other than the true God revealed in Jesus Christ may be the price that one pays.

When there is little or no operational trust in the loving God as the initiator of atonement, one has to find a variety of atoning strategies for oneself. This twin idolatry, which is necessary for survival in childhood, often becomes a fixed pattern in the pastor and later threatens the marital and family relationships.

The level of maturity in the minister's object relationships based upon human relationships in childhood tends to persist into adulthood unless there have been therapeutic and healing interventions. Thus the idolatrous images of God and the resulting patterns of defensive coping are the model for life, even into adulthood. When they are transferred into marriage and family life, there will usually be anguish for all in the family. The pastor will experience a sense of a vicious cycle in which one is caught by a painful consistency of the old defensive patterns of behavior. If the pastor tries to avoid being exposed to the problems, conflicts, feelings, and needs of the family by being busy

102

with the work, then the pastor takes the risk of avoiding intimate dialogue with God in struggling and wrestling with these difficulties.

Most clergy may be unaware of an implicit religious drama being played out in the minister's marriage and family, because the whole family may have an idolatrous sense of ultimate reality. Those involved may attempt to live out their own messianic deliverance from the situation. They make terrible sacrifices of themselves, including various kinds of emotional sickness and social deviance in the minister's family, in order to find salvation in their imprisoned worlds. So, it is imperative for ministers to struggle for the liberating experiences of the Divine Love that affirms the freedom to be themselves in the context of a loving family.

4. Coping with the Cacophony of the Church
For some clergy, ministry can be challenging, fulfilling, and satisfying. For others, it is just a series of battles, disappointments, and disillusionments. For all, there are problems to be surmounted, decisions to be made in which everybody cannot be pleased, and a host of other issues and wearing pressures. The contemporary minister faces unusual challenges in that the knowledge explosion demands continuous learning in order to maintain professional competence; the complexities of a changing technological society in the nuclear age seem at times so overwhelmingly difficult for the pastor to be the shepherd and the prophet of God's people; and the diverse and competing roles and functions of ministry in which one can hardly be an expert can really tear the minister apart. While there is often a grandeur and fulfillment in ministry, there is also agony and frustration. It takes an unusual amount of maturity for a minister to chart and sail the waters of ministry without serious damage to the role as marital partner and as parent.

Ministers seem to have inexhaustible pressures and problems that confront them in the context of the church. While other professions may share some of the same vocational hazards, the minister seems to have a unique configuration of issues and concerns bearing heavily on the marriage and family life. The tip of the iceberg of pressures and problems that can be a significant factor in upending a minister's marriage and family include the following:

1. Owning of one's own home with the opportunity for building equity and making decisions about one's home without consultation with church officials versus the use of a parsonage without the problems of down payments and reselling but with the potential conflicts of the minister and/or the spouse in having to negotiate any home improvements and changes with church officers who may or may not be sympathetic and helpful.

2.   Unrealistic expectations by the congregation of the roles and functions of the minister. The minister has diverse expectations from a heterogeneous congregation. Church members in one parish may vary widely in their theological beliefs and in their priorities for the work of their minister. The minister can feel trapped in trying to be all things to all people. Parish ministry has such permeable boundaries and rarely, if ever, is there a sense of the job being done. The minister has to have solid ego strength to be able to choose and to mediate between competing responsibilities and expectations. In addition to the superhuman expectations laid on the pastor, there are sometimes ideal roles and functions that the minister's spouse and children are supposed to perform. Life in a fishbowl with numerous congregational "bosses" over the minister and his or her family can add to the normal tensions of marriage and family life. Marital and family conflicts for a minister often involve issues of competing loyalties between profession and home with tough decisions to be made in one's use of time and energy.

3.   Reasonable and realistic ego satisfactions from the ministry. In contrast to other professions, the ministry is relatively underpaid. While denominations have been working to upgrade salary scales for their clergy, the financial rewards for the majority of clergy are minimal and many clergy families are seriously hurting economically. It has become imperative for many clergy and their spouses to work. They have little money available for leisure time and recreation. Planning for college tuition seems ridiculously hopeless on the budgets of many families of clergy. Women in ministry still can expect radically lower salaries than their male counterparts. Women ministers can also still expect in most instances to find more barriers and blocks in their way to moving upward into church positions that would be more gratifying and rewarding. The itinerant quality of ministry often poses marital and family problems for mates and children who may not be ready to move when the minister is finally called to do so. Enjoying vacations, days off, and leisure time without guilt and without undue financial worries or criticism from church members are too rare experiences for clergy and their families.

The minister needs a great deal of evolving maturity in order to cope with so many of the issues and problems that have an impact on the marriage and family. The pastor needs to be able to utilize skills in communication, conflict resolution, time management, planning, and goal setting to orchestrate a symphony out of the potentially discordant notes that are often present in the cacophony of the church.

In brief, for most clergy the pilgrimage to maturity within the family requires lifelong learning as ministers and family members go through the various stages of life and its vicissitudes. The perils for the minister are many and great on that journey, but the rewards and joys can be rich and fulfilling.

Notes

1. Maxie Dunham, Gary Herbertson, Everett Shostrom, *The Manipulator and the Church* (Nashville: Abingdon Press, 1968), p. 81.

2. Erich Berne, *Games People Play* (New York: Grove Press, 1967), p. 48.

3. Charles Duell Kean, *The Inward Cross* (Philadelphia: Westminster Press, 1952).

4. Howard M. Halpern, *Cutting Loose* (New York: Bantam Books, 1978), pp. 4, 6.

5. Karen Horney, *Neurotics and Human Growth* (New York: W. W. Norton, 1970), p. 191.

VIII. Maturity, Ministry, and Midlife Crises

Margaret Gorman

Is there any relationship between burnout and midlife crises for ministers? What are the similarities and the differences? Are ministers' midlife crises different in kind or degree from the midlife crises of other professionals or business persons? In dealing with these I hope to examine briefly the following aspects of midlife crisis and maturity as it might affect the minister:

1) Levinson's description of the midlife crisis.
2) Identification with the persona to the neglect of the self dimension in midlife.
3) The nature of burnout as it might affect those in ministry.
4) The distinction between vocation and ministry in midlife.
5) The nature of the dream for those in ministry in coping with midlife crisis.

1. Levinson's View of the Midlife Crisis (As a Religious or Meaning Crisis)

As Levinson describes, the questions asked in the midlife transition are no longer the question of "How do I make it to the top?" but rather the inward questions: "What have I done with my life? What do I really get from and give to my wife, children, friends, work, community—and self? What is it I truly want for myself and others? What are my central values and how are they reflected in my life?"[1]

One gets the impression that Levinson's subjects, as they entered young adulthood and even as they settled down, had never reflected upon nor examined their values or their beliefs about the meaning and purpose of life. They simply plunged into the work world determined to make it to the top. They lived and thought on a highly external level. They sought only to develop the proper *persona* and to fulfill the appropriate role prescriptions. There was little or no consideration or

107

examination of who they were, their values, and their beliefs. The need for a transcendent reality outside the material world was just not there.

So at midlife, faced with the experience of their own limits (physical, intellectual, and emotional) as well as the limits and limitations of their work, family, and social world, most people are forced to look both within themselves and beyond the temporal and materialistic values they had so unquestioningly and naively espoused. Is this a moment for religious questions to be asked?

At one point, soon after his book was published, I did write Levinson to ask him whether the midlife crises he described had a religious component or whether he had ever probed that dimension. He did not answer.

As we know, however, Jung was outspoken in this matter:

> Among all my patients in the second half of life— that is to say, over thirty-five, there has not been one whose problem in the last resort was not that of finding a religious outlook on life. It is safe to say that every one of them has been really healed who did not regain his religious outlook. This of course has nothing whatever to do with a particular creed or membership of a church.[2]

If then the persons in Levinson's sample had ignored the religious, spiritual, or value dimension in their young adulthood, that dimension would have forced itself upon them in midlife.

But ministers, it seems to me, would have examined those values and recognized the spiritual dimension as the basis of their commitment. Of course, one can say that the midlife crisis is a developmental one and that even the faith commitment of young ministers is an immature one. But it would seem that the commitments of ordinary business and professional persons are challenged at midlife by the limits of their material aspects and satisfactions. Human beings are by nature spiritual and yearn for a transcendent reality. This can be avoided in young adulthood by the sheer busyness and novelty of engaging in the challenge of the work world. Eventually its attractions can be seen as failing to answer the deepest needs of human beings.

Ministers, however, by their commitments to a spiritual dimension would have deliberately chosen to put material possessions and advancement lower on the hierarchy of their values. They would have already recognized the limits of material possessions. It would seem then that they should not experience midlife crises unless there is another approach to midlife crises and unless the midlife crises of those not ostensibly engaged in the competitive endeavor of becoming one's own man have other sources.

2. Persona and Self

Kao does speak of ministers who seem to have had midlife crises: "It was around the age of fifty-five that I preached from the gut level for the first time." As he says, "Midlife crisis calls for further individuation, by integrating world views and an ultimate commitment to reaching a state of authentic living . . , ."[3] Sanford presents an interesting insight into one of the dangers or occupational hazards of ministry: "The ministering person must function a great deal of time on his *persona*."[4] Both the notion of authentic living and the notion of persona may give helpful insights into the midlife crises of ministers not in the sense that the midlife crises of nonministers are not also concerned with authenticity and persona but in a different way.

Sanford points out two aspects of the excessive pressure of being a persona for the minister: (a) because one is called upon to greet persons at the church door and other impersonal functions, one has difficulty relating on a deeper level to two or three hundred people; (b) not only is there a great danger in ministers themselves taking on persona but also a great danger present in the fact that people impose persona on ministers as well.

Now, business and professional people also have their personae thrust upon them, but the situation is slightly different. The personae in business and professions are precisely those of their work world. The greater danger for ministers lies in the fact that the personae thrust upon them are less of their profession and more of being a perfect person, an authentic person (when they know they are not). This pressure to be before the world what they know they are not can result in self-deception or in hypocrisy. Is part of the midlife crisis for a minister an awareness of the futility of being what others expect, not only as persona but as a person? We recall Jung's statement: "These identifications with a social role are a very fruitful source of neuroses. A man cannot get rid of himself in favor of an artificial personality without punishment . . . . The social 'strong man' is in his private life often a mere child where his own states of feeling are concerned; his discipline in public . . . . goes miserably to pieces in private."[5]

Kao's model of differentiation, integration, and transcendence describes the three levels on which these processes take place as the physical, mental, and spiritual. He also implies that transcendence would include transcending the roles chosen by oneself or imposed by others. Somehow, ministers at midlife must struggle with the personae imposed on them, personae that imply they are, by choice of their "career," authentic persons.

Kegan's model also speaks somewhat to the task facing the minister of distinguishing between being a self *derived* from others and being a self *relating* to others: "If one no longer is one's institution,

109

neither is one any longer the duties, performances, work roles, career which institutionality gives rise to. One *has* a career; one no longer *is* a career."[6] Thus, there can be a subtle difference between the confusion about one's identity and one's role a experienced by those in the business world and those in ministry. Both either have their personae thrust upon them or they themselves totally identify with their personae. But, while the persona of the business executive is a work persona, the persona of the minister seems to be one of authentic selfhood. Although this seems a contradiction in terms, we are not talking about the actual self of the minister but about the persona of authentic selfhood that is often perceived as a role prescription for those in ministry either by themselves or by those whom they serve. How can one adopt or accept the *role* of authentic selfhood? Does not this, at its very inception, contain seeds of confusion that at midlife may bring forth in the minister the bad fruit of disillusionment with oneself?

3. The Nature of Burnout

While burnout can come at any period in one's life, it is often associated with the midlife crisis. Does burnout precipitate the questioning of life's goals? The burnout of executives often follows the BOOM period of young adulthood during which they have plunged into making it on the corporate scene.

But usually the syndrome is applied to those in the caring profession and ministry: it belongs, par excellence, to those in this category. In fact, Maslach specifically defines burnout as characteristic only of those in the caring profession: "Burnout is a syndrome of emotional exhaustion, depersonalization and reduced personal accomplishment that can occur among individuals who do 'people work' of some kind."[7]

We have shown above that there is a difference between the minister and those in business or professions in the manner and mode in which they identify with their personae and in the type of personae they adopt. So, too, there can be subtle difference between the burnout of executives and that of the caring professionals. Powerlessness is an essential component in the syndrome of both groups but for different reasons. The motivations of those in business are usually those of salary, benefits, prestige, and power over things and persons, power to effect change in the business, legal, or political world.

Those in the caring profession seem to choose their careers from altruistic and selfless motives. However, there can be other motives such as the need for approval as given by the appreciation of grateful recipients. Others may wish to expiate a vague feeling of guilt. Others, who may have difficulty in establishing close personal relationships, use the caring profession as a way of satisfying their need for intimacy.

Thus, those in industry might feel burnout when they experience the limits of the satisfaction they sought in material accumulation. Now, since those in the caring profession do not, at least initially, seek such material evidence but are motivated by desire to help persons in need, the cause of their burnout may differ. The possibility of visible evidence of success is far less for those in ministry than it is for those who seek material possessions and advancement.

In Levinson's sample, we might say that burnout, which often includes a recognition that an intense pursuit of material possessions and power does not really satisfy one's fundamental desires, can precipitate or accompany the midlife crises of those in business. But those in the caring profession are not primarily seeking material possessions. Are their midlife crises or burnout experiences even deeper and more traumatic since they seek for signs that their dedication to others has borne fruit and there are few such signs? These questions lead us to another distinction and discussion.

4. Vocation and Ministry

An important distinction is to be made between one's vocation and one's ministry. I do not think that there is such a parallel or analogous distinction for those in business. Vocation in ministry is a call to be a certain kind of person, a follower of Christ in complete dedication. For some, that dedication includes vows of poverty, obedience, and chastity. For those in Christian ministry, theirs is a call to follow most especially the Gospel values, which do not describe what one should do but whom one should strive to become.

Now, some enter the ministry to serve the poor, to educate the young, or to care for the sick. The *ministry* is primary. There may be various motivations for choosing a life of service. But the immersion in activity for the first twenty years of their service may well be similar to the immersion in the work world of those in business. They may even seek prestige and power of recognition in some way. When such recognition is not forthcoming, burnout or the questioning of midlifers may ensue, and they may "leave" the ministry for other occupations. Since their roles or personae fall upon them (or do not bring sufficient satisfaction), this change can be a severe identity crisis similar to the midlife crisis of those in business who also find that their persona identity is insufficient, unsatisfying, and superficial.

Those who originally felt called to God, in the form of vocation, may feel the same disillusionment with their caring occupation. They, too, may leave their ministry, but they will not leave their vocation. They still feel called to a life of commitment to God but change the way they will do that service without changing their vocation. For example, having been teachers, they may now work in hospitals. Or, having served in parishes, they may now work with prisoners. If they

111

have a midlife crisis or experience burnout, that does not alter their vocation. They will change their ministries or ways of serving, but not their commitments.

If one were to look at this from the point of view of role and persona, or from Kegan's model, they have changed their roles or careers but have only deepened their self-identity, which, as Jung would say, is rooted in a "relation to an extra-mundane reality."[8] It would seem, then, that such a reexamination of one's ministry would lead to a planned change but not to a midlife crisis. The only time it might be a midlife crisis is, if the identity had been limited to the ministry.

Does this mean that those not in the ministry are doomed to have their identities only from their careers and roles? Does this mean that they will always experience midlife crises if that is defined as a reexamination of the limits of one's physical powers and the limits of one's career? It would seem true for many. There are some, few perhaps, in government who have had or do have such commitment to a goal larger than themselves, for example, the commitments of Gandhi or Dag Hammarskjold.

5. Reflections on the Dream

A man's Dream is his personal *myth*, an imagined drama in which he is the central character, a would-be hero engaged in a noble quest. . . . The youthful Dream is prime example of the ground in which illusions develop. It is a vision of the adult self living the good life.9

The Dream described by Levinson is quite different from the Dream that calls some, if not many, to the ministry. I would propose that, even though he does state that "the outcome has portentous consequences for that entire world," the Dream of Levinson's men is highly personal and involves "success" in one's chosen career or avocation. The novelists dreamt of becoming writers; some of the businessmen wished to become the head of a major corporation. As the boy-man begins his entry into adulthood, he imagines exciting possibilities for his adult life and struggles to attain the "I am" feeling in this dreamed-of self and world.

I would propose that the dream that calls some to the ministry is a dream of working to establish or spread the Kingdom, the Kingdom of peace and justice described in the Judeo-Christian Scriptures. Although one's personal success may be part of the Dream, still the Dream is not forged by one person, nor achieved by one person. It is given. The Dream is lager than any one person's success in any given field. It is a Dream described by and ascribed to by many people over thousands of years. Does this make a difference in midlife when the Dream must, according to Levinson, be modified and "de-illusionment" (Levinson) must take its place? I think it does.

In the case of a young woman who enters religious life "to convert the world," at midlife she may well recognize that her Dream had many illusions. She may have to recognize that the limits of reality mean that she cannot convert the world and, perhaps, cannot convert anyone. But she can witness to that kingdom of justice and peace. And in the small area where she is, she can contribute to that kingdom. Since her Dream lay not so much in personal success but in a goal outside of her, she can be at peace with herself. She is not alone in her Dream, and the Dream is the Dream of people of the past and of the future.

In a similar way, Martin Luther King spoke of his Dream, and it was not of personal success but of peace and justice. Commitment to a Dream larger than oneself and shared by others, then, might mean that the reexamination of the Dream at midlife need not be a crisis. It can be a recognition once again that the Dream will be realized eventually, and one is not alone in working for it.

Thus, because the dream of those in ministry is larger than themselves and is shared and will be shared by many across the centuries, the "de-illusionment" of midlife need not be so harmful. True, one does not realize the Dream, but someday it will be realized for it is shared by many of all ages and continents. While Levinson recommends that those in midlife sublimate their "de-illusionment" by becoming mentors, those in ministry have a much greater strength in their faith that others share their vision and seek to bring it about. They ar not alone and that should diminish the regret that ministers might have about their personal limitations. The Dream is too large for anyone, and ministers are a part of a larger Whole. "And the gates of hell will not prevail against" the Kingdom.

6. Ministry, Midlife, and Maturity

Let us look again at Kao's model of differentiation, integration, and transcendence. Although he proposes that these processes occur at all three developmental levels, the physical, the mental, and the spiritual, it would seem that ministers, early in their lives, give primacy to the spiritual. Therefore, they would seem to have the characteristics of maturity by their transcendence once they commit themselves to a life of service to God. By that very commitment they should be autonomous and independent of the limits of career and role. It follows, therefore, that they should be less susceptible to those midlife crises described by Levinson.

However, by their very commitment to a caring profession, ministers belong to the group who are more susceptible to "burnout." Burnout, as we have proposed above, often precipitates the midlife crisis. The question arises: are ministers more or less susceptible to midlife crisis by virtue of their commitment and their susceptibility to burnout?

Let us look again at the distinction between *vocation* and *ministry*. In the case of ministers, vocation is a commitment of the self to a transcendent Being. Having committed themselves, they then choose the ministry or manner in which they will serve. When the service no longer seems appropriate, they can change it without abandoning their vocation which is derived from the identity and selfhood. However, if they have chosen the ministry for itself and not as an expression of their vocation,then when the ministry fails or ministers fail, they lose their identity and are susceptible to both burnout and midlife crisis.

7. Summary and Conclusions

This has been a series of reflections on maturity and midlife crisis. I hesitate to state anything dogmatically, but certain insights have emerged:

1. The role and personae of those in business do not imply some kind of authentic selfhood while the personae of ministers often do.

2. While those in business at midlife recognize the superficiality of their personae, those in ministry at midlife might have a different awareness. It is an awareness, less of the paucity of the persona and more of their failure to live up to the persona.

3. Thus, both groups are forced to accept their finitude and the limits of anything material. But those in business are forced to recognize the finitude of the persona as well as of their own physical strength, while those in ministry may well come to recognize a deeper finitude of their own selves in a recognition of their failure to fully take on the persona of authentic selfhood that is often thrust upon them by those to whom they minister.

4. The rewards sought by the two groups are also different. Those in business seek prestige, power, and accumulation of material possessions as signs of their success. While some in the ministry may seek power and prestige, avowedly they reject the pursuit of material possessions and for the most part have little visible signs of their "success."

5. The commitment of some in ministry is to a particular type of service. The commitment of others is to God expressed through service. The former may at midlife, or because of burnout, leave their ministry, whereas the later may change their ministry but keep their vocation. Those ministers who feel they have a vocation should, it would seem, better survive the vicissitudes of burnout and midlife.

6. Because the dream of those in ministry is not of personal origin, is larger than any personal success, and is shared by many of all

ages and continents, there can be great faith and hope because they are not alone in the vision and in working at its realization.

7. Finally, as Kao points out, transcendence of the here and now is a vital component of maturity for both groups. Thus, there are certain key differences between the midlife crises of those in business and those in ministry. Whether that can really make the crisis more painful or more bearable depends on the type of commitment of the minister. It behooves the community to discern the difference.

Notes

1. Daniel J. Levinson, *The Seasons of a Man's Life* (New York: Ballantine Books, 1978), p. 192.

2. Carl G. Jung, *Modern Man in Search of a Soul* (London: Routledge and Kegan Paul, 1933), p. 229.

3. Charles C. L. Kao, *Psychological and Religious Development: Maturity and Maturation* (Washington, DC: University Press of America, 1981), p. 14.

4. John A. Stanford, *Ministry Burnout* (New York: Paulist Press, 1982).

5. Jung, *Two Essays on Analytical Psychology* , trans. by R. F. C. Hull (Princeton, NJ: Princeton University Press, 1966), p. 194.

6. Robert Kegan, *The Evolving Self* (Cambridge, MA: Harvard University Press, 1982).

7. C. Maslach, *Burnout: The Cost of Caring* (Englewood Cliffs, NJ: Prentice-Hall, 1982), p. 3.

8. Jung, *The Undiscovered Self* (New York: New American Library, 1957), p.34.

9. Levinson, *The Seasons of a Man's Life*, pp. 246–247.

IX. Maturity, Spirituality, and Suffering

John L. Maes

One day I sat working in a quiet office on the night side of a mental hospital ward. All of the patients, save one, were in the dayroom along with the rest of the staff. I was writing reports on testing and patient interviews. The one patient, who was diagnosed as having a schizo-affective disorder, was confined to a seclusion room because of his state of agitation and the danger that he might hurt himself. During a long afternoon the silence was rent by incredible cries of pain and terror. After more than thirty years, I can still hear that patient crying out, "Oh, God, I'll give you anything if you make them stop shooting me."

This incident raises several questions about the nature of suffering. Since there was no one near the patient and he appeared to be in good physical health and since there was no furniture in the room, only a mattress on the floor, and he was not hurting himself, what caused the suffering? Is suffering simply a matter of perception? Is it an illusion? The patient's cries of agony were accompanied by obvious physiological signs of agitation. He was pacing, twisting his hand, with his face distorted. There were tears along with the cries. What is the relationship between perceived (mental) suffering and physical agony? This patient placed the dialogue about his suffering in the context of his relationship with God. Is all suffering spiritual?

I propose to respond to these questions under three general headings: "The Nature of Suffering," "Nuances of Suffering," and "Responses to Suffering." I will then conclude with a section titled "Suffering and Maturity" in which I will attempt to apply these understandings to a mature and positive approach to suffering.

1. The Nature of Suffering

The word *suffer* comes to us through French from the Latin. It combines two words—*sub* meaning *up* and *ferre* meaning *to bear: to bear up*. Its first meaning in Webster's is "to submit to or be forced to endure." Other supporting meanings are "to put up with, especially as inevitable or unavoidable; to endure death, pain, or distress; to sustain loss or damage; to be subject to disability or handicap."

Surprisingly, the definitions of sufferings listed above emphasize duration rather than intensity as the key to its meaning. Suffering is defined as bearing up, enduring, putting up with, sustaining, and being subject to. It is not defined by sharp pains or moments of intense terror. Suffering is a state rather than an incident. To prove that this can be seen in human experience and not simply as a construct, one need only go to the midway of a fair or carnival. There may be seen human beings delightedly frightening themselves by riding the monstrous inventions intended to provide brief periods of sheer terror.

Looking up the etymology of the word *suffering* has helped me to focus something that I have subliminally known for a long time. Suffering is closely related to the fundamental conditions of existence. Waiting and boredom, ordinary conditions of our human existence, lie at the basis for despair and, hence, suffering. We are aware that suicides mostly happen in attempts to terminate states of despair and not in response to short-term crises, however terrible. It is when the pain of terror, loneliness, or physical illness seems interminable that death appears to be a welcome relief.

> Let the day perish wherein I was born, and the night which said "A man-child is conceived"; Let that day be darkness! May God above not seek it, nor light shine upon it. . . . (Job 3:3–4).

> Why did I not die at birth, come from the womb, and expire? Why did the knees receive me? Or why the breasts that I should suck? For then I should have lain down and been quiet; I should have slept; then I should have been at rest, with kings and counselors of the earth who rebuilt ruins for themselves, or with princes who had gold, who filled their houses with silver (Job 3:11–15).

It is enduring the unbearable that is the real definition of suffering. Experiencing mutilation is terrible but living with it is worth. As all persons with handicapping conditions or long illnesses know, it is the boredom, limitation, and humiliation that are often the greatest pain. They are often more difficult to bear than physical suffering. Even the intensity of physical suffering is modulated by these psychological factors. Both the thresholds and intensity of pain are related to the elements of terror and despair that we discover in the writings of Kierkegaard and Becker.

Kierkegaard has made the point that physical suffering and even death are not the ultimate suffering. The ultimate suffering is despair. In this sense the loss of faith (or hope as it is variously expressed by these writers) is the real death. As Kierkegaard wrote in discussing the raising of Lazarus by Jesus:

> So then Lazarus was dead, and yet this sickness was not unto death; he was dead, and yet this sickness is not unto death. . . .

> For humanly speaking, death is by no means the last thing of all, hence it is only a little event within that which is all, an eternal life; and Christianity understood there is in death infinitely much more hope than merely humanly speaking there is when there not only is life but this life exhibits the fullest health and vigor.[1]

> Yet in another and still more definite sense despair is the sickness unto death. . . . the torment of despair is precisely this, not to be able to die. So it has much in common with the situation of the moribund when he lies and struggles with death, and cannot die.[2]

From these writings we might arrive at the following working definitions: pain is the immediate experience of intense physical, emotional, or spiritual discomfort. Because of the interactions of the human organism, all three of these elements may be present at the same time. Suffering is a state, rather than an incident, in which one is being forced to bear the unbearable. The unbearable may take the form of pain, terror, boredom, or loneliness. Despair is an attitude toward or belief about life that often interacts with suffering. It may appear to be the result of long periods of suffering, or it may intensify suffering by adding hopelessness to pain, loneliness, or boredom. As Kierkegaard has said, despair is the sickness unto death. Despair is the failure of hope, trust, and belief and as such is a spiritual attitude.

Those of us who have attended the bedsides of dying patients or parishioners are aware of the phenomenon pointed out by Kierkegaard, Kübler-Ross, and Becker in various ways; that is, that despair is worse than dying, and the terror of death is worse than death.[3]

Thus, we must arrive at the conclusion that suffering, although it may be caused by interpersonal or physical circumstances (as in the cases of pain or loneliness), is a highly subjective and ultimately spiritual experience. In this use of the word "spiritual," I mean relating to God, ultimate Spirit. We must also conclude that suffering is intimately related to our existential state as human beings and need not be caused by trauma, terror, or violence but can be caused by more mundane and ubiquitous situations such as boredom, loneliness, and waiting. We may also conclude that suffering, to some degree, is not uncommon to most human beings. It is only a small step to conclude that if despair often follows suffering, faith is its greatest antidote. Hence, it is easy to understand why religion and religious practice are so avidly sought by suffering persons. Why then do we not simply open our hearts to God and our minds to faith as an antidote to suffering?

From a psychological point of view, it is because the defenses that are built against suffering the daily slights of shyness, loneliness, humiliation, and feelings of inadequacy wrap us in layers of neurotic protection that keep us from being able to solve the common existential problems of monotony and boredom that lead to despair. As Becker has written, "Freud summed it up beautifully when he somewhere remarked that psychoanalysis cured the neurotic misery in order to introduce the patient to the common misery of life."[4]

Becker goes on to say,

> I like the way Perls conceived the neurotic structure as a thick edifice built of four layers. The first two layers are the everyday layers, the tactics that the child learns to get along in society by the facile use of words to win ready approval and to placate others and move them along with him: these are the glib, empty talk, "cliche," and role playing layers. Many people live out their lives never getting underneath them. The third layer is a stiff one to penetrate: it is the "impasse" that covers our feeling of being empty and lost, the very feeling that we try to banish in building up our character defenses. Underneath this layer is the fourth and most baffling one: the "death" or fear of death layer; and this, as we have seen, is the layer of our true and basic animal anxieties, the terror that we carry around in our secret heart. Only when we explode this fourth layer, says Perls, do we get to the layer of what we might call our "authentic self": what we really are without sham, without disguise, without defenses against fear.[5]

It seems to me that all three of these theorists: Freud, Perls, and Becker are saying that layers of "neurotic defenses" are built by most persons as a way to reduce the anxiety (psychic pain) experienced in response to slights, humiliations, terrors, and physical pain but by so doing them make it less possible to deal with the more existential causes that lie at the root of suffering such as the "denial of death" and the lack of faith. Becker has written a major treatise in explanation of the former and Kierkegaard has done the same for the latter.[16]

2. Nuances of Suffering

In this section of the paper I will attempt to deal with suffering as apprehension, suffering as perceived punishment, suffering as sorrow or repentance, and suffering as physical pain.

Suffering as Apprehension

The patient in the incident with which we began this discussion was in an acute anxiety state. Such a state is truly psychophysical in nature. There would have been measurable changes in the patient's autonomic reactions. Such conditions as elevated blood pressure, increased heart rate, altered vascular activity, changes in perspiration and salivation, altered digestive processes, and changes in the activity of the endocrine glands would all have been measurably present. It is such a state that translators of Freud called anxiety, from the German word *angst*.

But the subjective experience that accompanies such anxiety states is often labeled apprehension or, as Kierkegaard called it, dread. This word, which so often appears in his writings, was translated into English from the same word, *angst*. Thus, we have two famous observers looking at the same phenomenon from two different points of view, one starting with the physiological evidence and the other starting with the subjective feeling.

The sense of apprehension that is so often a part of anxiety attacks has been described in various ways, using such phrases as "the feeling that something awful is going to happen," "like a big black cloud hanging over my head," "a great big black hole ready to swallow me up." Robert White gave a memorable account of apprehension in one of his books. The patient is speaking:

> I stand looking out over the silent and vacant water, in the blue midday. I feel a sinking loneliness, an uneasy, a weird isolation. . . . Then on the tracks from Eagle Heights and the woods across the lake comes a freight-train, blowing its whistle. Instantaneously diffused premonitions become acute panic. The cabin of that locomotive feels right over my head as if about to engulf me. . . . I race back and forth on the embankment. I say to myself (and aloud): "It is half a mile across the lake—it can't touch you, it can't. . . . I smash a wooden box to pieces, board by board, against my knee to occupy myself against

121

panic. I am all the while mad with terror and despair
of being so far from home and parents.7

Persons who have experienced acute anxiety over a period of time
first attempt to find objective solutions to their problems. They may
seek advice, look for community support, attempt to form dependent
relationships, and use other sensible means to attempt to reduce
anxiety. But the intensity of the anxiety often drives them to adopt
neurotic defenses. While these may succeed in repressing the anxiety-
provoking material that is so painful to bear, all neurotic defenses are
expensive in terms of the energy they consume and the personal
freedom that must be surrendered in order to maintain them. All
neurotic defenses are expensive in terms of the energy they consume;
some more than others. For example, conversion hysterics must
surrender freedom of bodily movement; phobics must surrender freedom
of location, while obsessive persons must give enormous energy to the
time-consuming countermeasures that have become part of their life-
styles. Neuroses have only one useful purpose: the temporary reduction
of anxiety, which is accomplished at great cost to freedom of thought,
feelings, and action.

An even more serious problem with neurotic defenses is that they
seal off the intellectual and emotional material that lies at the base of
the real suffering in the lives of suffering persons. Neither the questions
arising from the fear of death nor the ultimate meaning of life can be
responded to openly and effectively. Of course, intense anxiety can be
reduced by the use of prescription drugs, but the underlying existential
questions and problems may remain unresolved and may lie in wait to
cause further suffering. Therapeutic means, such as drugs, supportive
therapy, even short periods of hospitalization, can be used to reduce
apprehension temporarily, giving an opportunity for the suffering
person to join a spiritual support community where ultimate questions
may be judiciously entertained and faith building may proceed.

Suffering as Punishment

An impedance to the overcoming of suffering has been the feeling,
deeply imbedded in human history, that suffering is the result of
wrongdoing and that the proper corrective is punishment This has been
conditioned into human beings through archaic childrearing practices
and through formal and folk theologies. In a history ranging from Job's
comforters to Calvinist theology, the wages of sin have been death. In
the individual psyche the wages of low self-esteem have been self-
punishment. Freud explained this phenomenon as the internalization of
negative parental evaluations and prohibitions directed toward the
developing child.8 He wrote, "The superego seems to have made a one-
sided selection, and to have chosen only the harshness and severity of

122

the parents. . . . while their loving care is not taken up and continued by it."

In more recent writings,[9] Kovacs and Beck have developed a cognitive theory of depression that states that many depressed persons have "negative tapes" in their minds that can be triggered by any failures or problems in the conduct of life. These negative tapes consist of a triad of somber views on the self, the world, and the future. It is as if a "button" of memory is pressed and the whole tape plays. This negative rumination is part of the suffering for many persons.

The presence of an archaic self-punitive superego is a heavy factor in maintaining the psychological side of suffering. When these negative self evaluations are reinforced by negative cognitive tapes that "play" at a moment's notice, they defy grace and become impediments to faith.

Surprisingly enough, punishment sometimes seems to help. This is especially true when considerable clinical depression is present. It has long been considered possible that the salutary effects of electroshock therapy for psychotic depressive patients may have as much to do with the sense of having been punished as with the temporary disconnection of neural connections in the brain. The archaic superego seems to "forgive" the person, thus alleviating depression.

The problem with punishment as an alleviation of feelings of guilt and worthlessness is that it may become part of a masochistic cycle that reinforces the sense of worthlessness. This may be true not only for depressed adults but also for normal children. The phrase "whom the Lord loveth he chasteneth"[10] when applied by the child to the lord or lady of the house can come to mean "you don't love me if you're not cruel to me."

We are learning from object relations theorists that consistent presence, modeling, and response with appropriate limits applied to the relationship is the developmental strategy that seems to help children develop constancy and self-esteem. It is also an effective therapeutic tool for helping persons with faulty character development. So grace in the form of acceptance, relationship, and honest mirroring appears to be triumphing over punishment as a form of treatment.

Well-trained spiritual directors have been effective in sorting through this complex layering with the persons whom they have assisted in their spiritual journey.

Suffering as Sorrow and Repentance

There are two causes for suffering that should be discussed briefly in this context. The first of these is the unavoidable suffering of grief. The loss of loved ones is an occasion for suffering that in the long term cannot be avoided. Sometimes the suffering of bereavement is so intense that it is difficult to differentiate from severe depression. A wide range of "abnormal" behaviors are normal during periods of intense grief. Grief reactions are often defended against by perceptual narrowing and blocking and by regression. In healthy personalities this serves to reduce complexity and allow the sufferer the space needed to recover integration. Occasionally the prodromal personality is fragile, and the regression results in a psychotic episode. In another context, I have discussed this subject using Freud's "Mourning and Melancholia" as a springboard for the understanding of the differences between depression and sorrow.[11]

A second cause for sorrow is guilt over one's sins. We have already discussed the false guilt and suffering created by poor superego training and the negative self images that result from this. But both Herbert Mowrer and Karl Menninger have pointed out that all guilt is not neurotic. Some of it is real because it relates to behaviors that were morally or ethically wrong. In such cases, suffering will not cease until the acts of contrition are used, and a sense of forgiveness is experienced. Such religious practices as confession and restitution can be very helpful, especially if they are set in the context of the religious community.

Suffering as Physical Pain

The complexities of this subject can be illustrated by introducing you to a person with whom I worked years ago. She was a petite, middle-aged woman who had been beautiful before her accident, which occurred during an operation when there was a brief cardiac arrest. As a result of this accident, there was considerable neurological damage. While she appeared mentally alert, her mobility was impaired. Her face was drawn, she was clinically depressed and was close to despair. The most painful symbol for all the agony of her condition was the catheter she was forced to wear. It was a source of continuous unhappiness. Not only did she have recurring infections from the use of the catheter, but it was a source of great humiliation. It represented the death of what she had been for so long—a vivacious and attractive woman. She was loaded up on medication and simply never felt well. In the course of therapy, she recovered enough energy and self-respect to see a new urologist who had come to the area in which she lived. The urologist used a new procedure that restored the use of her urethra obviating the need for the catheter. Seldom have I seen such a transformation in a person's attitude. She became cheerful, began to be more mobile since she could travel in a car again without fear of accident or without paraphernalia. Very soon after this transformation took place, gradual termination of therapy began.

This story illustrates the complex interaction between attitude and pain. The intensity of pain is generally not explainable in physiological terms alone; it is modulated by attitude, outlook, focus of attention, loneliness, and many other psychological variables. [There is a summary of theories of pain and a consideration of the ethnocultural, developmental, and personal factors interacting in the management of pain in an article by Edelstein in the *Israel Annals of Psychiatry and Related Disciplines* (Volume 12, 1974).] The response to suffering caused by physical pain is not simply to medicate. Pastoral care, whether provided by clergy or others involved in the care of the patient, can be an essential factor in understanding the psychological and spiritual elements of the suffering. Emotional and spiritual support may be as effective as medicine or may greatly enhance the effectiveness of medicine.

Considerable progress has been made in teaching patients to control or diminish the effects of pain through behavior therapy.

3. Responses to Suffering

Most persons do not have a stereotyped response to suffering. As I suggested earlier, it depends on a number of physical and emotional factors as well as life space circumstances. However, there are some variables that come to mind when one thinks of suffering. The most compelling of these is suffering and suicide. Killing oneself is a response to perceived suffering that runs across the entire range of wellness and pathology. It is our tendency to label suicides as emotionally disturbed, no matter how compelling may be the reasons for their behavior in terms of personal pain or unfavorable circumstances. When I am tempted to believe that only disturbed persons commit suicide, I always remember a parishioner I once had whom I shall call "Grandpa Woodling." Grandpa Woodling was in his eighties, long since retired. He lived by himself in a converted summer cottage near a beautiful lake. He was not isolated, having neighbors around him. He was universally loved and appreciated by the community. But one winter day Grandpa Woodling took his shotgun, went to the outhouse, held the muzzle to his stomach, and shot himself. As you might imagine, it was difficult for me, as his pastor, to explain to myself and his friends at his funeral what had happened.

I never knew what caused Grandpa Woodling to take his own life. He may have had bad news from his doctor. He may have decided that life was no longer worth the daily struggle it cost him. But of one thing I feel sure. By any conventional psychological measurements, he was sane.

Fortunately, most sufferers signal increasing despair before attempting suicide. In most cases, proper psychiatric and spiritual care will tide them over the self-destructive crisis, giving them an opportunity to work out new understandings of life.

Suicide is an extreme and statistically infrequent response to suffering. The more normative responses to suffering are as varied and widespread as are other human behaviors. However, I have dared to believe that most of them fall into four major patterns. See if these patterns make sense to you.

1. Surrender and Withdrawal

Some persons surrender themselves to the condition and mechanics of suffering. They narrow their frames of reference to disinclude vital, contemporary life events. Often such persons develop a personal litany that may take one of three forms. It may consist of complaints about the injustice of life, stressing their own unimportance and the perception that no one cares about their existence (especially such key figures as spouses, children, or clergy). The liturgy may take the form of an endless recitation of the medical bulletin of the day. This may include medications, bowel movements, and endless intimate nuances of physiological minutiae. Or it may take the form of memorializing the past. In this case, a ritual is developed wherein past relationships, triumphs, and occupations are remembered and embellished while the present possibilities are ignored.

When surrender and withdrawal become severe, the perceptual cues for maintaining social awareness in the contemporary situation may be reduced to the point where behavior becomes bizarre and inappropriate. It is apparent that while surrender and withdrawal may numb the awareness of suffering, they also make life joyless and empty. They reduce the possibility of meaningful involvement in relationships and destroy the possibility of hope, anticipation, and, yes, faith. Hope is like a teleological pull that gives meaning to all our lives, and its opposite is despair which Kierkegaard called the sickness unto death.

2. Counterdependency and Aggression

Another major pattern of response to suffering is counter-dependency and aggression. Many patients suffering from physical illness mobilize enough energy to become crotchety, reactive, or even hostile. Such counterdependency is usually more mobilizing to the personality than surrender or despair. However, it is alienating to other persons, tending to keep them at a distance. It is better than surrender and despair, but it is "immature." But sometimes the energy in this approach can be turned into redemptive effort. Mwalimi Imara tells the story of just such a patient:

> I was told that the patient, Miss Martin, was recovering from rather extensive abdominal surgery for cancer, and the more she healed the more demanding, abusive, foul mouthed and cantankerous she became. The Chaplain's office was called in as a last ditch effort to sweeten her up a little for the staff's sake until she was well enough to be sent to a nursing home.[12]

Through the patient daily ministry of pastoral care, this patient's story unfolded. She had been competent, successful, and increasingly lonely throughout her lifetime. When her serious (ultimately terminal) illness was discovered, she responded with incredible bitterness. But through careful spiritual direction and group work she was transformed into a woman who said to her group, "I have lived more in the past three months than I have during my whole life." Just like any major change in life, serious illness, with all of its suffering, is an opportunity to evaluate, reconsider, and start in a new direction.

3. Mastering Pain and Staying in Touch

"Bear as much as you can, use medication when you must, be as active as possible, and stay in touch with your friends."

That is the nature of my own heroic fantasy as I think of the suffering that surely awaits me. For those of us who intend to meet suffering in this manner, Freud is an heroic figure. One can see him in London in the late thirties refusing medication for cancer of the jaw so that he might complete the book he was writing. He chose his own *raison d'etre* over relief from pain. Meaning was more important to him than comfort.

Such an approach to suffering requires an intact ego and considerable courage. It requires contemporary involvement with the world and human relationships. Such a sufferer's activity focus can be on unfinished work: money management; friendships that require cards, letters, or phone calls; journals to be written or uncompleted manuscripts. All of these are good reasons to stay alive, as are blue skies, golden sunsets, and green plants.

Sufferers are not always haunted by illness. Sometimes they are haunted by old age. The painful loss of energy, colleagues, sexual vitality, employment, and interpersonal acuity cause great suffering. Relationships and contemporary involvement are the best antidotes for aging.

4. Acceptance and Faith

All of us who have worked in pastoral care have at least one person etched in our memories who simply worked through and rose above suffering. Such persons are uniquely at peace; uniquely open to others and uniquely honest. Let us return for a moment to Imara's chapter in *Death, the Final Stage of Growth*. Readers of the Kübler-Ross books are aware of the five stages of "growth" after one becomes aware of one's own impending death. These are denial, anger, bargaining, preparatory depression, and acceptance. Imara wrote,

127

Is it so hard to think of a dying patient as having a direction, as having a life plan? Moving and living our days with a sense of coherence is the dividend that the terminally ill patient receives for moving through the five stages. The stage of acceptance, the final stage in the transcendence of the patient is the time when the person's life becomes recentered and more self sufficient. This is quite often a very difficult reality to face for close friends and family of the patient.13

A person need not be involved in a terminal illness to learn to accept the reality of suffering, work out the meaning of life in this new and painful context, recast the sense of time in a new and eternal framework, and begin to live more presently and fully. Suffering, a cruel and unrelenting schoolmaster, can teach us to value the present moment, to savor beauty and friendships. It can help us shift our values away from competition and material success. There is a perfection of spirit and attitude to be derived through suffering.

This does not mean, however, that it is good per se to suffer. Suffering by itself does nothing but hurt. If suffering is the independent variable in our discussion, then the dependent variables are: the developmental history of the person; the prodromal ego structure and personality integration (or, in object relations terms, the completeness of the self); the presence or absence of a satisfying faith; and the existence (or non-existence) of a support community.

The more of these variables that are present, and the more completely developed each of them is, the greater the likelihood that suffering will enhance humanness, grace, and maturity in the person. But suffering like any crucible will reveal imperfections of all kinds. Thus, if the dependent variables are lacking, suffering can leave a person brittle, fragmented, and empty.

The four modes of response to suffering presented here are on a continuum with regard to maturity. Each successive mode, moving from surrender and withdrawal to acceptance and faith, requires a more mature response pattern and, in turn, creates more growth. Sometimes suffering persons, like Mwalimi's Miss Martin, move from one response level to another during the process of suffering. In her case, she took two giant steps; she moved from counter dependency and aggression to acceptance and faith.

In the last few sentences, I have slipped the word "maturity" into the text three times, so it is time to define it. Let us accept as our definition of maturity: a being fully grown or fully developed, rather than the more forbidding definition: a being perfect, complete, or ready.

Like Methodists of yore, we are "going on to perfection" but have not gotten there yet.

4. Suffering and Maturity

In this presentation I have defined and discussed the nature of suffering as ranging from physical pain to spiritual despair. I have responded to physical, psychophysical, psychological, and spiritual aspects of the sufferers' struggles. I have explored several nuances of suffering, including suffering as apprehension, punishment, sorrow and repentance, and physical pain. I have framed four major responses to suffering which I called surrender and withdrawal, counter dependency and aggression, mastering pain and staying in touch, and acceptance and faith.

Throughout the presentation I have tried to suggest ways in which friendships, pastoral care, and various therapeutic methods impinge upon the suffering person in positive ways.

Finally, I wish to share some thoughts that have become clear to me as I have worked with the relationships between maturity, spirituality, and suffering. I have discovered two important continua. The first is the continuum in human experience between adjusting to the short-term stresses and crises of life at the one end and the deeper, more continuous struggle with meaning and ultimate termination of life at the other end. I have come to believe that despair has more to do with the inability to resolve suffering about ultimate existential issues than it has to do with short-term crises such as illnesses, accidents, and fears—no matter how intense or dramatic. In fact, I believe that the inability to come to a satisfactory view of the ultimate meaning and purpose of life is at the root of despair for persons sick or well. I also believe that suicides occur because of this irresolution even tough they may have been triggered by traumatic events. As mentioned earlier, we are all layered with protective levels that are more or less "neurotic" in nature. These must be understood and penetrated in order to reach the real battleground of the sufferer, for the struggle is ultimately spiritual and can only be resolved by an understanding self-acceptance, world acceptance, and faith in the love and goodness of ultimate being.

The second of these continua is different from but related to the first. It is that which exists between the professions that attend to the symptoms of "sickness" and those that respond to the underlying existential concerns of human beings. On the one end is the medical profession and its growing coterie of handmaiden professions who care for the "sick." On the other end is the ancient profession of ministry (dating back through the priests and priestesses to the shamans) expanding itself along the continuum with such specialized ministries as hospital chaplaincies, pastoral care and counseling, and a newly psychologized approach to spiritual direction. The medical profession is becoming more "holistic," which is a euphemism for paying more attention to the spiritual side of human beings, while the ministry is learning more and more about the emotional and physiological facts of human existence. Perhaps the cultural segmenting, the battle over what professions own what parts of the human being, is about to end. In terms of personality development, segmenting (splitting) occurs as a result of anxiety. Institutionalized segmenting perpetuates the dilemma, making it harder for human beings to see themselves as being whole and complete. Clearly a team approach to suffering persons, with open dialogue about all aspects of the "patient's" experience, is indicated. Professional "secrets" have kept us from being effective too long.

For too long persons in ministry have not known how to deal with the "neurotic" layers of the personality, confusing existential struggles with psychopathology. But medical technology and professional psychotherapy have not understood the centrality of spiritual issues to the health and well being of their patients. They have often stopped short of a willingness to deal with questions of life's meaning, death, God, and faith—thus leaving the essential problem described so well by Kierkegaard and Becker untouched.

1. S. Kierkegaard, *Fear and Trembling: The Sickness Unto Death* (Garden City: Doubleday and Company, 1954), p. 144.

2. Ibid., p. 150.

3. See E. Kübler-Ross, ed., *Death, the Final Stage of Growth* (Englewood Cliffs, NJ: Prentice-Hall, 1975).

4. E. Becker, *The Denial of Death* (New York: Macmillan, 1973), p. 57.

5. Ibid.

6. Becker, op. cit.; Kierkegaard, op. cit.

7. Robert White, *The Abnormal Personality* (New York: Ronald Press, 1956), p. 209.

8. S. Freud, *New Introductory Lectures in Psychoanalysis* (New York: Norton, 1933), p. 89.

9. M. Kovacs and A. Beck, "Maladaptive Cognitive Structures in Depression," *American Journal of Psychiatry*, vol. 135 (May 1978).

10. Hebrews 12:6.

11. John L. Maes, "Grief and Loss in Fathering," chapter V in Edward V. Stein, ed., *Fathering: Fact or Fable* (Nashville: Abingdon Press, 1977).

12. E. Kübler-Ross, op. cit., p. 152.

13. Ibid., p. 159.

X. Maturity, Spirituality, and Ethical Decisions

Arthur J. Dyck

1. Introduction

Albert Speer once thought of himself as first and foremost an architect. That conception of himself did not prevent him, as the second most powerful man in Hitler's Third Reich, from approving and accepting the use of slave labor in Germany's factories and mines. For that, he was sentenced at Nuremburg to twenty years in prison. While at Spandau Prison, Speer wrote his memoirs. He speaks of how disturbed he was that

> I failed to read the physiognomy of the regime mirrored in the faces of those prisoners—the regime whose existence I was so obsessively trying to prolong during those weeks and months. I did not see any moral ground outside the prison system where I should have taken my stand. And sometimes I ask myself who this young man really was, this young man who has now become so alien to me, who walked through the workshops of the Linz steelworks or descended into the caverns of the Central Works twenty-five years ago.[1]

Speer tries to account for being then a self who is alien to him later, upon reflection: "Before 1944 I so rarely—in fact almost never—found the time to reflect about myself or my own activities, that I never gave my own existence a thought. Today in retrospect, I often have the feeling that something swept me off the ground at the time, wrenched me from all roots, and beamed a host of alien forces upon me."[2]

Speer's recognition that, during the height of his involvement in atrocities, he did not take time to reflect on himself, his own activities, and his own existence is a significant insight about the nature of moral experience. The psychologist Gordon Allport observed, "I experience 'ought' whenever I pause to relate a choice that lies before me to my ideal self-image."[3] We may fail to experience an 'ought' force because we do not pause and because we do not imagine how an ideal self would choose between the alternatives before us. Being too busy to reflect can lead to grossly unethical conduct, as Speer notes. But who was that self who could be too busy to reflect and too insensitive to see the vast human suffering he helped to perpetuate?

Speer, when he joined with Hitler, professed to have a dominant image of the self he should be—an architect in the glorious rebuilding of German cities. Clearly this self-image was insufficient to prevent Speer from violating well-known moral norms on an enormous scale. As a youthful architect, Speer's image of himself allowed him to regard some lives as unworthy of the protection and opportunities he coveted for his own life. We could say that he lacked the equal regard for himself and others, the impartiality, demanded by the Golden Rule. He did not love those prisoners of war as he loved himself.

Shall we say, then, that he was simply immature? Perhaps he was, but even if he were mature in the sense of being a fully qualified professional architect, even the best of his kind, he might still have an image of himself that would lead him to tolerate or actively condone a gross disregard for the preciousness of every human life. Maturity, or the full development of a particular ideal of selfhood, does not guarantee that human life will be deeply valued and that each human life will be equally valued. To see why this is so, I will examine competing ideals as to what are mature expressions of impartiality: first, with regard to the Golden Rule; secondly, with regard to the decision-making process. But I do not wish simply to illustrate that differing ideals of selfhood will yield differing ethical decisions. I wish to argue as well for an ideal of selfhood that recognizes our interdependence as human beings and that links us spiritually with the divine powers within and beyond as human agents. Mature expressions of spirituality take the form of cultivating love for all human beings as equally God's children and, as such, equally precious and equally loved by God. It is this ideal of selfhood for which I shall contend in the face of its currently strong competitors.

2. Ideals of Impartiality

1. Impartial Moral Norms—"The Golden Rule"

John Stuart Mill, defending utilitarianism against its assailants, invokes the Golden Rule as an ideal expression of impartiality:

> The happiness which forms the utilitarian standard of what is right in conduct is not the agent's own happiness, but that of all concerned; as, between his

own happiness and that of others, utilitarianism requires him to be as strictly impartial as a disinterested and benevolent spectator. In the golden rule of Jesus of Nazareth, we reach the complete spirit of the ethics of utility. To do as you would be done by, and to love your neighbor as yourself, constitute the ideal perfection of utilitarian morality.[4]

Mill's formula for deciding what is ethical is to assess which of two or more possible choices will result in the greatest happiness of the greatest number or the best balance of pleasure over pain. In calculating total amounts of happiness expected to result from each alternative action being contemplated, the pleasures and pains that may result for each person affected are to be counted.

I will not dwell on some of the widely recognized shortcomings of the utilitarian calculus, such as the fact that what would bring happiness to any one person or group may not be the action or policy that would lead to the happiness of the greatest number or to the best balance of pleasure over pain; individual rights or the rights of minorities are not predictably protected by this formula. Indeed, no moral norm has predictable weight in a calculus that considers all preferences and aversions, moral and nonmoral alike.

But it is Mill's conception of the self that renders the Golden Rule problematic as a standard of impartiality. When Mill asks what reason can be given for the desirability of general happiness—the aim of the utilitarian calculus—the only reason is that each person "desires his own happiness."[5] Mill offers no reason why people should desire the happiness of others as much as they do happiness for themselves; nor even why they would find it desirable to count each person as one.

However, even if we grant that people do seek the happiness for others that they seek for themselves, happiness as a standard does not distinguish desires that are ethical from those that are not. And, what is more, people differ markedly with regard to what brings them happiness; one's person's desire may be another person's aversion. If then the biblical version of the Golden Rule represents "the complete spirit of the ethics of utility" as Mill understands it, that rule is subject to these same two criticisms. Indeed these criticisms of the Golden Rule are duly discussed by the contemporary philosopher Alan Gewirth.[6] He notes that in the biblical version of the Golden Rule, "Whatever you wish that men would do to you, do so to them,"[7] the Greek word *thelete* (translated "wish") has a very general desiderative sense. For Gewirth this means that what agents wish for themselves may not accord with how recipients might wish to be treated. He cites Bernard Shaw's famous quip, "Do not do unto others as you would that they should do unto you. Their tastes may not be the same."[8] Thus, we have the unfortunate result that, for example, persons who like to quarrel or fight may think themselves authorized by the Golden Rule to engage others in these ways, much to the dismay of those on the receiving end.

To illustrate the second difficulty of a rule based on what we may wish for ourselves, Gewirth refers to the philosopher Henry Sidgwick's observation that "one might wish for another's cooperation in sin and be willing to reciprocate it."[9] And so, for example, someone who bribes a corrupt policeman may be acting toward the policeman as he wishes others would behave toward him.

Gewirth, after considerable further discussion, concludes quite correctly, "If the Golden Rule is to be saved, then, its criterion of rightness must be separated from the contingency and potential arbitrariness which attaches to desires taken without qualification."[10] Gewirth's solution is to limit the Golden Rule to *rational* desires for oneself and others and to use rational in a morally neutral, strictly logical sense. How does he argue his case for a so-called Rational Golden Rule?

Gewirth begins by pointing out that each of us is an actual and prospective agent, seeking to realize certain aims and purposes; each of us as agent wants to attain things we regard as good. There are certain conditions necessary to attaining anything we require as good, and hence, these are also seen as goods. They consist in: freedom to control and initiate goal-directed behavior without interference; and the well-being—life itself—to enable goal setting and achievement. Freedom and well-being, Gewirth regards as generic rights; they are necessary and generic conditions of our purposive activity. It is contradictory to deny that one has such rights. To do so is, on the one hand, to affirm that freedom an well-being are necessary goods as the conditions of my acting for the sake of any other goods and, on the other hand, to affirm that people may be permitted to stop me from having these necessary goods. And to be rationally consistent, agents must follow the Golden Rule, as now reformulated: "Act in accord with the generic rights of your recipients as well as of yourself."[11] For, logically, every person who is a purposive agent has these same rights and to deny any purposive agent such rights is to deny them for oneself as a purposive agent. The Golden Rule, as Gewirth has formulated it, is a call for rational consistency, the content of which is to ask each agent to refrain from coercing and harming other persons and to "preserve a rationally grounded mutuality or equality between his generic rights and those of his recipients."[12]

In spelling out the content of the right to well-being enjoined in the Golden Rule, Gewirth includes the following prohibitions: interference with basic goods through killing and physical assault (except in self-defense), lying, stealing, and promise breaking. These are prohibited because they diminish one's level of purpose-fulfillment.

Also required by the Golden Rule are positive actions where inaction would cause or permit the occurrence of basic harms, and also parental care and social arrangements for raising levels of purpose-fulfillment, those of children, for example.

We see, then, in Gewirth something like an affirmation and restatement of the Mosaic Covenant, at least insofar as it applies to the "Second Table of the Law" or "neighbor love." Insofar as Gewirth sticks to what is logically requisite for purposive action, he remains on a parallel with what biblical norms require of us. This makes sense from the biblical perspective of Judaism and Christianity: the law is written on our hearts; everything is expected to be able to discern right from wrong. However, Gewirth's case for moral restraints is based upon the desires of autonomous individuals to act freely for their own purposes, without interference from others. In the end, individuals reign supreme over their own lives, to dispose of them as they please. There is no higher power to which they are beholden. In the last analysis, they are not beholden to others, either. We see this in the way in which he justifies suicide. Gewirth asserts that agents act in accord with their own generic rights by maintaining their own freedom and well-being in ways that avoid any interference from other persons to which they do not consent. The would-be suicide is no exception, Gewirth argues.[13] Such individuals seek to be in control of their behavior and to prevent others from interfering with their freedom and well-being without their consent. But do they not by committing suicide relinquish irrevocably both freedom and well-being?

With regard to the right to well-being, Gewirth contends that there are circumstances when the act of suicide is purely an act of harming the one who does it. To qualify as such, the persons committing suicide must have no one dependent on them for economic or other support.

What about the freedom of a would-be suicide? Do not others have a responsibility to rescue them and, hence, to interfere with their freedom? Gewirth suggests that in cases of a would-be suicide, other persons should express concern to such individuals over the contemplated act. Secondly, persons should interfere with the project temporarily to test whether it is a voluntary undertaking. However, the third step is to discontinue interference, if and when the conditions for voluntariness have been met. Gewirth argues that if one interfered with the would-be suicide's action, then that individual will not be able to act; and if that individual does carry out the act of self-destruction, the ability to act is also ended. It follows, for Gewirth, that there is, in such an instance, no justification for interference with freedom. You should not be the one who ends a person's freedom. Those who commit suicide voluntarily do not violate their own generic rights, says Gewirth, since they do not allow other persons to interfere with their freedom of well-being without their consent.

But if I am morally forbidden to prevent individuals from committing suicide, what happens to my "duty to rescue," a duty Gewirth has strongly endorsed? Clearly, Gewirth has qualified the duty to rescue: rescue only those who consent to it.

Suppose someone, Cal, who meets Gewirth's criteria for noninterference from others, has just turned on the gas jets in his locked apartment for the purpose of committing suicide. Gewirth, who approves of what Cal is doing, has said goodbye to him and is about to leave for home when he notices me breaking the basement window. Gewirth grabs me and demands to know what I am doing. I explain that I am going to turn off the gas for Cal's apartment. I know from a neighbor's call what Cal is trying to do, and I am going to try to save his life. What, now, should Gewirth do? If he permits me to shut off the gas, he has, in effect, deprived Cal of his right to noninterference. (I am assuming that Gewirth has the karate skills to stop me with a minimum of force and that he risks nothing, except a few moments of time, for this purpose). If, however, he does forcibly stop me, and it would take force, he has deprived me of the freedom to carry out what I consider to be a strict moral responsibility. Whose freedom should be respected in this instance? Frankly, I am not certain what Gewirth would do, nor do I find guidance from his thinking on rights and duties as to what he should do. I would expect Gewirth to try to persuade me not to turn off the gas, but why should I listen until I have made certain that, for the time being, Cal would continue to live and would enjoy the freedom to consider again the value of his life. After all, in this case, the infringement of Cal's freedom is temporary; its purpose is like any other rescue, namely to save his life. The complexity of determining when people with suicidal tendencies are to be hospitalized or otherwise recommended for treatment is not at issue in this example. The issue under discussion is that, for many individuals, the duty to rescue includes the prevention of death from suicide, even suicides in some sense voluntarily chosen and intended to harm no one. To prevent a suicide is, after all, to prevent a killing and save a life.

So far then, Gewirth's own thinking has generated certain questions he has not explicitly addressed nor resolved, given his premises. First of all, Gewirth gives us no explicit basis for choosing between Cal's freedom to commit suicide and anyone's perceived responsibility to prevent it episodically whenever possible. If Gewirth chooses forcibly to block someone's efforts to stop Cal's suicide, the loss of freedom of the person blocked, in cases of this kind, is permanent: one can never again prevent Cal's death. (The example assumes that Cal will die unless the gas jets are turned off by someone other than Cal.) Secondly, why should not Gewirth consider the freedom of all agents in this example as equal? All agents require freedom to carry out their purposes, and, in this example, these are aimed at preserving life, which is among what Gewirth calls "genuine rights." Strictly, then, is there any logical reason for Gewirth, given his own premises, to prefer Cal's suicide, someone's prevention of it, or someone's prevention of interference with Cal's actions?

Gewirth could well accuse me of a strange inability to grasp his thinking: "Have you forgotten," he might say, "that individuals have a right to freedom when they are engaged in activity that harms no one but themselves? If you can show that Cal is harming someone other than Cal, then you have a duty to rescue him, but otherwise you deny his right to freedom, provided, of course, he is acting voluntarily."

I think I am beginning to see why Gewirth and I are talking past one another. We have a different view of the relations individuals have a responsibility to cultivate toward others, and toward themselves. Gewirth believes that Cal can achieve a detachment from all other persons, such that no one *should* be harmed by his death. But Cal is powerless to achieve a self-inflicted death that harms no one if I, or anyone else, wish him to live, something he cannot predictably suppress in me or others. Gewirth has to show that my desire to see Cal live is morally irresponsible, given Cal's desire to detach himself from all relations to others. Gewirth does not recognize a moral responsibility to seek that one's own life and the lives of others continue to their natural end. Nor does Gewirth recognize a responsibility to improve one's moral character as long as it is possible to strive to do so. Autonomy in the form of detachment has become an absolute right for Gewirth, including as it does an approval of suicide, the approval of seeking permanent detachment even from one's own self as a living being.

What Gewirth is justifying is not a heroic act or an act of martyrdom in which a person gives up life to save the lives of others— for example, smothering a bomb about to explode and thereby saving the lives of one's comrades or children. Gewirth is precisely justifying taking one's life to serve one's own purposes and being able to do so ethically because one has no responsibilities to anyone else and presumably none to any other being but oneself. This is a far cry from the context in which the Golden Rule occurs in the New Testament portion of the Christian Bible.

In Matthew, chapter 7, the Golden Rule is not only linked to the law and the prophets, and so to the prohibitions Gewirth also notes in part, but also to the knowledge we have of what to expect in the way of good gifts from God. As parents, even though we are evil, we know enough to meet the needs of our children; we do not give them stones, for example, when bread is being asked for. In the light of our ability to know what is good, rather than evil, to give to our children, we are told in verse 11 that our "Father who is in heaven" will—much more "give good things to those who ask him." And then verse 12 follows with,

"So whatever you wish that men would do to you, do so to them; for this is the law of the prophets." The context for our wishing is that of being children of God, wishing from God, our parent, what is good. And the good things we can expect from God and wish from others are what we seek to provide for others. What we wish for ourselves and others are those good things that a perfect parent—a parent who is not at all evil—would bestow on us as children.

In the biblical version of the Golden Rule, it is not the wishes of an ideally autonomous, detached individual that provide the standard of our behavior toward ourselves and others; rather it is the wishes of ideally loving parents in relation to their children that provide the standard. Ironically, Gewirth's own method of reasoning should have led him in this direction.

Gewirth takes autonomous individuals as his starting point and considers rights to be the necessary conditions for their actions. But he never considers what is necessary for there to be agents at all, and given what is necessary, no agent is ever autonomous in the sense of being actually or potentially responsible to no one.

To begin with, as human agents we exist only because other human agents cooperated to conceive, nurture, love, and instruct us and to prevent and rectify potential and actual harm to us. This original gift of life is daily reaffirmed and rendered possible by the responsible behavior of all those who refrain from killing us, who protect us from those who would harm us, and who stand ready to save our lives whenever it is necessary and possible. Even the remotest hermit is not without a history of parental love, for without love in the form of some attention and fondling, no human will live and grow in infancy; food is not sufficient. And no hermit can live alone and have the space and resources to do so unless others permit it. Hermits are also here at everyone's mercy and, like others, share the responsibility to ask themselves how to use the gift of life in ways that honor and express gratitude to those who nurtured them, both family members and that larger protective and sustaining community and communities. At the very least, one may reasonably exact from hermits that they value their lives to some degree commensurate with the restraint, protection, and institutional aid, such as health facilities, fire-fighting equipment, and police forces, with which we in the surrounding community envelop them. When someone commits suicide, it is a direct repudiation of all past and present responsibilities for that life assumed by a number of individuals, groups, and social institutions. In turn, to ask all those persons to experience no harm whatsoever to their well-being is itself a repudiation of the attachments, the moral bonds that make community possible. However devoid of friends, relatives, and attachments Cal manages to become in his own mind, when Cal commits suicide, Gewirth has given no substantive reason to obligate us to be unharmed

140

by it: if we think we, or someone else, might have prevented it, that will be discouraging—it could even be utterly depressing; if we think that Cal had more to live for than we do, his suicide could push us in the same direction. This happens! If we think that our efforts on behalf of life are already too onerous, each suicide weakens our fading resolve and the upkeep of the resources necessary to sustain and protect others. But quite apart from these contingent relations to Cal's death by suicide, there is the sheer responsibility all of us have to prevent someone like Cal from breaking the parental and community bonds expressed in the wishes and efforts to have him live and to have everyone else, ourselves included, live as well.

Gewirth, like so many others, has not been very thorough in his investigation of the necessary conditions of individual agency; like so many of his contemporaries and predecessors, he has not taken into account the agent's dependence upon communities, and the actions that made, and make, them possible. Life is, to be sure, a necessary good for actual and prospective agents. But life as a right cannot simply be attained by the claims of individual agents on others; life as a right cannot simply be attained by claims on others to avoid killing, to rescue and heal, and to provide legal protection and enforcement agencies; the right to life cannot simply come to be as a claim of an individual agent at all. For human life to be, survive, and flourish there must be, as necessary requisites, some procreation, some nurture, and some sharing of time, resources, and energy and restraint against killing. Every living human being lives on the basis of these activities on the part of others. The right to life, from this perspective, is the expectation that the relationships (responsibilities) requisite (universally necessary) for life to come to be and to be sustained will apply to every individual human being as such: I have a natural right to life if, and only if, everyone naturally has the ability to recognize, and the will to take on, responsibility for what will perpetuate human life and the communities needed for that purpose. Rights, then, are natural expectations regarding natural responsibilities. Rights and responsibilities are moral insofar as they are universally and necessarily requisites of community, and insofar as these are seen as such from some specific impartial point of view. Rights become claims, as well as expectations, when our expectations that someone act responsibly are asserted. Rights, then, are rendered actual by the responsible, caring actions that make communities, cooperative behavior, and our very lives possible. Sometimes we use coercive powers of law, or of police enforcement, for example, to assert or try more nearly to assure a right, such as our right not to be the target of an intentional homicidal project.

I have spoken of natural rights based on natural responsibilities. The word *natural* here does not preclude the presence of the divine.

141

Before there are procreative, nurturant, and otherwise caring human selves, there are those power that make all that activity possible and render it actual, and that continue to work in that direction. Before there are genes, there are the forces that make the selves and communities possible for the transmission, nurture, and protection of those genes. The existence of genes and their limited altruism in seeking to perpetuate themselves in others does not explain *that* they are nor what moves them. You cannot obtain something from nothing. Before we favored life by procreating, the forces making that possible favored life enough to actualize it. Those of us open to the logical necessity of all this, and who feel awe and gratitude before these powerful, eternal forces, consider ourselves to be religious and speak of God, finding that a loving force, favoring individual life, seems best understood on the analogy of a superperson of some kind.

Given the acknowledgment of God as an absolute requisite of community, someone like Calvin regarded our powers to recognize and live in accord with the Mosaic Covenant as that which identifies us as made in the image of God.

Why does Gewirth fail to see that to identify the requisites of individual action logically entails the requisites of community as we have described them? Of course I do not know all the reasons, but the one close at hand is his adherence to a particular conception of the self as an autonomous actor.

In the final analysis, Gewirth equates rational autonomy with an absolute right not to be interfered with. His notion of freedom is essentially the one we find in Mill and commonly in modern rights theorists: if it were not, then surely Gewirth would have to think of suicide as the surrender of the right to freedom rather than an expression of it.

Gewirth is advocating detachment from human relations in one of its most extreme forms and depicting it as a necessary good and as a right. Gilligan's research and theory is explicitly a critique of this common tendency in Gewirth and other modern analysts of rights. From Gilligan's perspective, the ideal of becoming evermore free of interdependent relations is a false view of human moral development. It condones a failure to cultivate or sustain caring relationships, and hence, also condones the suffering or moral nihilism that may be induced in individuals affected by such failures. Gewirth's argument for the right to commit suicide presupposes the neglect or rejection of any continuous responsibility to cultivate and sustain human relationships.

Gewirth has rendered the right to life without substance. What value life has is the value I give it as an autonomous agent. Though logically I should value life in myself and others up to the moment of accomplishing my voluntary purposes even in seeking death, since I need life for that also, nevertheless, it is the case that if I no longer value my life enough to sustain it, why should I value anyone else's any more than I do my own? Certainly it is unclear why I should on Gewirth's premises. If killing myself is somehow better than living, why should it not be so for people I regard as similarly situated? Indeed, this argument is in the literature. The Presidential Commission on Bioethics speaks of considering the net benefit of the life for someone seriously ill in order to decide for them whether it should be sustained.[14] Of course they say those who are competent should make just such a determination for themselves. The value of life is what I, the individual agent, decide it to be. No question is raised by the commission about how my life may be of value to others nor of how my life should be valued by others, regardless of how I value it.

In the end, Gewirth has equated the right of freedom with the right to individual autonomy as a form of separation. But autonomy does not have to take the form of severed relationships. Insofar as autonomy is a capacity and power to make choices, it may be expressed in ways that foster attachment and human relationships. Consider friendship. As Aristotle noted, friends are those who wish for their friend what they wish for themselves; one thing we wish for our friends is that they exist.[15] To die without harming anyone else is to die without friends; to seek a death in which no one is harmed is to seek to be without friends. We can function autonomously, then, as those who recognize and favor our interdependence. We can and do choose to be interdependent. We do procreate, nurture, and protect life. The biologist E. O. Wilson regards any contribution made to the survival of the species as an expression of the highest ethic.[16] Christians have long regarded procreation and nurture as human participation in God's loving intentions for us and for life in this world. That some churches have issued statements that completely individualize procreative decisions is very much a sign of the times; the tendency to equate autonomy with separation from others is strong and pervasive.[17]

And so the equal value of life is logically and theologically a requisite condition for us not only to achieve our purposes as moral agents, but also to come into existence and develop as moral agents. But our interdependent efforts on behalf of life are complicated because our efforts to prevent harm to one another and to protect life cannot be done without inflicting harm and causing suffering. Medical interventions, when justified at all, as for example in removals of diseased organs, such as the appendix, cause suffering, however temporary, and subject persons to risk of death.

But what are we to do when, to the best of our knowledge, an intended benefit in the way of life sustenance is a source of additional harm or suffering but does not remove a lethal condition and the suffering that accompanies it? Is the failure to extend life to a dying person morally the same as killing? If so, it would be killing akin to murder, and not akin to self-defense or other forms of protecting human lives against aggression that are not judged to be murder, at least not generally.

Some have argued that the failure to sustain a person's life is morally no different from an intentional act to kill or murder that person. Rachels, a philosopher, has argued for this position.[18] He contends that there is no difference between deliberately drowning someone in a tub of water and making it look like an accident and deliberately doing nothing while someone, accidentally knocked unconscious, drowns in a tub of water. He supposes, of course, that the deaths are desired both by the one who actively drowns someone and by the one who refuses to help the drowning person, in circumstances where such aid could obviously be given without risk to anyone.

Now Rachels is right that failing to save life where it can be saved and removed from the life-threatening situation is morally the same as intentional killing of an innocent person. However, this example does not clearly or necessarily apply to the situations that obtain when persons are dying and no remedy exists to remove the cause of death.

Reflect with me on a situation that is like those faced in terminal illness by health care professionals and their patients. Think of someone stranded on a rock in the midst of a very remote wilderness, a rock surrounded by rapidly rising floodwaters. Once these swift and powerful waters reach the person on this slippery rock, that person will be carried to his doom down a very steep waterfall. There is no question this person is going to die. I am on the shore, but I can't rescue the person. I don't have a long rope, and I can't possibly step in the water without being carried away myself. There is no one around. So there is nothing I can do.

Now, if I have a rifle and I am a good marksman, and if this person is in pain, I could shoot him and put him out of his misery. I could do that, but even if asked, that would be killing akin to murder morally and legally. I would be the agent of that person's death.

However, if that person asked to be shot with a tranquilizing drug, I would not be responsible for his death. I would be responsible for his being out of it, but not for his death.

Suppose, however, that this person is on a jagged rock that is higher and wants to get to a lower rock that is smoother and more comfortable. If I have a short rope to help the person reach that smooth rock, he could ask me for that rope. Now, if I give him that rope, it won't rescue him, but it will help this person to lower himself to the smoother rock. That person will die sooner rather than later, but that person will be more comfortable and that is what the person wants. If I give that person the rope and he dies sooner rather than later, have I killed him? I would argue that I have not. What has happened is that I have agreed to help this person live in greater comfort. He will die anyway, but he wants to live in greater comfort, and I have acceded to his wish.

What I have done is not different morally from certain decisions we make all the time. When we are not patients, are constantly deciding, sometimes without even knowing it, that we will die sooner rather than later, and we have that freedom. Some people smoke, some people talk too much, some travel too much, and some work too hard. What do we mean by working too hard? We mean so hard they risk shortening their lives. But if what they do is important, we may even praise them or encourage them to work harder. Some of us will even agree that someone should work too hard if we think, for example, that the whole nation will be safer as a result.

With competent persons who are seriously ill, we can negotiate. We can encourage them to live where there is hope; we can do what makes them comfortable where no treatment will save their lives. But when patients are incompetent what process of decision-making will help assure fidelity to an ideal of impartiality?

2. Ideals of Impartial Decision-Making

The decision-making process in both Mill and Gewirth is informed by the notion of an ideally rational individual self. In Mill, the "Ideal Spectator," the person most informed and experienced, is the model of impartiality for calculating the best balance of pleasure over pain. This tends to suggest a process of becoming experts as individuals and, in some circumstances, relying on experts. This was Mill's view of himself as an elected public official; he ran for office on the condition that he did not have to represent the views of those who would and did elect him to parliament. Gewirth also links decision-making to what individuals do in their own heads. Ideally what they do is informed by sheer logic and no other consideration. But this divorce between cognition and feeling, and this separation from others in decision-making, will not do.

Harvard philosopher Roderick Firth has proposed an ideal observer theory, in the form of an ideal, impartial self, to describe the basis for moral decision-making.[19] This account includes sensitivity to how it is for others. Ideal conditions for moral decision-making would be achieved by someone who is omniscient, with regard to nonmoral facts, omnipercipient—that is, able vividly to imagine how it is for everyone affected by a contemplated action—and impartial—that is, uninfluenced by particular passions and interests. This theory suggests relevant criteria for moral decision-making quite like certain conceptions of God as an ideal moral judge, but yet different in important, problematic ways.

The ideal observer theory, unlike Christian conceptions of God, is not concretely helpful in suggesting processes for improving our ability

145

to perceive and do what is morally required of us. Omnipercipience is not only something no human being can attain, but it describes an attainment, not a process, of attaining. Since we are not perfectly able to vividly imagine how others are affected by our actions, we need to know how to become better at it; and certainly, to the extent that we wish to be moral, we also do not wish to become worse. Our Christian account of God does describe some characteristics of a perfect moral judge which are, at the same time, processes in which we as human beings can and do participate.

God is portrayed as loving particular human beings, both as creating them and, in human form, going to the Cross for them. And this love is for all human beings—all children of God and all bearing God's image. Now as David Davis has pointed out in his book *The Problem of Slavery in Western Culture*, those beliefs were powerfully operative in defeating slavery and the slave trade; it was not philosophical ideas held at the door or previously that helped defeat slavery. You neither will have the will nor the ability to imagine what someone else is experiencing unless you love him or her. And a person's life has no value for you if you do not love him or her, nor if you do not love yourself. We are to love our neighbors as ourselves, are we not?

Gewirth has utterly struck out in this regard. Where is love for life in Gewirth? Where is the love that wishes others into being and wishes to be there for them, providing the nurture and protection every human being needs to live? The responsibilities we take on out of love for our children, and the responsibilities they take on for us as their parents, never cease—unless love ceases.

Love for all particular persons obviously guides our moral sensitivities in other kinds of relations and processes. I have time only for a few examples. Slowly, but finally, we have recognized the importance of positive human sympathy as a cognitive factor in trying to obtain justice in our courts. We have learned that blacks should not be judged by all white juries; that females should not be judged by all male juries, particularly in rape cases. Love for all particular persons means black presence, female presence, as well as white and male presence, in every significant sector of our communities, whether economic, cultural, familial, educational, political, or religious.

Returning now to the case for the dying incompetent, what should an impartial decision-making process look like? I will take as an example someone inflicted with Alzheimer's disease, a fatal, incurable ailment that gradually robs persons of their mental abilities.

When it comes to the facts, health professionals play a key role. Their integrity and skill has to be relied upon, largely, if not exclusively, to know whether someone has Alzheimer's disease or some other irreversible, fatal disease, as the problems of how to care for persons increasingly unable to care, or care well, for themselves begin to emerge or mount. What medications best relieve pain, what nourishment is needed, what may improve certain functions, what may prolong life, and the risks to health and well-being of each and all of these measures will again require reliance on expert medical judgment to a very high degree, if not entirely. In such medical judgments, I include physicians, nurses, and other staff who are in close attendance of those committed to their care. In all of this, the changing responses of the incompetent, beyond the measurable physical and vital signs, should not be overlooked. That is why the facts of behavior seen by family members or close friends, and by caretakers in daily contact with patients, are to be taken seriously. Individual care for incompetents requires information from everyone concerned and in close contact with them.

As we think of vividly imagining how everyone is affected by the care being given to incompetents, the point about being in touch with every person significant to the lives of incompetent patients becomes even more urgent. Health professionals have a special responsibility to walk a tightrope between resisting premature requests, from weary relatives or staff, to stop all life-prolonging efforts and applying overzealous efforts up to the last breath of life. Because life is a moral requisite of community and because relatives and friends do not want to be seen as abandoning a loved one, situations in which health professionals are uncertain about what is best should be resolved in favor of extending life where possible. The same policy should apply where friends or relatives strongly urge it. They will have to live with these decisions, in a way that health professionals do not, after the death of their loved ones. However, despite a philosophy biased toward sustaining life, not all circumstances call for continuing to do so for dying incompetent patients. Impartiality demands a more nuanced care.

Impartiality means, among other things, that the right to life is equally a right for all human beings, and by itself, incompetence should not diminish that right. At the same time, competent human beings have the right to refuse medical treatment, and as dying persons to choose comfort, even if that means foregoing some chance to live somewhat longer. Some incompetent persons, therefore, may be among those who would prefer being more comfortable or less subject to the side effects of certain types of life-supporting technology or medication. But how should we determine which incompetent individuals belong to this group?

Some would argue that relatives, an appointed guardian, or a living will made out while competent take care of the matter. But in a slowly progressing, incurable disease such as Alzheimer's, there are various points at which judgments will need to be made as to whether the next life-sustaining effort, for example, inserting a gastrostomy tube, is the

147

one the dying patient would like to avoid. How close is death? What joys or satisfactions, however primitive, remain to a given patient? These judgments are relevant and cannot be made impartially from simply one perspective, whether that of a relative, a close friend, a guardian, an attending physician, or a nurse. Some consensus about how the patient, stoutly refusing food, might best be served is surely needed. All those who care will have to live with that death, and any one of the caretakers, family, or friends may not think the time has come, given their observations of that patient's refusing food. Any individual concerned with a dying patient as family, close friend, or caretaker should be able to insist upon continued life sustenance. Life is a shared moral value and should always receive preference over less than totally informed judgments about what medical interventions a patient may or may not find desirable. Where there is an unresolvable conflict over care, the courts are there as a last resort. Presumably, they are there to protect life and to make impartial judgments about fairness, by giving everyone the care considered professionally standard for the case in question.

What I have argued for, then, is that a decision for comfort only, such as withholding nutrition, something which should occur only when death is imminent, requires a consensus of those lovingly caring for a dying incompetent patient. Even one voice on behalf of life-sustenance should suffice in the face of such uncertain medical and ethical judgments.

3. Summary

In this essay, I have illustrated some ways in which concepts of ideal selfhood affect ethical decisions and decision-making. I have concentrated on certain competing conceptions of impartiality and what these imply with respect to how much life is valued. I have argued for an ideal of impartiality that views the self as interdependent and spiritual. The spiritual quality for which I argued is that of seeing ourselves and others as God's offspring, and as equally loved by God. A mature expression of this spiritual quality gives substance to the Golden Rule and reflects its spirit. Mature expression of this spiritual quality treats the life and agency of each individual as equally precious. While an architect for Hitler, presiding over enslaved laborers, Albert Speer did not exhibit this quality.

Notes

1. Albert Speer, *Inside the Third Reich* (New York: Avon Books, 1970), p. 480. I have taken these citations of Speer from James W. Fowler, *Stages of Faith* (New York: Harper & Row, 1982).

2. Ibid., p. 64.

3. Gordon W. Allport, *Becoming* (New Haven: Yale University Press, 1955), p. 73.

4. John Stuart Mill, "Utilitarianism," in *The Philosophy of John Stuart Mill,* Marshall Cohen, ed. (New York: The Modern Library, 1961), p.342.

5. Ibid., p. 363.

6. Alan Gewirth, *Human Rights* (Chicago: The University of Chicago Press, 1982).

7. Ibid., p. 132.

8. Ibid., p. 128.

9. Ibid., p. 128.

10. Ibid., p. 132.

11. Ibid., p. 134.

12. Ibid., p. 138.

13. Gewirth, *Reason and Morality* (Chicago: The University of Chicago Press, 1982), pp. 136–137.

14. President's Commission for the Study of Ethical Problems in Medicine and Behavioral Research, *Deciding to Forego Life-Sustaining Treatment* (Washington: U.S. Government Printing Office, 1983).

15. Aristotle, *Nicomachean Ethics,* Book IX, ch. 4.

16. Edward O. Wilson, *Biophilia* (Cambridge: Harvard University Press, 1984), p. 121.

17. Valerie DeMarinis and Arthur Dyck, "Procreation," in *The Westminster Dictionary of Christian Ethics*, James F. Childress and John Macquarrie, eds. (Philadelphia: Westminster Press, 1986), pp. 499–502.

18. James Rachels, "Active and Passive Euthanasia, *New England Journal of Medicine* 292:78 (1975).

19. Roderick Firth, "Ethical Absolutism and the Ideal Observer," *Phil. and Phen. Research* 12 (March 1952).

Part III

Maturity and Meaningful Ministry

XI. Maturity in Pastoral Counseling

John L. Maes

Like a blossom displayed at the Chelsea Flower Show, this chapter has had a long period of germination. It has had several transplantings, thinnings, and prunings; a period of steady, sturdy growth; and a little forcing when being prepared for display. It has sprung from the soil of thirty-five years of pastoral ministry, seminary teaching, therapeutic practice, training, and supervision. It is from this soil of accumulated experience that the ideas have blossomed.

At the outset we should recognize that maturity is really a process rather than a state. In human beings it is a process terminated only by death (which may be an opportunity for a new process to begin). Thus, attempts to evaluate the maturity of persons are descriptions of phases or states selected from that continuing process. The moments for measuring maturity are like motion picture sequences frozen in time. Tomorrow the scene will be different. Any description of maturity must leave room for growth and change, since we are always "becoming"[1] as long as we're alive. Even dying can result in new and positive phases of maturity, as pointed out by Kübler-Ross in her book, *Death: The Final Stage of Growth.*[2]

There are several aspects of maturity that will be touched upon in the course of this discussion. Among these will be the maturing field of pastoral counseling as a specialized ministry; maturity in the practice of pastoral counseling; the personal maturity of the pastoral counselor; training pastoral counselors toward maturity and mature awareness of the social contexts in which pastoral counselors function.

Pastoral counseling has arisen as a new form of ministry in response to ancient existential human needs. Every human being of all generations must live through a series of critical events. These include birth, dependency, puberty, courtship, marriage, child bearing and rearing, accidents, illness, old age, and death. These events have great significance to human beings. They carry with them the potential for death or for powerful new experiences of growth. Such events disturb the equanimity of human beings and create what Tillich[3] has called *urangst,* anxiety about being. One need not be neurotic to feel increased tensions while passing through these events. They are stressful for healthy human beings. But when basic personality structures are fragile, any of these existential crises may become triggers for failures of adjustment. These failures may take the forms of loss of faith, physical illness, or psychopathology.

Clergy persons have always been seen as primary resources in existential crises. Therefore, they have always been drawn into areas of pastoral care where spiritual, psychological, and physical problems meet. As awareness of the intricate balance of mind and body has developed, it has become clear that sicknesses of the soul and sicknesses of the body are interactive and intercausal. The "psychopharmacological bridge"[4] between mind and body has been almost closed by recent research on hormones and neurotransmitters. This research indicates that both mind and body must be treated in any attempt to assure or restore mental health. These new understandings of the nature of human beings have already had profound effects on the theory and praxis of pastoral care, resulting in changes in the theological education and clinical training.

The value of applying psychological theory to the ministry of pastoral care was first recognized by such pioneers as Boisen[5] and Dicks.[6] Their experiments led to the formalization of clinical pastoral education for ministers. This training was intended to help clergy use psychological insights in performing pastoral care activities. It remained for a new group of theorists, which included Hiltner, Johnson, Wise, and Oates, to expand upon the use of clinical interviews by ministers until they became the base for a new ministerial specialty, pastoral counseling. This specialty attained considerable independence from the parish ministry under the next generation of theorists, which included Clinebell,[7] Jaekel,[8] Patton,[9] Thornton,[10] Strunk,[11] and others. About that time, writers began using the term *pastoral psychotherapy* to mean psychotherapy as practiced by a clergyperson, regardless of whether such practice took place within the confines of a church or in a private office.

This discipline, in its training at the doctoral level, is about equally religious and psychological in its context. Normally it subsumes first degree theological education, clinical pastoral education, and ordination as prerequisites, then goes on to advanced academic and clinical training. This training has allowed many persons with initially pastoral identities to practice psychological healing at a level of sophistication and competence roughly commensurate with well-trained psychiatrists and psychologists who are inheritors of a more secular and scientific tradition.

It can be said, then, that pastoral counseling has attained a certain maturity of theoretical and practical explication, resulting in a reasonably clear and unique identity. Pastoral counseling has become established enough and secure enough to form its own profession-defining national organization: the American Association of Pastoral Counselors. It has also begun to examine its own implicit values and their relationship to their origins in the church and theology. This may be seen in the recent writings of Gerin,[12] Browning,[13] and others. Perhaps we can agree that this represents a reasonable measure of maturity in the sense of full development or professional ripeness.

Let us now turn to a consideration of what constitutes a mature pastoral counselor. I have decided to treat this topic under the following headings: the human given, the vision (calling), the theories, and the vocational experiences.

1. The Given

Those of us who annually select students for training in pastoral counseling programs must evaluate the quality of the "givens." What kind of psychological animal is this person who asks to be trained? What is the family background? The academic background? What are the major sources of motivation? How emotionally healthy and ready is the applicant? Since training is often translated into dollars, energy, and time, we trainers who seek to reinforce our *raison d'etre* through professional progeny must calculate whether our investment in the learner is worth a piece of our lives and a chunk of our funding.

We seem to think that the most promising trainees should be intellectually bright and able but reasonably humble about their gifts. They should be healthy enough not to work out their personal problems through their caretaking relationships. They should have suffered enough to be empathic without being emotionally impaired. They should be tenacious, organized, and dedicated without being too compulsive. They should be confident and assertive without being too aggressive or manipulative. They should be warm and accepting without generating inappropriate intimacy or dependency in their counselees. We like them to be deeply spiritual without being subject to religiosity.

Perhaps it is not surprising that candidates seldom appear to have all of these qualities. Like all of us, these supplicants for growth and training carry within themselves the scars of humankind. They know loneliness, deprivation, sorrow, and brokenness. Thus, they have within them the potential for understanding the cry for freedom, release, and growth that will come from their counselees. It may come in ritualized, garbled, or muted forms. It may be the cry of the disenfranchised or disempowered pleading for justice. It may be the disconnected murmur of the mentally ill looking for an island of reality on which to stand. The trainable instrument through which the pastoral counselor learns to respond is his or her own being. How can this marvelous instrument be trained to understand, evaluate, and respond in ways that enable those who ask for help to step outside the prisons of their neurotically transformed fear and rage, their obsessions, their confusion, their toxemias to learn new problem-solving actions?

2. The Calling

Most pastoral counselors start the journey toward maturity with what Becker[14] called a sense of cosmic specialness. As with ministers who feel called, they have a sense of mission and direction, a sense of being instruments of healing. This inner commitment may initially be awkward, misdirected, or grandiose, but its impetus can be used as a force to move the novice counselor through the pains of trial, error, correction, and trying again that are necessary for growth. This calling will be tempered by time, corrected by failure, and informed by the limits of reality, but it is an essential beginning.

3. Theories

But this vision of the future, if it is to be sustained and fulfilled, carries a heavy pack upon its back. First of all, there is the development of theories.

There must emerge a theory of cosmic reality. What is the relationship of human beings to the universe? What is the direction of human existence in the universe? And as Christians to whom do we and the universe belong? In his declamation of a "faith in Man," Teilhard de Chardin described the future direction of human beings on earth as follows: "Mankind (humankind) as an organic and organized whole possesses a future: future consisting not merely of successive years, but of higher states to be achieved by struggle. Not merely survival, . . . but some form of higher life."[15] He further observed that this human trend toward a state of higher being in its deepest origins is as old and universal as the world itself, and that "the advance of Life, however spurred on by the sheer hard necessity of continuing to exist, has always been inspired by an expectation of something greater."[16] This sense of human longing for transcendence was recognized by Maslow and Rogers, who used the term "self-actualization" to describe the phenomenon known to every mature therapist. This vital urge to grasp all things and transcend oneself is the willingness of a counselee to move forward into the face of one's deepest and most repressed fears, facing the awful truth about oneself in order to become whole, a single act of faith. Without this life force, pushing toward wholeness, there would be no impetus for psychotherapy.

Jung saw these urges toward wholeness and self-actualization as inherited archetypal forms within us. He wrote, "if there the flow of instinctive dynamism into our life is to be maintained, as is absolutely necessary, then it is imperative that we remold these archetypal forms into ideas which are adequate to the challenge of the present."[17]

Here the tasks of psychotherapy ad theology meet. It is not enough for the pastoral counselor to help the counselee adjust to a cynical world in which there is no hope for redemptive change, but to understand to *Whom* the world and human beings belong, to know that it is not only the power or instincts that move human beings to transcend their shadow selves, but the pull of teleology calling us to greater harmony with ourselves, each other, and God.

Mature pastoral counselors have come to know the eternal context of their task. They have come to know why human life is ultimately valuable. They have humbly come to know the Source from which all energy flows, including the energy of the counselee to change.

But the task of moving from the now to the possible *then* requires more theoretical specificity than these philosophic and theological generalizations. It requires an understanding of human development as well as an explicated theory of therapy. Theories of therapy are informed by theories of human development, which are informed by ontological and cosmological assumptions both philosophic and theological in nature. It is not really "elephants all the way down" as the Hindu swami is reputed to have said when asked upon what the world rested.

Humanistic rather than analytic theories of therapy appear to have been particularly congenial to pastoral counselors. As Gerkin pointed out in his recent book: "Carroll A. Wise and Paul E. Johnson, both of whom were educated and found their theological home in the personalistic theories of Borden P. Bowne and Edgar S. Brightman, drew their early counseling theoretical framework largely from Rogerian theories."[18]

The ideas of Rogers were especially congenial to pastoral counselors for several reasons. First, because of the sense of holy uniqueness surrounded the discussion of human beings. Nomothetic generalizations across persons were at a minimum. Freedom of choice and the right to grow were emphasized. The concept of self-actualization had an almost teleological sense to it. It was only a small step for a Christian to believe that this might be a secular euphemism for "the leadings of the Holy Spirit" or "the presence of God." Carl Rogers' early years at Union Seminary may have built an unconscious bridge to theological language.

Rogers' somewhat incomplete theory of human development, with its strong phenomenological flavor, was essentially congenial to persons with theological orientations. Perhaps the theology of Tillich, deeply affected by psychological insights, made the easiest match with client centered theory.

However, there may have been a more practical reason for the early popularity of the client centered approach. As pastoral counseling eased its way into the American scene, ministers did not have the social mandate to be analytical, interpretive, or case managing in their counseling activities. They did have a mandate to be caring, available, and spiritual in the hospitals or other orthoprofessional settings in which they worked. Client centered therapy had the appearance of being a "no harm" kind of approach. In his adaptation of client centered therapy, Paul Johnson used the term "responsive counseling." This meant that the pastoral counselor did not take the initiative, set the parameters, or do the digging. The pastoral counselor simply provided a safe environment and responded with understanding to the counselee's presentations.

Since these early beginnings, widely ranging theories of therapy have found their way into the practice of pastoral counseling. Freudian and Jungian analytical approaches provided venturesome pastoral counselors with vehicles for greater depth and acuity in their counseling. Gestalt approaches provided vehicles for the expression of the repressed anger that was so often a block to the growth of clients in religious settings. Some of the "body language" approaches such as Bioenergetics have provided vehicles for the release of sexual and aggressive tensions so common to persons with repressive religious defenses. Pastoral counselors, in their greater professional maturity, are now free to master and invoke a wide range of theories of therapy once considered to be beyond their expertise.

The most promising recent development appears to be in the area of Object Relations theory. Not only is it particularly helpful in understanding and treating the problems of narcissistic and borderline personalities, once seen as beyond the ken of pastoral counselors, but it also explicates human development in language and images that are congenial to theological thinking. A concept such as "holding introjects," the internalization of warm and loving thoughts and memories as ways to make being-in-the-world existentially bearable, even positive, is a way of taking goodness into one's self. The importance of clear, consistent (loving) modeling so that positive internal images may sustain the growing child has an aura of incarnation about them. It could almost be said that it is not so much what we do but what we introject that makes us whole.

Whatever the basic thread, psychoanalytic, Client Centered, Interpersonal, Gestalt, Object Relations, or Bioenergetic, the mature pastoral counselor will have developed an effective tapestry that explains human development, relates it to ultimate cosmological beliefs, and provides a clear sense of how therapeutic interventions can be made to enhance growth and wholeness in the counselee. It is important that training centers provide appropriate theory-to-practice continua that demonstrate the relationships among theology, psychology, and clinical practice.

158

4. Training

Training provides the groundwork for the professional maturation of the pastoral counselor. This task has become more complex, expensive, and time consuming as pastoral counseling as a discipline has moved toward greater clarity, autonomy, and responsibility. In recent years, there has been a tendency to blunt the meaning of ministry while enhancing the meaning of psychotherapist. The clinical side of training programs has become increasingly compelling. In order for pastoral psychotherapists to stand shoulder to shoulder with other mental health specialists, the following developments should take place.

1. *More theoretical training* is required in advance of clinical placement. Such psychological subjects as psychodynamic theory, developmental theory, assessment techniques, psychophysiology, psychopharmacology, and psychopathology have found their way into curricula. These have been added to such conventional requirements as theories of pastoral care; clinical pastoral education; group, family, and marital counseling; existential life crises, and so on.

2. *More religious training* is required because what gets lost in all of this is continued involvement in the prophetic and sacramental aspects of ministry. The uses of prayer and symbolic religious acts related to the therapeutic process are hardly mentioned.

This bias often follows through in the model of supervision and consultation designed for the training of pastoral counselors. There is often a strange embarrassment around corporate worship, theological dialogue, or personal witnessing to one's faith in the settings where pastoral counselors are trained. The training emphases tend to be on such subjects as intake and diagnosis, establishing therapeutic contracts, case management, intratherapeutic evaluation, termination, referral transference, and countertransference. Such sustaining religious concepts as the Source of healing, the Grace that surrounds therapeutic work, the qualities of sin and redemption, the importance of religious symbols, and the values of corporate worship are usually implicit if present at all.

In order for a pastoral counselor to mature as a minister while engaged in the therapeutic task, these important elements of religious life should be explicated in such a way that they remain as natural as the more psychological aspects of the training experience. Human beings are motoric creatures. We learn by doing. To a great extent we become what we practice. The task of pastoral counseling can be seen as an expression of ministry and, as such, as a means to the redemption of fragmented human beings who have become alienated from themselves, from significant others and from God. While it is seldom appropriate for the therapeutic task to be evangelistic, it is appropriate for it to open the counselee to deeper experiences of religious meaning and theological understanding. As St. Paul has indicated, among

159

ministerial husbandmen some sow the seed, others tend the vineyard, but only God can cause the grapes to grow.

5. Experience

Maturity requires time and experience. This is what leaps to one's mind when discussing maturing. For many years, the skills of pastoral counselors were truncated by their limited access to a wide variety of clinical cases. Often experience tended to be filled with a repetition of the same types of human problems. Marriage problems, religious obsessions, and depressions were three favorite categories. It is now possible for pastoral counselors to work as major therapists, with children, families, characterological problems (narcissistic and borderline personalities), and schizophrenics. Well-supervised experience over a wide range of cases is essential to professional maturity. But growth does not simply occur through repetition, nor simply through aging. "Older" does not necessarily mean smarter, and "experienced" does not always mean skilled. Continued reading, open peer dialogue on one's cases, and continued consultation can turn experience into growth and learning.

Maturity comes from the continued emotional growth of the pastoral counselor, whose ability to face existential limits, to negotiate life's passages, and to surrender infantile fantasies and wishes must also grow. The control and appropriate direction of impulse and the delay of gratification are essential qualities of a mature and successful therapist. In order for this to happen, there are two conditions that seem to be essential. One of these is a stable and satisfying support system. Warm and continuous personal relationships outside of therapy, respect from professional colleagues, appropriate outlets for physical exercise and sexual gratification, and reasonable freedom from financial worries are all part of such a support system.

It is also essential that the therapist develop interests outside the emotionally debilitating demands of the counseling profession. Rest, health, humor, variety, and exercise keep people sane. It is easy to encounter empty, tragic, depressed figures who have spent a lifetime giving forty to fifty hours a week to listening to the problems of other human beings. Worship and meditation are important restorative exercises for pastoral counselors. One cannot mature without being renewed; one simply ages.

However, time cannot be dismissed as a matrix for maturity. As the more insistent juices and urges of youth become physiologically tempered and ambition is placed in perspective by experience, there is a certain mellowness that enriches the therapist's life. This becomes a time, as Erikson has said, to become less self-absorbed and more generative.[19] Training in pastoral counseling is wisely based on an apprenticeship model. The tribal myths as well as the techniques are taught to the youths by the elders. To share the richness of insights, to shape the eager energy for bright young persons, is both generative and regenerative. Pastoral counseling is a profession in which the elders are still respected.

6. Conclusion

So the mature pastoral counselor is one who has paid the price for credentials, given endless hours to the healing task, learned from experience, stayed open to peer evaluation, developed a workable philosophy, lived a human and decent life, shared the fruits of experience with younger colleagues, retained a deep sense of ministry, and attempted to be a good human being above all other things. Such a person shall be "like a tree planted by the rivers of waters, that bringeth forth his (her) fruit in season; his (her) leaf also shall not wither; and whatsoever he (she) doeth shall prosper" (Ps. 1:3).

Notes

1. Gordon W. Allport, *Becoming* (New Haven: Yale University Press, 1955).

2. Elizabeth Kübler-Ross, *Death: The Final Stage of Growth* (Englewood Cliffs, NJ: Prentice-Hall, 1975).

3. C. W. Kegley and R. W. Bretall, *The Theology of Paul Tillich* (New York: Macmillan Co., 1961).

4. S. Snyder, *Madness and the Brain* (New York: McGraw-Hill, 1975).

5. Anton Boisen, *Out of the Depths* (New York: Harper & Row, 1960).

6. Russell Dicks, *Pastoral Work and Personal Counseling* (New York: Macmillan Co., 1949).

7. Howard Clinebell, *Basic Types of Pastoral Counseling* (Nashville: Abingdon Press, 1966).

8. C. Jaekel and W. Clebsch, *Pastoral Care in Historical Perspective* (Englewood Cliffs, NJ: Prentice-Hall, 1964).

9. John Patton, *Pastoral Counseling: A Ministry of the Church* (Nashville: Abingdon Press, 1983).

10. E. Thorton, *Theology and Pastoral Counseling* (Englewood Cliffs, NJ: Prentice-Hall, 1964).

11. Orlo Strunk, ed., *Readings in the Psychology of Religion* (Nashville: Abingdon Press, 1959).

12. Charles Gerkin, *The Living Human Document* (Nashville: Abingdon Press, 1984).

13. Don Browning, *The Moral Context of Pastoral Care* (Philadelphia: Westminster Press, 1976).

14. E. Becker, *The Denial of Death* (New York: Free Press, 1973).

15. Pierre Teilhard de Chardin, *The Future of Man* (New York: Harper & Row, 1964), p. 185.

16. Ibid.

17. Carl G. Jung, *The Undiscovered Self* (New York: The American Library, 1959), p. 82.

18. Gerkin, *The Living Human Document,* p. 14.

19. Erik H. Erikson, *Identity and the Life Cycle* (New York: International Universities Press, 1959).

XII. Maturity in Teaching and Preaching

John H. Snow

1. Culture, Characters, and Professions

There is a curious and fairly recent obsession in American culture with a reductionist understanding of human life, both corporate and individual, as either growing or dying. Anything, or anyone, who is not growing, we are told, is dying. Growth or death is held up, along with win or lose, success or failure, as a total value system. Anything or anyone who is growing, winning, or succeeding is good; anything or anyone who is not growing, winning, or succeeding is dying, losing, or failing, or in the language of business, sports, and politics, is dead, a loser, or a failure. The concept of growth, a biological concept, is taking the place of progress, a historical concept. Americans are fast coming to believe that history is the setting in of inexorability, is a kind of meaningless burden that keeps us from growing, from developing as we should, from reaching our full potential.

My topic is maturity as it relates to the two professions of preaching and teaching. I guess I was chosen to take this topic because I have been a preacher most of my adult life and a professor for the past twelve years. Although the two professions in some ways complement each other, they are basically quite different things, even for someone like myself who is a professor in a seminary which permits me to preach regularly in the chapel to those whom I also teach in the classroom.

I suppose that if one is going to speak of maturity in these professions one should address first the choice of these professions. Alasdair MacIntryre, in his wonderful book *After Virtue*, maintains that the moral philosophy of a particular historical era reaches cultural assimilation and expression through what he calls "characters," groups of public personages who most widely reflect in their professions the moral philosophy of their times.[1] He suggests that the three major characters of the Victorian age were public school headmasters, explorers, and engineers. For our time he suggests therapists,

165

bureaucratic managers, and aesthetes. For rich aesthetes I would substitute celebrities, but never mind.

My theory is that something of the same process goes on in the postadolescent individual. One is exposed to an array of characters in one's own life—teachers, doctors, professors, military officers, ministers—whom one actually sees in the performance of what they do and whose performance directly affects one's life. One is exposed as well to media characters: politicians, performing artists, newscasters and various celebrities, who for increasing numbers of people can become more real and important than characters who are known. Where people feel a real vocation or calling to a profession, rather than the *pro forma* acceptance of a profession as a safe thing to do, they are most often moved in a particular direction by some character in that profession who has caught their imagination. The character who has this effect is usually mature or *has* been in the past. An important social function of maturity is in its power to catch the imagination of the young and contribute to their hopeful vision of the future. "Some day I would like to be like that person. There is a human being; in some respects I would like to be like that person. There is a human being in some respects like myself anyway, who was perhaps once *very* like me, who is now fully formed, whose identity has been settled in part by a public commitment to a profession," the young person says.

I am not talking about a mentor here. I am talking about a distant, subtle, transferential relationship with a lot of room for fantasy and a great deal of freedom. It is far more intellectual than having to do with affect. This role becomes more important than the individual who acts the role. Nothing like this ever happened to me as an undergraduate. No professors caught my imagination. My undergraduate's life was more like a tollbooth on a superhighway than an education. I wanted the degree, and I wanted out.

I went to Columbia at the age of twenty-five with no idea of getting a doctorate, or becoming an English professor, or for any good reason beyond the availability of G.I. Bill money and a vague dream of writing a novel someday. I really had no idea of what I wanted to do with my life or what I wanted to become.

When the academic year had sorted itself out, I found myself along with half the graduate students at Columbia in the humanities fastening on Mark Van Doren. Many of us needed father figures in the worst sort of way. We cut and combed our hair like Mark Van Doren; we cultivated a mild stammer. We imitated his hand gestures. The lecture course, "Tragedy and Comedy," contained at least three hundred students, and from time to time during the lecture students would stand up suddenly, be recognized by Van Doren, and would comment in an animated way upon some point Van Doren had made. Van Doren would listen carefully, expressing sheer delight in what was being offered, and then would comment on it, carefully fitting it into his rather loosely organized lecture. When the comments were particularly apt or brilliant, he would rub his head and say, "Why, that's wonderful. That's absolutely wonderful." In a way, that was truly extraordinary, the most participatory class I ever attended.

What was the case with Van Doren was really the style for Columbia professors in general. So far as one's work was concerned, the professors were remarkably accessible, truly interested in one's ideas, and respected one's seriousness about one's ideas, but they were careful to ignore the charms of particular students. What Martin Buber sees as the Eros Model between teacher and student—the reaching out of the professor to particularly gifted, creative, imaginative, or even beautiful students to form a close personal relationship that will radically change and reshape the student in the image of the professor—was surprisingly lacking at Columbia. In its place was a passion for the whole intellectual enterprise, the whole life of the mind that was reflected in the superb lectures, the accomplished teaching styles, and also in the professors' participation in the intellectual and political life of New York City. All of these professors were at that time mature, certainly in their fifties.

The professor as character, then, has a lot to do with people choosing the academic life, and an awareness of this is a part of becoming a mature professor. One is not simply, by becoming a professor, becoming a conduit for information about one's professed field. One will, by how one goes about one's teaching and indeed by how one goes about living one's life, make a statement in time about the importance of the life of the mind. Great professors leave their students free to understand that it is not necessary to join the academy to live the life of the mind.

2. "The Finished Man Among His Enemies"

The choice to be a professor, then, is influenced by the imprint of certain professorial characters. The movement from then on towards maturity seems to follow stages. W. B. Yeats is helpful here. In his late sixties, looking back over his eventful life he wrote the poem, "A Dialogue of Self and Soul." It goes in part like this:

> What matter if I live it all once more?
> Endure that toil of growing up;
> The ignominy of boyhood, the distress
> Of boyhood changing into man;
> The unfinished man and his pain
> Brought face to face with his own clumsiness;
> The finished man among his enemies?

167

The unfinished man and his pain . . . .
The finished man among his enemies.[2]

I know no more vivid picture of career than that. I can still remember the pain of being unfinished. The seemingly endless academic preparation for career, the politeness of it, the intense ambivalence, the moments of sheer doubt, and the nagging suspicion that one's identity as a person was being forced into a professional persona and that this process would end in the utter loss of self.

And then as one moved into the profession itself, one remembers how quickly one's attention and energy were removed from inner concerns and focused upon the outside world, the world of colleagues and students and administrators, until one day one realized that one was perceived by others as complete, as a person with a history, a verifiable narrative, a predictable person who believed certain things and behaved in certain ways and had to be met and dealt with as one who was, in the Yeatian sense, "finished." One realized that the cost of being finished was to be among enemies. "Enemies" here is a strong word, a poetic word, but I suspect it is used in the sense that Jesus used it when he told us to love our enemies. The finished public person, the tenured, published professor, the lawyer who becomes a partner in the firm, the military officer who reaches flag rank, the politician who reaches high office, the parish minister who becomes a bishop or moderator will practically find his or her definition in conflict.

Again Yeats:

The finished man among his enemies?
How in the name of heaven can he escape
That defiling and disfiguring shape
The mirror of malicious eyes
Casts upon his eyes until at last
He thinks that shape must be *his* shape?
And what's the good of an escape
If honour find him in the wintry blast?[3]

Or as Mark Twin said of being tarred and feathered and ridden out of town on a rail, "It would be a terrible thing if it weren't for the honor of it."[4] The public, the political, the career life of professors, when they reach maturity, differs hardly at all from the public life of other professionals. It tends to be entrepreneurial, competitive, and concerned with power. One has only to live in Cambridge for as long as I have to see the waves of professors follow each new administration to Washington as the professors from the last administration quietly return to their academic posts. The role of the university has radically changed during my lifetime and, along with it, the role of the professor.

168

The late Gregory Bateson liked to point out the purpose of a university as being in part the passing on of the traditional knowledge of a culture from one generation to the next and in part the discovery of new knowledge.[4] Bateson maintained that these two functions were not necessarily compatible; that the discovery function could radically disrupt the passing on of traditional knowledge.

I think this has happened. However, universities may want to see their purpose, the culture increasingly expects them to teach strategies for surviving in a time of rapid social changes. Some time ago a university dean at a highly respected institution of higher learning said, "What we are trying to teach undergraduates is not so much a lot of stuff as how to learn." The role of the university in its relationship to culture is no longer so much to maintain and enrich and pass it on, as to prepare the young to deal with it adaptively as it changes. Czieslaw Milosz stated it more harshly when he suggested in the Norton Lectures a few years ago that in the West we are substituting biology for culture. In this kind of environment, professors find themselves following the path prepared for them by research scientists. Suddenly their field has value only as it can be applied to the problem of human adaptation and survival. As scientists become engineers, even history professors become consultants or political advisors. Their stuff has no particular value beyond the adaptive skills to be derived from it, and these are marketable.

For individual professors, this change in role presents a great danger that he or she will never go beyond a maturity seen as "the finished man among his enemies." He or she may discover some honor in the wintry blast, some extra degrees or other prizes, the guarantee of a prosperous retirement, but the very finishedness of the entrepreneurial professor may keep him or her from reaching a different and quite other level of maturity that Yeats also describes:

> I am content to follow to its source
> Every event in action or in thought:
> Measure the lot: forgive myself a lot!
> When such as I cast out remorse
> So great a sweetness flows into the breast
> We must laugh and we must sing,
> We are blest by everything,
> Everything we look upon is blesst.[5]

It seems to me that particularly for professors true maturity will be found in the life of the mind and that quite separate from career. Even that obsession with power that so often comes over us as we become finished is for us most often a new way to make sense out of life. What we most often seek in power is truth, not just power for its own sake, but I must add ruefully that we seldom find it there. As Yeats said, we find instead an image of ourselves we do not like mirrored in the eyes of the resentful.

The essence of maturity in professors is their willingness to use that mind so carefully trained and intensively put to work to make sense out of their own lives. This means in maturity moving beyond the limits of one's field, indeed, being willing not to be up on all the literature of one's field (one has, after all, *done that*) and beginning to read and think extensively even to the point of examining the significance of one's own field in a larger historical and philosophical matrix. Therefore, it is very important for professors at the peak of their maturity, not as they are about to retire, to ask, "What have I been doing all this time? Why have I been doing it? What is the value of all this? Where is it leading? What is its end?"

3. Maturity of the Professor

When one has a history, when one begins to deal with the consequences of early choices, one is in fact in danger of becoming a hostage to those consequences. For professors, this can become particularly unnerving. We tend to commit ourselves as we mature to a particular school or viewpoint or paradigm in our field, a particular approach to our field, and to be strong advocates of this approach. We find ourselves, as Yeats says, among our enemies, defending a position in which we have a considerable investment of time and work, and for which we are on record by books, articles, and lectures. Younger professors in our fields may be wedded to new paradigms and full of downright scorn for our work. We find that we can defend ourselves adequately or even brilliantly, but increasingly it becomes ourselves, rather than our work, that we are defending.

For too many professors, this becomes a time of preservation. We begin to improvise on good old themes that won us acclaim. Accepting the biological model, we try to make our work more adaptive: we become increasingly concerned with our own survival. We fear that if we show any openness to the new approach, we shall sacrifice our integrity. We get trapped in a reductionist win-lose bind that so often ends in cynicism and despair, a struggle to maintain some shreds of integrity as we wait for retirement. One is haunted by a bitter sense of unfairness as one suspects that the rest of one's professional life has been determined by a few critical choices made in the past. And as Yeats saw, there is the guilt, the pain one caused, the damage one did in the absolute assurance that one has it right.

Perhaps the hardest part of maturity for the professor in times like ours is the slow realization for some of us that we miss some of the ideas and thought forms that we opposed ideologically and succeeded in doing away with. Indeed, we grieve. We find ourselves paying lip

170

service to ideas that we once held passionately. We hear our enemies, the young Turks, going after our ideas with the same passion we felt in originally putting them forward, and their arguments do not sound altogether implausible to us. Perhaps we did *not* have it right. Perhaps this whole world of ideas is an illusion, a kind of random biological arena where the fittest ideas of one generation simply succumb to the power of the ideas more fit, more adaptive, yet certainly no more true, which pop up randomly in the next generation. Perhaps, through all those years of *sturm und drang,* we were simply, as the young say, playing games.

The crisis of maturity for professors is the overwhelming cloud of ambiguity that settles upon any reflective person whose historical experience is long enough to demand accountability. Where one's ideas no longer account for one's own experience, and one's intellectual life is full of anomalies and inner contradictions, there is bound to be considerable pain.

When Sophocles wrote at the end of *Oedipus Rex*: "Call no man happy until he's dead," he meant, as Alasdair MacIntryre suggests, that the last word cannot be spoken about until that life is completed. Like a play, or a novel, a human life follows a narrative form. It can be told, and if it is a good life, a happy life, it will, in its completion, be coherent and make sense. I do not think Yeats had it quite right when he said:

> I am content to follow to its source
> Every event in action or in thought:
> Measure the lot; forgive myself the lot.

For professors, at least, this is too simple.

One must certainly measure the lot, examine the lot. But forgiving the lot sounds too much like letting it all go, as though all those events in action or in thought were so many sins to be forgiven and even forgotten. It sounds as though it were all illusion. I think it is better to examine the lot for a deeper structure of coherence and intention, to find out what it was that one was, at the deepest level, trying to accomplish, and from that to find out how one should live during the remainder of one's life with idea and action working together to complement each other.

Above all, the adversary role is no longer appropriate in maturity. In this society where it is assumed that all relationships are adversary relationship, moving out of an adversary role is not easy. Yet if there is anything that a professor learns in maturity, it is that it is precisely one's role as adversary that blinds one to ambiguity. One can talk about ambiguity as an abstraction when one is young and then ignore it. But on maturity, ambiguity ceases to be an abstraction and grabs one by the throat. One must come to terms with it, or one begins to lie, one becomes false to one's self.

One way to deal with ambiguity is to reflect upon the context of one's specialty and to broaden that context as much as one can. In my own field, pastoral theology, one can get as specialized as in any other. We have our commitments to particular models of pastoral counseling, or parish administration, or preaching, and we will occasionally fight and die for them. We often, in our specialization, neglect even the theological implications of our models, to say nothing of their cultural, sociological, or historical context. For example, if I have been teaching pastoral counseling for many years on a Freudian-Rogerian Model and suddenly I am faced on every side by a new counseling method called Neuro Linguistic Programming (N.L.P.), a totally different model, I can think about N.L.P. on the level of psychotherapeutic theory and decide whether to oppose it or accept it. As a mature professor, I have seen a fair number of theories come and go. Most of them were easily assimilated into my basic model. Others were off the wall and could be ignored. This one is neither. The choice at this level may appear to be between joining the old curmudgeons defending the classical pastoral counseling model or joining a bunch of trendy youngsters who currently seem to be winning the day. But supposing instead that I look at this dilemma on a different level than psychotherapeutic theory and academic survival.

I might ask: what statements do these two models make about human nature? To what extent does the conflict between these models reflect a change in cultural assumptions? What are the ethical implications of this change? Can I trace the historical development of pastoral counseling since 1940 in such a way as to show increasing numbers of anomalies and inadequacies in the Freudian-Rogerian model as its cultural environment changed?

Perhaps I could develop a course or write a book on pastoral counseling during a time of shifting cultural assumptions about human nature that would involve historical, ethical, theological, and sociological perspectives. Perhaps I could provide a larger and more sophisticated context within which to judge new theory in my field of specialization. It seems to me that it is in this kind of contextual course or book that one is able to deal honestly with the ambiguities while giving guidance to a new generation in one's field and interpreting one's field to others outside it. The most vivid example seems to be the article, now a book by Freeman Dyson, in the *New Yorker*, where he puts his work as physicist and mathematician into a larger context and attempts to make sense out of it as he works at providing some useful modes of thinking to avoid nuclear war.[7]

4. Maturity and Preaching

Well, so much for professors and maturity. Preachers are another matter. I was brought up an atheist, and it was not until I was twenty-six that I started churchgoing. I was not very moved by the preaching I heard. If it had anything to do with human existence at all, it seemed to be sentimental nonsense. Purely theological or biblical preaching was better. It was at least intellectually interesting. I became fascinated with the preaching process, the structure of sermons, the place of the sermon in the liturgy, the use of illustrations and the choice of illustrations, and the rest, but the context of sermons seemed to end up with some sort of reassuring good news, the Gospel, a cure-all for everything usually presented more as a necessary ritual at the end of a sermon than as having any logic of its own.

At the same time, I started comparison shopping the churches for sermons. Adlai Stevenson appeared on the national political scene. For the first time I saw that strange phenomenon, i.e., one person rose up out of a mass of people to articulate his experience and give it significance. Roosevelt was able to do that, of course, but with far less depth. When one finished listening to Adlai Stevenson, one felt that there was something fine and purposeful and hugely important about being human, something which I had come to doubt during World War II and needed to hear.

Providentially, a preacher came to town at roughly the same time Stevenson was running for office, and I began to have an experience at church that was of the same magnitude as hearing a speech by Stevenson. No longer was the Gospel added as a kind of overlay at the end of a sermon, it was discovered by the preacher in the midst of the life he so vividly presented to us in words. What he did was simple. He discovered in his own life those things that tended to be universally experienced. The life he described had an uncanny resemblance to life as we, the congregation, experienced it. The result was a profound trust on the part of the congregation. He never told us what life was supposed to be like, or how we were supposed to feel it. But once we were firmly ensconced in reality, we were willing to let the preacher give this life the significance that is to be found in the light of the Gospel. I began to see how necessary it is for there to be public figures who can with a kind of inner assurance articulate what it is like to be a human being, and to do it in such a way as to make human beings seem important, significant, and, on the whole, good.

I discovered in seminary, though, a great distrust of preaching. The assumption was that preaching was a narcissistic exercise that ministers indulged themselves in rather than doing the real work of the church, which was either pastoral or concerned with community organization in the city. This was exactly what I needed to hear at that moment of my life, mainly because it is an assumption with a lot of truth in it. For

173

many of my classmates who had no interest in preaching it was exactly the opposite of what they needed to hear, because it was all they heard.

It is right here that the road to maturity in preaching is most likely to be blocked. If one simply assumes, despite all scriptural warrant to the contrary, that preaching is a kind of minor liturgical task, an assumption that haunts the Episcopal Church, then one's preaching never matures. It remains a dutiful rehearsal of Scripture and inappropriate illustrations made up slightly before the service begins. If the preacher has never been warned of the danger of preaching becoming precisely an exercise in narcissism and an excuse to neglect the parish and the community, the preacher may end up with forty minutes of elegant rhetoric that does not really communicate anything of significance.

Maturity in a preacher can be spotted in a moment. Almost all preachers, when they leave seminary, have some sort of theology, but it is usually an intellectual overlay covering the more primitive assumptions by which they make sense out of their lives; assumptions learned from their ambient culture by a kind of osmosis, by a process largely unconscious. The process of maturity in preaching depends on the willingness of preachers to let themselves feel the tension between the theology they profess and the deep structures of the unconscious paradigm by which they really make sense out of their lives. To do this, one must become deeply engaged in the parish as pastor and in the community as advocate. The maturation process depends, then, on existential engagement with the larger community, professional engagement with the parish, and a kind of reflective prayer life tied closely to one's preaching.

Maturity in preaching itself depends on preachers assimilating their theology in such a way that their professional and political lives are not in public contradiction to it. This assimilation reveals itself in sermons that promise with assurance nothing that preachers themselves have not experienced. If one suggests that the Gospel promises more, as one should, one should at the same time communicate that one does not claim for oneself the fullness of the promise. The mature preacher always presents the Gospel as one who is himself or herself engaged seriously, prayerfully in the process of sanctification, in the process of moving toward the fullness of the Gospel promise.

Young preachers will often bravely attempt to do this by relating in some detail their crisis of unbelief, sometimes when they are in the midst of such a crisis. The mature preacher, simply by the way he or she presents life in a sermon, reveals a vision at best only partly redeemed, only partially free of ambiguity, an understanding of life that in many areas of life admits to being far from having reached conclusions. At the same time, mature preachers will speak of those aspects of the Gospel promise that have been realized in their lives with great power and assurance.

A second thing that one notices in mature preaching is a deeply felt understanding of the scientific world view, which the preacher neither accepts nor rejects but examines and questions constantly in the light of the Gospel. One of the most difficult things for any mature Christian preacher to face is the extent to which his or her way of looking at things is dominated by the scientific world view rather than by Christian revelation. The same is even more true of the listening congregation. This world view is called in the scientific community "evolutionary naturalism," which Karl Peters describes in the following terms: "The realm of nature is all there is: There is no 'supernatural' . . . . nature is dynamic; it evolves. Change is not merely an appearance . . . . but is essential to the way things are . . . . the evolution of nature is best understood by updated Darwinian mechanism."[9]

I do not regard as mature any preacher who rejects this world view and preaches, as pure Gospel, sermons that do not address it at all. Neither do I regard as mature preachers who mindlessly, with no conscious choice, accept this world view and work hard at bending Scripture to conform it.

This does not mean that mature preachers address this whole paradigm in every sermon, but simply that they will be aware that when they consider any issue from nuclear war to abortion, from world hunger to feminism, their congregation and probably they themselves will first think of such issues from the viewpoint of evolutionary naturalism, simply because this is the way we have been taught to think in the mainstream of American society. The same holds for theology. If one preaches on salvation, one should understand that one's congregation and possibly oneself believe that those with the best genes or the optimal environment will be saved.

If one decides to preach on the doctrine of the atonement, one will most likely be misunderstood no matter how one goes at it, but the concept of sacrifice, where the immediate, identifiable benefit for self or others is not clear, fits very badly into the world view of evolutionary naturalism as it is most commonly held. People may be moved by the rhetoric of atonement, but most of those moved will still lack any ability to assimilate the concept of sacrifice into their way of making sense out of life.

5. Maturity and the Preacher

But what of the preacher as person? Is there a peculiar kind of psychological and spiritual maturity that is common to preachers who have become mature in their craft? The only mature preachers I have known have been anything but well adjusted by usual standards of mental health. Most of them have tended to be moody and unpredictable

175

out of the pulpit. At times they will preach to you, or lecture you, or tell you a great deal more than you want to know about something obscure and perhaps boring. At other times something you say will interest them, and they will begin to question you in a very perceptive way until you yourself become rather eloquent. The best of them do not carry note books in which to enter any brilliant thoughts or significant events they might come across. Neither do they see everything in life as potential sermon illustrations. They read a lot, including a great deal of secular stuff. All mature preachers I have known have been obsessive about understanding the culture from which, in which, to which they preached. All have, at times, seemed to me to be distant, and some have seemed to me more than normally anxious. Most of them seem to be people who do not find existence at all easy. They are seldom once-born. Yet they are far from unhappy people. They just find their happiness in unexpected places.

The spirituality of mature preachers can be quite different from the spirituality of mature parish ministers in that mature parish ministers tend to be disciplined and consistent in their prayer lives. Preachers tend to be idiosyncratic in their prayer lives. For preachers, prayer and sermon preparation tend to overlap, the pen or the typewriter or the word processor may for them be the key to prayer as well as to sermons.

The professional life of the mature preacher is not always an easy one. In my own denomination a mature preacher may be the rector of a large, or as we call it, a cardinal parish, but most often not. One of the ironies of our time, at least for Episcopalians, is that parish administration and preaching do not necessarily go together as vocations. For Episcopalians a mix of administrative and pastoral skills is regarded as the most appropriate requirement for leading large parishes. As a result, one will find more mature preachers scattered around in unlikely places than one will find in cardinal parishes.

Those preachers destined to become mature tend to be rebellious in seminary. Their sermons will often seem to lack form, be discursive, seem to tackle too many issues, to say too much. Their delivery may be uneven, with poor eye contact, or clumsy gestures, or lacking in gestures. Yet from the beginning, a kind of assurance and excitement in the delivery will be evident. There will not be that subtle or even terribly noticeable distancing from the context of the sermon, as though the preacher's attention were on a mirror rather than on the Gospel. They may approach the pulpit in a fever of anxiety, bur shortly after they begin to preach, a great calm will descend, not only on them, but on the congregation as well. Even where the sermon is theologically shallow or scripturally questionable, one thing will be unquestionable, and that is that all present are caught up in something serious, something important, something that cannot be trivialized at any level.

A humble being is trying without pretense to make sense out of human life in the light of the Gospel. The worst thing a teacher of homiletics can do is immediately to submit such an event to rigorous critical analysis. The teacher should only thank God. The criticism should come later, and it should be sensitive and positive and full of care.

For preachers destined to become mature in preaching are often destined as well to remain unfinished, vulnerable. Their pain does not leave them as they move into their professional career. Like biological mutants, they may seek a niche, a noncompetitive place of existential turf where they are free to develop towards maturity at their own pace and in their own way. At the same time, they are not like poets or painters in that a condition of maturity is a purposeful involvement in the main currents of the life of their time. (One thinks of Eliot at his bank or Stevens at his work in insurance or Williams as a pediatrician.) No recluse will ever reach maturity in preaching, for no recluse can speak to the day-to-day experience of a congregation.

It is hard to get at the essence of mature preaching, but the great raconteur of National Public Radio, Garrison Keilor, gives some insight into what it is about. Keilor has constructed an imaginary town known as Lake Wobegon in rural Minnesota. He has done this over many years by telling stories over the radio every Saturday night. His stories are full of surprises. It turns out that this tiny village is far from a predictable place. Seen through Keilor's eyes, Lake Wobegon becomes a microcosm, a metaphor for the rich varieties of experience to be found in human corporate life, a life where Sin and Grace abound.

Mature preachers do not create an imaginary village, but over the years, their sermons will tend to provide an alternative vision for understanding the corporate human life that surrounds the place where they are preached. I am convinced that mature preaching requires a faithful commitment to a place and to a community. This does not mean that the preacher spends his or her life in one place, but that wherever the preacher is, the preacher identifies with, becomes a part of, shares the history, and cares about the future of that place. Preaching does not mature when the preacher regards one parish as a stepping-stone to another parish, hopefully more grand. Mature preachers give their undivided attention to where they are. Their sermons assume a certain, distinct, historical place.

When Paul wrote to Corinth, he wrote to the Corinthians not to the Ephesians. If the actual context of preaching is ignored, sermons may become great literature; but, as sermons, they will lack authenticity because they lack context. As George Buttrick used to point out, this is why a collection of sermons by a great preacher is so incredibly dull. You were not there. You were not a part of the community to which they were preached. In preaching to this particular community, one does not fill one's sermons with anecdotes from the real life of this community, but one addresses one's apprehension of the Gospel to what is in the mind of the community or being celebrated in the community. Slowly in the minds of the congregation an alternative vision of the community will grow. It will be an ecumenical vision, not only in the ecclesial sense of the word, but in the larger sense of ecumenical. The congregation will begin to see its community as a metaphor for the world as God's household, God's *oikos*.

As the preacher's longitudinal, historical apprehension of the community grows and becomes more and more inclusive, the preacher's sermons will contribute to a growing congregational consensus about the significance of their corporate life within this context, its significance to them, its significance in its relationship to the lager household of the world, and, most important, its significance within the household of God. Mature preaching provides a vision of corporate human reality where Grace comes to be understood as a constant, accessible, vividly real agent in one's day-to-day life, exactly as that life is, requiring no denial, no false consciousness, no self-deception. This vision grows, becomes more welcoming and authentic with the years as an alternative to the vision of life lived as one damned thing after another. It is not as if the congregation—or the preacher, for that matter—live their lives within the happy confines of this vision. It is only there as an increasingly trustworthy alternative, on occasion to be lived in with a kind of quiet joy, on occasion to be found most painfully missing.

Our task is to make history a home for man. For this to happen there must be a vision that we can enter into where in Yeats' words we can cast out remorse and "so great a sweetness flows into the breast.

> We must laugh and we must sing,
> We are blest by everything
> Everything we look upon is blest."9

Preaching has matured when it is keeping this vision alive and vivid and accessible to the world.

1. Alasdair MacIntyre, *After Virtue* (Notre Dame, IN: Notre Dame University Press, 1981), ch. 3.

2. Peter Allt and Russell K. Alspach, eds., *The Variorum Editions of the Poems of W. B. Yeats* (New York: Macmillan Co., 1973), pp. 478–479.

3. Ibid.

4. Gregory Bateson, *Mind and Nature: A Necessary Unity* (New York: E. P. Dutton, 1979), appendix.

5. Allt and Alspach, eds., *The Variorum Editions of the Poems of W. B. Yeats*, p. 479.

6. MacIntyre, *After Virgue*, ch. 11.

7. Freeman Dyson, *Disturbing the Universe* (New York: Harper and Row, 1981).

8. A. R. Peacocke, "The New Biology and Nature, Man and God," in Kenneth Hare, ed., *The Experiment of Life* (Toronto: University of Toronto Press, 1983), p. 6.

9. Allt and Alspach, eds., *The Variorum Editions of the Poems of W. B. Yeats*, p. 479.

XIII. Ministerial Maturity and Person-Centered Administration

William R. Rogers

As children, we wanted someone to show us and let us in on the secrets of the world of grown-ups. But in adulthood, once educational preparation and initial success are behind us, we seem to feel that we will age gracefully in our skills and personal style. Occasionally, identity malaise or an organizational crisis will call up questions of confidence or direction. Rarely do we stop and give serious, focused attention to what it means to be a *mature* professional administrator. That meaning is exactly what animates this chapter.

As ministers, we ask, "What characterizes a maturity that is worth striving for, especially in dealing with my administrative responsibilities?" As professionals, we need to understand the principles or guidelines that lead to informed and coherent action in helping individuals and communities. And as Christians, we want to confirm those theological grounding points that give ultimate purpose and faithful coherence to what we do.

One assumption here is that "maturity" does not simply come with age. Another is that *descriptive* analyses of adulthood must be differentiated from normative statements of the features of maturity. Our concern will be with the latter, attempting to state some of the principles on which such qualities might be based. A critical dimension of the nature of maturity must be that each professional will refine and extend his or her own fundamental perspective. Hence, the ideas presented here will be designed to foster such reflection. It also is pertinent to suggest that maturity, especially in administrative dimensions of ministry, has more to do with finding a good *mentor* and developing a trusted, honest, and resourceful consultation group than with theoretical analyses, discussions, and readings—no matter how brilliant.

What follows is more a theoretical and constructive statement than an empirical research. After a brief preliminary look at some key thinkers who have shifted the contemporary discussion of administration in the ministry, I shall introduce two interrelated issues of principle in organizational theory and theology. From there we will move into a discussion of characteristics that might give shape to a view of maturity in ministerial administration. What enables maturity, and what impediments are there in this formation process? Overall, there is an attempt to demonstrate that "administration," sometimes maligned as less substantive or creative than teaching, preaching, or counseling, can in fact be what the word implies: "toward ministry"—a set of thoughtful sensibilities and skills that enable both individual spiritual growth and the effective prophetic engagement of the organizational church in meeting broader social and global needs.

1. A Modest Paradigm Shift

Among other characteristics, maturity is marked by the restless, creative transposition of mental sets in which intellectual schemes that had seemed satisfactory for generations become questions and a new scheme of organizing perceptions flashes into view. A paradigm that had appeared to be satisfactory is strikingly revised. It is sometimes as though a diagonal slice is cut through a series of stratified columns that had previously been viewed only from a vertical perspective. This sort of shift has occurred in the very understanding of ministerial functions themselves. Whereas for generations the self-understanding of Christian ministry consisted of a series of roles, parallel columns, if you will, the two important studies in the 1950s cut a diagonal slice showing the interpenetration of several central perspectives crossing through virtually every task of ministry. That slice directly affects our current exploration of administration in ministry.

Previously it made sense to speak of preaching, teaching, pastoral care, evangelism, and church administration as relatively discrete roles in ministry. These appeared to be organized by task, by traditional expectation, by time allocation, and so on. But Seward Hiltner, in *Preface to Pastoral Theology*, pointed out that it would be much more compelling to look at basic perspectives that a pastor has in caring for people, no matter what the specific role.[1] Role separation can lead to fragmentation, inconsistency, and ineptness in observing the broader opportunities for ministry, no matter what the setting. Hiltner named the components of this diagonal slice "healing, sustaining, organizing and guiding."

In this way, Hiltner intended to show that a concern for healing could be expressed as well in preaching, or even in a conversation in the grocery story, as it could in traditional pastoral care. Similarly, organizing could become as much a part of a pastoral ministry to a family in difficulty as it would be in setting up church committees or an annual budget. His basic hope was to identify the perspective of Christian "shepherding" that might be germane in any and all acts of ministry. And of particular importance to this chapter is the way in which he reconceived of administration as *NOT* a set of specific tasks such as calendar preparation, financial analysis, fund raising, personnel management, maintenance, schedules, etc., but rather an organizing or sustaining perspective that should inform the entire spectrum of a minister's caring interaction with people.

Shortly after Hiltner came the important work of Niebuhr, Gustafson, and Williams also reconceiving the tasks of ministry into a central unifying theme: "the Pastoral Director."2 This, too, was a theme that took administration and converted it from a discrete role to a dimension of all pastoral work, basing this conception on the biblical image of the "equipping of the saints" such that all could increasingly become ministers to one another.

Being appreciative of this kind of paradigm shift, I intend to follow a similar course in suggesting that administration as it is to be viewed in the following discussion will be conceived broadly as a set of skills and perspectives that cut across virtually all tasks of ministry, calling for sensitivity to the enabling of structures that enhance the richness of maturation of individuals and groups in the life of faith.

2. Theory Z and All That

There are several developments in contemporary organizational theory that may be helpful in defining what these skills or sensitivities might be. Insofar as they are compatible with basic theological principles, they may strengthen our frame of reference in eventually constructing some of the characteristics of maturity in relation to administration.

In contrast to the typical pyramidal or hierarchical organizational designs that have characterized most businesses and many nonprofit institutions in the past few decades, vigorous attention is now being given to the emergence of collegial or democratic models. Though the latter has the intrinsic appeal of a humane interpersonal style, it is only recently that research has demonstrated the increased productivity, reduced absenteeism, reduced errors, stronger organizational identification, and improved profitability that comes with shared decision-making, open evaluation systems, shared ownership, and democratic procedures. Taken together, these dimensions of shared participation, greater mutuality of authority, and open involvement in decision-making have been termed Theory Z.

The application of Theory Z within an analysis of nonprofit organizations has already been undertaken by people such as McQuillen.[3] It would seem thoroughly fitting to explore this model in conjunction with religious organizations and the specific roles of a mature minister.

It should also be pointed out that similar emphases on democratic structures and the seeking of consensus in decision-making have been highlighted in research on "Type B" organizations by Argyris and Schon.[4] The current interest in Japanese management styles further strengthens attention given to participation, loyalty through involvement, respect, collegial decisions, shared leadership, etc. A thorough bibliography on both research and theory in democratic management has recently been prepared by Stevens.[5]

Within a discussion of maturity, these emphases seem especially appropriate since they represent many factors that human development theorists have noted in human maturation. I refer to a noteworthy transition from (a) external locus of authority placed in a relatively inaccessible other, (b) external locus of control, (c) clearly accepted and handed-down definitions of right and wrong behavior, (d) inability in taking the role of the other; to (a) locus of authority in shared experience, (b) internal locus of control, (c) acceptable behavior mutually defined within the social contract or a loyalty to some higher good, and (d) increased ability to take the role of the other and to be committed to areas of mutual benefit.

3. Guiding Theological Principles

A consideration of maturity in administrative style, whether or not involves ministerial functions, should be interconnected with a worthy underpinning in theological principles. Because our attention here is directly with ministerial maturity, it becomes all the more important. There are four principles that I find to be especially relevant: (1) the interrelatedness of all human functions within an ultimate context, (2) the centrality of incarnate love, (3) the hallowing of every moment in an openness to the Spirit, and (4) the profound givenness of mutual transcendence in the structure of life.[6]

1. The Interrelatedness of All Human Functions Within an Ultimate Context. This is already apparent in the commitments discussed above, concerning a paradigm shift. All functions, including all ministerial functions, are held together in the structure and process of being. All relationships affect other relationships. Each act is intertwined both with ultimate possibility and with the limits of facticity and time. One implication of this for administration in ministry is, as Hiltner suggests, that administrative functions not only organize the work of the church, they also may be healing and sustaining. Budgetary work, for instance, may identify cost centers, predict inflationary pressures, establish annual giving goals, etc., but it may also be the opportunity for an entire congregation to establish a sense of cohesiveness around significant priorities, to affirm a sense of care for those in need, to identify and eventually bridge divergent individual assertions of self-interest, to establish a sense of mission, and so on.

2. The Centrality of Incarnate Love. This is perhaps the heart of our faith. God's love is not only manifest in Christ, but it is also made available through the Christian community in meaningful forms of reconciliation, nurturance, forgiveness, support, enablement, and caring. We affirm our capacity to embody love in spite of the times of brokenness and felt limitation, or perhaps because of them and the grateful sense that we have been healed and renewed by that reality of love. One implication of this central affirmation is that *ALL* people, within and without the church, are embraced within the redemptive actualization of this love. Effective administration is consequently realized more appropriately in the careful inclusion and nurture of each one, rather than in some authoritarian or patronizing attitude that "takes over" without listening to the real yearnings and perceptions of the other (in spite of the fact that some might call that "benevolent paternalism"). Real benevolence takes the concern of the other as its own! It suffers long and is kind.

3. The Hallowing of Every Moment in an Openness to the Spirit. This suggests that no church organization, no special committee, no particular time, no influential person is somehow more sacred or worthy of concern than another. Each decision, each person, each committee, each moment may be an occasion for the realization of spiritual depth. One cannot orchestrate the politics of decisive action on the basis of a biased power base. To do so leads not only to disharmony but to a betrayal of the vision of incarnate love. Maturity in the Spirit enables the minister to risk attention even to the seemingly minor or unsettled or incongruent contribution, even to the inarticulate wince or troubled silence, knowing that there may be the seed of a new insight or the broadening of the whole gathered community.

4. Mutual Transcendence in the Structure of Life. This is the theological awareness in which we perceive the transcending structure of inconclusiveness by which individuals are enabled to move beyond the more infantile forms of dependence, and even beyond the somewhat adolescent pretenses of independence (which all too often betray a counterdependence: protestations of freedom which in fact are driven by opposition to expectation). Mutual transdependence is a way of acknowledging that we are interdependent, neither fully dependent nor independent. Furthermore, that mutuality is sustained by our oneness in a more profound reality. Acknowledging that, we may be released from the anxiety and drivenness by which some would try to establish an individual mark in the way that Tillich so aptly described as "self-sufficient finitude." Within the awareness of mutual transdependence, the administrative implication of collegiality and nonhierarchical consensus-building is given even further theological significance.

185

4.   Characteristics of Mature Administration

Based on these four theological principles, and with a view to the importance of understanding administration as a transverse slice of virtually all the specific tasks of ministry, we can point to several characteristics of mature ministerial administration. Some of these characteristics demand explication; others will be listed more briefly for the sake of brevity.[7]

1. Developing an Enabling Climate for Personal Participation. Mutual transdependence and the experience of incarnate love carry practical implications for guiding a church structure in which all persons feel supported, involved, and potent in shaping the decisions of the church. A ministry of compassion is expressed not only in sermons and lecture, but in thousands of daily interactions with people throughout the community. It is organizationally expressed by a committee structure and a communication network that enables people to know when decisions are being made and invites their participation. Families in the Sunday School, for instance, should have a chance to discuss Christian education principles and the character of curriculum development for their children. Young people should have a chance to design retreats and special projects that will express their sense of urgency and religious concern. More broadly, people not only within a church but within a wider community may be involved in critical issues of the church's witness in race relations, urban planning, problems of poverty and hunger, and so on.

Almost inevitably critical decisions and strategic planning within the church and community involve contrasting points of view. People with economic, personal, and ideological matters at stake will feel a need to be taken seriously. This suggests that an enabling administrator and a caring minister will face a difficult mediating function when he or she seriously includes in the decision-making process people whose lives will be affected by those decisions. It is a challenging and unsettling task and sometimes collapses under pressures for either efficiency or autonomous control of some strong and more hierarchical leaders. In the long run, both the theological significance of mutuality and love and the organizational effectiveness of an inclusive base of personal involvement in decision-making are worth every ounce of effort in helping those with diverse judgments come together in the seeking of consensus on programs and action strategies.

2. Enabling Clarity of a Shared Vision. Not only immediate projects but a broader view of the mission of the church and of a particular congregation can engage broad personal participation. The development of a longer perspective on the nature of the Kingdom has traditionally been the function of the church. But, again, the actualization of a long range view of the mission of a particular congregation is not always an easy task. Even matters of salvation and redemption, the transformation of human life in relation to the love of God, take on strikingly different characteristics. There may be those who see the primary mission as one of deepening individual spiritual life. There may be others who see a central importance in the power of God working toward social justice, organizational change, economic and political realignments. Bringing such diverse visions of a central mission of the church together may call for recognition of not only the legitimacy of both, but also a clarification of the significant ways in which the varying views interpenetrate and support one another. That certainly is the case with individual spiritual development and social action.

3. Openness and Consistency in Procedures. Enabling genuine participation in the life and decision-making of a church necessitates a clarity of understanding regarding how things are done. It is not enough to be simply dedicated to the characteristics of Christian community and of seeking consensus in the building of a spiritual and social vision informed by theological principles. The mature minister must also take responsibility to work with the various procedures and in following those procedures in making decisions on everything from establishing religious curricular priorities through setting major fund goals for an annual budget.

Openness in procedure matters involves two main components. One is a pattern of communication that announces publicly and in advance the issues, committees, responsibility flow, and agenda that will be followed in shaping policy. The other involves clarity in articulating the timetable, the points of reference, and the criteria of judgment used in deliberations. Both the structure and the process should be spelled out as clearly as possible, including modes for reconsideration or reevaluation of decisions should there be substantial groups within the church who feel uncomfortable with the steps that are being taken.

Since churches function as "voluntary associations," and since leadership in various committees turns over with considerable regularity, it may be advisable to have some of the major planning groups in the church developing a handbook of procedures—when and how in the church calendar various programs get organized, when and how nominating procedures take place, when and how financial consultation is undertaken related to annual budget planning, and so on.

Since religious institutions also frequently experience patterns of power dominance on the part of several members who become invested either implicitly or explicitly with particular authority, it would be all the more important for a minister who seeks to build genuine community and mutual involvement to be sure that procedures are followed consistently. That may be one of the surest ways of confirming the openness of the process, avoiding what otherwise could be manipulative and preemptive decisions made behind the scenes.

4. Availability. Our corporate leadership in the ministry of the church must include the principle of personal availability—availability of time, of concern, of professional leadership in all phases of the life of the church. Such availability should include not only the minister's willingness to respond to the needs of parishioners and of the community, but also a willingness to generate a climate in which people can be available to one another, both in times of joy and in times of need.

While most ministers are committed to the importance of being available, the practical exigencies of a heavy schedule of responsibility sometimes make it difficult to keep an "open door" policy. There is a tension between the administrative wisdom of "effective time management" (which implies clearly scheduled events and resistance to interruptions) and the importance of availability. Clearly a minister needs time for a life of reading and prayer, of sermon preparation, and counseling uninterruptedly with people in times of stress. But the key to retaining availability in spite of the stress of multiple demands on one's time lies in careful organization of calendar, and in the incorporation of volunteer assistance in responsibilities that can be appropriately delegated to others. In the final analysis, availability is a quality of genuine interest and a "willingness to be known." With an attitude of genuine compassion and involvement, we can maximize the time spent with any individual group and still remain open to the distinct and unexpected expressions of need.

5. Empathic Understanding. The attitudinal significance of understanding deserves special attention. It is the direct outgrowth of our own religious experience insofar as we find ourselves to be understood and supported by God. And it is suggested also by the best that we know regarding a healing and sustaining pastoral ministry to others—a set of relationships that are more often characterized by empathy than by interpretation or advice.

But it is equally important in administration that the mature minister do more than look at facts and figures, more than plan overall institutional structures and budget procedures. One must undertake the more specific organizational and quantitative analyses of the church with a clear and overriding concern that each of those structural and financial decisions respond specifically to an abiding and comprehensive concern for the genuine feelings and needs of the people. Unless there is empathy for the places of hurt and confusion in individual lives, of acrimony and suffering within families, of bewilderment and ambiguity at various stages in the life process, the programs and organizational efficiency of a church would completely miss the mark in being the vehicle for divine compassion and inspiration. Just as preaching is a two-way matter, attention to the Word and to the needs of the specific congregation in a specific time, administration is a two-way process, attending to the mechanisms by which things get accomplished but at the same time insisting that the things that do not get accomplished are genuinely responsive to an empathic understanding of the people for whom one cares.

6. Alertness to Hidden Agenda. Expressions of human understanding are both an outgrowth of our concern with incarnate love and our willingness to recognize that such love cannot be actualized if we remain at the level of surface appearances. Human need, partly, because it is painful and often the result of ambiguous forces that play in one's inner life, cannot be easily articulated. For that reason, the mature and sensitive minister must be particularly alert to the more subtle feelings that are often obscured through oblique anger, or silence and withdrawal. In a sense, the task of pastoral counseling and the task of ministerial administration are identical. They both have to do with hearing the urgent but partly concealed messages of people who know only in part how to express the reality of their predicament.

Recognizing hidden agenda is important within small group and committee work as well as within the total life of a religious community. It is important to "listen between the lines," to nonverbal as well as verbal messages, to inflections and the literal positioning of people in relation to one another. I am reminded of the example of members of a discussion group who came down very hard on a middle-aged man who was reprimanding an unmarried young woman who had become pregnant, only to discover through the gentle questions of the minister that much of that moral outrage had been driven by the man's own struggles for some fifteen years with the problem of infertility and childlessness in his own marriage—a situation which called for as much compassion as judgment. Ginnott cites the case of a child being taken to a day school for the first time and boisterously asking who had broken a toy that was lying on the floor—a question driven not so much by unwillingness to cooperate, or even by curiosity, as by an apprehension of what might happen to him if he were to make a mistake and break something. Listening to both children and adults, in settings that range from play to budget discussions, can be absolutely critical. Without acknowledging the hidden agendas, the minister as administrator could easily misgauge the priorities being expressed and could, over time, develop programs that would be irrelevant to the most important values and personal strivings of people within the church.

7. The Incorporation of Multiple Individual Concerns in the Development of Group Consensus. As a minister listens to both the expressed and unexpressed concerns of people, some attention must be given to the interweaving of these concerns into the broader mission and structure of the church. Sometimes a board of

189

committee, or a program development committee can be the vehicle by which these concerns are brought together. At other times it may be the minister's own vision, or perhaps more accurately a restless agitation in the middle of the night, which generates a constructive set of program suggestions.

The task of bringing multiple individual concerns together is always complicated by diverse political and socioeconomic allegiances. It may be the minister's task to strengthen communication, for instance, among individuals with quite divergent views of how justice may be done in areas of international conflict. There may be equally difficult tasks in helping people to bridge priorities between internal needs for church beautification or for a new organ, on the one hand, and a response to community needs in addressing poverty and unemployment, on the other. As both the spiritual quest and dedication to social action enliven the vitality of a church, they can also create dissension, misunderstanding, and anger. The mature minister, rather than wanting to squelch that misunderstanding and anger, must be prepared to create a forum both informally and sometimes formally for the open discussion of varying perspectives, being sure that that forum helps to nourish the ultimate commitment to the healing and reconciling power of the Spirit.

8. Respect for Both Individual Value Sensitivities and for Pluralism. Within the planning for specific programs of education, missions, youth work, and family life, a broad array of value commitments may be expressed. Hopefully these values will embody some of the common themes of Christian commitment—truth-telling, personal integrity, compassion for the disadvantaged, and commitment to justice and fair treatment for all, honesty, and forgiveness. But there may be a number of cases in which other values are expressed, or where the more central values of our faith are interpreted quite differently.

Part of the genius of a mature Christian perspective is in its recognition that no one human affirmation of what is right exhausts the truth. All human perspective is fallible and certainly culpable to the bias of self-interest and particularly of background. It is both theologically faithful and institutionally prudent to recognize the integrity and pluralism of an array of valued interpretations. But it is equally important to set some limits among those more belligerently expressed values that might threaten to end dialogue or to prejudge the ascendancy of one particular authoritarian position. At some point, the mature minister faces the subtle but significant task of interweaving respect for the values of an individual and the discipline of a community that must protect itself from being overwhelmed by forms of either dominance or diversion that might threaten to destroy the very process of the open, caring community. Again it seems possible that this difficult task may be accomplished only when there is a deeper sense of the "mutual transdependence" of all particular lives in the deeper, sustaining strength of divine love.

8. The Balance of Ministerial Maturity. The eight characteristics of person-centered administration enumerated above could easily be augmented by a series of other characteristics of maturity as they relate to ministerial administration. The following is an attempt to list some of the attitudinal characteristics that follow from both the theological and operational principles discussed earlier. Though briefly listed, the balance that is essential to these attitudes would be worthy of further reflection. They are:

1) Orientation towards service, without self-effacement.
2) Patience without weakness.
3) Loyalty to the institution, without idolatrous idealization.
4) Willingness to evaluate the strengths and weaknesses of staff members and key volunteers, without defensiveness or autocratic judgmentalism.
5) Willingness to take a stand on significant moral issues, without arrogance or moralism.
6) Energy and pace, without aggressiveness.
7) Enjoyment of tasks and humor about oneself, without glibness.
8) Financial savvy and fund-raising ability, without materialistic obsession.
9) Tolerance for ambiguity, without loss of moral passion.
10) Acceptance of limitations, without depressive withdrawal.
11) Confidentiality without secrecy.
12) Ability in arbitrating conflicts, without getting caught in the middle and becoming alienated from both sides.
13) Willingness to learn, without false modesty.
14) Willingness to be a sponsor of younger leaders, without ego aggrandisement of personal status.
15) Nurturing of the ideas of others, without deflective evasion of personal self-revelation.
16) Fairness in the distribution of resources, without compulsive legalism.
17) Joy in the celebration of significant events, achievements, and persons, without pompousness.
18) Competence in setting priorities and developing effective structures for following through on projects, without ensnarement within those structures.
19) Ability to plan for constructive purposes, without allowing the end to dominate the means and without compulsive attachment to those plans.

Every one of these characteristics is sustained by the theological perspective that what we are engaged in ultimately transcends personal effort and organizational effectiveness. Our devotion is to the deeper leading of the Spirit and to that power that transforms and matures human life, often "in spite of" our best efforts to understand and lead.

5. Practical Notes on Enablement and Impediments

Drawing both on research and common wisdom, it could be suggested that several specific conditions help enable maturity in ministry. The most central condition may well be the emerging maturity of the life of prayer, meditation, and worship in the minister's own spiritual pilgrimage. Also there are important matters of the appropriate fit, size, and denominational structure in which one's work is carried out. Personal conditions may include a richness and flexibility of thought, exercise, and relaxation, a trusted consultation group in which issues can be talked through in a nonthreatening way, sexual satisfaction, minibreaks in the rigors of routine work, and the provision for "a room of one's own"—a very personal place of refuge and reflection. Organizationally, enabling conditions include the cultivation of open relationships with a governing board, clarity regarding the structures for decision-making, the identification of proteges and sponsors within the organization, and the deliberate development of organizational and financial management skills.

Impediments to the development of ministerial maturity in administration include an inability to anticipate the effects of internal programs and the external environment and too heavy or too light a hand in areas of organizational leadership and financial planning. A loss of touch with key members of the organization, or withdrawal from stress, can lead to forms of regression that also would be an impediment. Clearly one's ego needs for personal recognition, or apprehension about not being liked, or playing favorites, or overidentification with pet projects that cannot be relinquished—all could lead to serious difficulty.

6. Conclusion

The foregoing reflections represent an attempt to define the principles, characteristics, attitudes, and conditions under which ministerial maturity may emerge. The focus of the discussion clearly is on the pastor as administrator but recognizes that administrative skill and institutional organization must stem from first principles of a theological order as well as from derivative management theory. Where that management theory deepens our sense of service and inclusiveness in working with the people of God struggling to understand and support one another, as well as to bring greater justice to the world, it may bring into actuality the spiritual maturity of the broader community.

Perhaps the notion of "person-centered administration" needs an ultimate disclaimer. In the final analysis, we center our work on personal expression, involvement, and fulfillment only as instrumental to a more ultimate center. It is the enhancement of profound relatedness to the *spiritual* center of all being that provides the most trustworthy guide for our ministry. And it is also, of course, that spiritual center that makes possible the very process of both aspiration and forgiveness of our own quest for maturity. Insofar as we can help to form a spiritually, socially, and politically effective organization that is responsive to the real needs of people, we can perhaps be an instrument of bringing the timeless into time.

Notes

1. Seward Hiltner, *Preface to Pastoral Theology* (Nashville: Abingdon Press, 1958).

2. H. R. Niebuhr, J. Gustafson, and D. Williams, *The Purpose of the Church and Its Ministry* (New York: Harper & Row, 1956).

3. C. C. McQuillen, "Universities as 'Theory Z' Organization," *AGB Reports* 24 (6) (1982), pp. 20–23.

4. C. Argyris and D. Schon, *Organizational Learning* (Boston: Addison-Wesley Co., 1978).

5. W. Stevens, "Bibliography of Theory and Research in Democratic Management" (Greensboro, NC: Guilford College, 1984).

6. Dietrich Bonhoeffer, *Life Together* (New York: Harper & Row, 1954); Seward Hiltner and L. G. Colston, *Context of Pastoral Counseling* (Nashville: Abingdon Press, 1961); Ronald F. Levant, John M. Schlien, *Client-Centered Therapy and the Person Centered Approach* (New York: Praeger Publishers, Inc., 1984); Niebuhr, Gustafson, and Williams, *The Purpose of the Church and Its Ministry*; Wayne E. Oates, *The Christian Pastor* (Philadelphia: Westminster Press, 1964); Ross Snyder, *The Ministry of Meaning* (Geneva: World Council of Churches, 1965); Paul Tillich, *Systematic Theology*, vols. 1–3 (Chicago: University of Chicago Press, 1951, 1957, 1963); Henry Nelson Wieman, *Man's Ultimate Commitment* (Carbondale, IL: Southern Illinois University Press, 1958).

7. Kenneth L. Callahan, *Twelve Keys to an Effective Church* (New York: Harper & Row, 1983); James D. Anderson and Ezra Earl Jones, *The Management of Ministry* (New York: Harper & Row, 1978); Alvin J. Lindgren and Norman Shawchuck, *Management of Ministry* (Nashville: Abingdon Press, 1977).

XIV. Ministry, Maturity, and Political Action

Walter G. Muelder

The Second Vatican Council praised participation in political leadership in these words: "The Church regards as worthy of praise and consideration the work of those who, as a service to others, dedicate themselves to the welfare of the state and undertake the burdens of this task."[1] From this general standpoint we may legitimately move to issues of the quality of participation by an ordained clergyperson who chooses to enter the political arena. From the general ministry of the laity we thus move to the dedication expected of the special ministry of clergy in politics as a functional vocation. Pope John Paul II has not satisfactorily justified his command that Father Drinan vacate his position as a congressman. For the purpose of this chapter I assume that the political activities of both the Pope and Father Drinan are legitimate and that this legitimacy extends to Protestants, Orthodox, and Jewish rabbis as well. I shall deal with questions of maturity in leadership of any and all clergy, not with the appropriateness of their participation as ordained ministers.

Parish clergy are inevitably involved in the political order because laity and clergy alike are citizens and because Jesus' Gospel of the Kingdom addresses both inner personal and social values and institutions. The moral agent is socially personal and personally social. In this general sense of communal participation, maturity relates to the courage of the minister in raising relevant political issues at the right time and with relevant wisdom. A sense of balanced responsibility among the many clergy roles in parish and community is clearly a mark of maturity. Yet general parish leadership is but one type of ministerial activity in politics. A greater intensity of involvement may occur at times of acute social crisis and in behalf of certain causes, as when Martin Luther King, Jr., became the leader of the Montgomery Bus Boycott while retaining his position as pastor, using the church as a source of ongoing inspiration, training the people in nonviolent action, and addressing the conscience of the nation from the pulpit and the rostrum of public gatherings. An even fuller political engagement occurs when a clergyperson is an elected national official. Moreover, there are the specialized officers of social action boards and agencies, lobbyists, seminary professors of social ethics, and the like. The range is very wide. To each a special accent of maturity is applicable. However, all face certain complex challenge.

A presumption of this chapter is that participating ministers be educated, professional, and ordained. We may elaborate this presumption in a threefold way: (a) that, as an educated person, the ordained minister is informed by Christian social ethics and the elements of political economy, i.e., knows the relation of justice to liberty and equality to be problematic or dialectical and that the goal of conflict among competing interests is reconciliation and the common good; (b) that, as a professional, the ordained minister is committed to social service as a good higher than personal gain, thus making of politics a vocation that transcends special and private interests; and (c) that, as an ordained minister, he or she is ready in both life-style and decision-making to be guided (as far as religious discernment and conscience allow) by denominational and ecumenical guidelines in ordering political action coherently. Without surrendering moral autonomy, the educated, professional, and ordained minister places political life within the ecclesial context of social ethics and the Kingdom of God as norm and goal. In these caveats I am not by definition sketching a paragon of political virtue but rather indicating benchmarks inherent in a topic that includes the meaning of ministry, the relevance of maturity, and the vocation of political life and action.

1. The Ubiquity of Religion in Politics

Religion is today everywhere involved in political life and often determines its shapes and goals. Though some religionists protest involvement in politics, the relative nonparticipation has political consequences. Limited participation is often determined and modified by what social or personal interests and rights are at stake. The worldwide varieties of mature and immature participation include the following settings: Orthodox Jewry in Israel; Pakistan; Catholic Ireland and Protestant Northern Ireland; the country of Poland, where a Roman Catholic nation is governed by the Communist Party; the civil war in Lebanon with its conflicts between sects of Christians and Muslims; the domination of Iran by the Ayatollah; the Liberation theologians in Latin America, particularly the Christians for Socialism; the Vatican state under the Pope; and, not least, the United States, where religious leaders pressure the president and the congress regarding school prayer and abortion and equal rights for women and a nuclear freeze, where the National Council of Churches is criticized for its liberal views, where

Jerry Falwell leads the Moral Majority, and where denominations lobby vigorously in the nation's capital. The list can be greatly extended.

These situations suggest the complex interpenetration of religion and community, both in nationhood and culture, as well as the embeddedness of religious institutions in the society. They pose the problems both of maturity of religious ethos and ethics and the maturity of religious leadership in the political sphere where particular religions dominate. It falls beyond the purview of this chapter to evaluate leaders and situations in particular, but it is humbling to reflect on the gap between ideals of universal humanity and the religion-in-politics scene. Whatever one says about maturity may seem remote from historical actuality. Yet, even the actual cannot be understood except in terms of models and norms of investigation. In what follows I shall have the context of the United States most explicitly in mind.

The church is one of the principal intermediary institutions that both join and separate people in the community to and from government. The family and the school are there also. In addition, tens of thousands of associations, clubs, and societies, each with its organs of control and governance, function as intermediaries between individuals and the state. There is, as Robert M. MacIver argued, a "web of government" that objectifies a "firmament of law" in the community as distinguished from the state. Society is held together by its myth structure as well as its technostructure. Its self-enforcing values give the community a habit of obedience and cohesion. Therefore, maturity within the participatory web of government of the subsidiary institutions of the community contributes to the level of maturity in the public realm. And *anomie,* or normlessness, in social order makes for disintegration. The church has a much closer daily interaction with this myth-structure of the community than with the formal political order and helps determine through family and education its ethos. As Chief Justice Earl Warren has observed, "Law floats on a sea of ethics." Religion's role in the interaction of state and community may be either destructive or constructive. In the struggle for justice, violence and nonviolence may depend on fanaticism or maturity.

2. Vocation and Pluralism

The minister in American politics must exercise one's vocation in a tense and pluralistic society. When one speaks of politics as vocation, one might well remember a dictum by Max Weber that puts the sense of vocation of politics at the intersection of an ethics of aspiration and an ethics of ends. The vertical line of duty and the horizontal line of goals often intersect in such a way as to create moral tension, requiring compromise in political life. To do the best possible in a historical situation means to discern the conflict among "rights" or "duties,"

197

among "goods," and between "right" and "good." The best and the feasible must be considered for both the short and the long term.

The church leaders in politics should understand the inherent ambiguity of leadership in a democratic society, the power of authentic personal example and character, and the limits to freedom of action because of entanglement in political, social, and economic interests. From a sociological perspective the church has generally been most effective in social change when it has mastered the dilemmas of leadership, has shown radiant power of authentic spirituality in its leaders, and has been most free of institutional entanglements. One reason that the witness of the churches has been relatively strong in America is the separation of church and state. No similar freedom exists in the church's relation to the economic order and the attendant structural involvement in sexism and racism. In fact, of course, no complete separation can exist between religious institutions (including their leaders) and the various modes of political and economic power.

In the early church there was a tendency to separate sharply the "church" and the "world," the two ways of light and darkness. There is also today a tendency and a temptation for some groups and their ministers to absolutize and to endow with literal biblical authority their political opinions, in strict doctrinal and moralistic terms. Thus an "authoritarian personality" tends to manifest itself. John Kater makes the following comment on the Christian Right today:

> It sees the world as a battle-ground between two absolutes, God and evil, and Christians know which side they are on. No skirmish holds any ambiguity or room for doubt; all is light and darkness, and the only choice that matters is which side we are on. It is a vision of the world, and of Americans and American Christians in the world, as warriors for the right—and for the Right.[2]

All religious leaders on all problems seek to bring an awareness of the ultimate conditions of human life, making social problems a subject of theological and ethical reflections. But this awareness of the ultimate aspects of political issues ought to illuminate the ambiguity of leadership and should relativize, not absolutize, social policies and values. There is a qualitative difference between saying "Jesus Christ is the light of the world" and saying "the church is the light of the world." At the same time, when an intrinsic value is at stake with respect to human rights and conscience, dedication to the ultimate conditions of human life will reinforce the defense of all persons created in the "image and likeness" of God.

The world as a whole is a pluralistic jumble at present, and the United States is a pluralistic nation that runs the gamut of ethnic minorities in its composition, the spectrum of denominations and sects, and boasts extremes of religiosity and secularism. In class patterns, it suffers a widening gap between rich and poor and a sense that the door to equal opportunity is closing.

Acceleration of social change and the pluralistic melange of minorities have heightened the sense of divisiveness and made many Americans feel anxious and powerless. They feed what Richard Hofstadter has called "the paranoid style in American politics" in a book by that title.[3] This style has afflicted religious as well as secular politicians. He says: the United States is "a country in which so many people do not know who they are or what they belong to or what belongs to them. It is a country of people whose status expectations are random and uncertain, and yet whose status aspirations have been whipped up to a high pitch by our democratic ethos and our rags-to-riches mythology." This is fed also by the bewildering images of the television media, its cheap advertising, its kaleidoscopic mixture of sex, violence, material success, death, fantasy, news, gags, and instant wealth—all perceived within minutes of each other and seldom with depth of perspective. Little depth of meaning sorts out recreation from serious news, which itself is offered up as entertainment.

Maturity is intimately related to the idea of responsible leadership viewed holistically. When crises arise, as in the racial strife of the 1950s, social injustices and weakness in leadership are exposed. A community that has not been prepared through years of training in justice and reconciliation cannot suddenly find a mature solution to earlier folly after the crisis erupts. The temptation for some clergy in strife-torn communities is to retreat into silence or otherworldliness. On the other hand, a prophetic voice can often call forth hitherto silent members to step forward, to find each other, and to rally constructive action.

Clergy participation even in a great civil rights demonstration, as in the March on Washington in 1963, may be a relatively immature substitute for needed leadership. Greater Boston clergy who went to Washington were evaluated by Harold Garman, who measured their responsibility by inquiring whether, perhaps, they were only unloading a feeling of accumulated personal guilt by a single act of protest. Had they been preaching regularly on racial issues? What interracial contacts did they cultivate for themselves and their parishioners? In what overt action groups locally had they participated? To what extent did they become involved in the social action of their own denominations and ecumenically? The study had many facets. Garman concluded that for many clergypersons their participation was a highly individualized event and episodic. Many had not even invited lay persons to join them as an act of Christian solidarity.

3. Mature Style of Gandhi and King

Our search for maturity for religious leaders in politics may be illuminated by the perspectives and styles of Gandhi and King. They have, of course, been roundly criticized for their methods and some of the consequences of their styles. However, there are ingredients in their religious and political behavior that have elevated them as well as the causes they represented in the eyes of the world.

Gandhi postulated a close relation between religion and politics. He said, "For me there are no politics devoid of religion. They subserve religion. Politics bereft of religion are a death-trap because they kill the soul."[4] He felt that no truly religious life was possible unless politics, "which encircles us like the coils of a snake from which we cannot get out no matter how one tries," was purified by and based on morality and religion. He did not mean religion in terms of a particular religion like Hinduism, Islam, or Christianity. He meant, as stated in *Young India* (December 5, 1920), religion that transcends all particular religions, "which changes one's very nature, which binds one indissolubly to the truth within and which purifies. It is the permanent element in human nature which counts no cost too great in order to find full expression and which leaves the soul utterly restless until it has found itself and appreciated the true correspondence between its Maker and itself."[5]

In order to be adequately involved in politics, religion has to be recalled, according to Gandhi, to its mission to serve selflessly. Hence, he had a critical attitude towards tradition and practices in religion that did disservice to the poor. Gandhi's religion was highly ethical and combated the spirit of communalism which an erroneous understanding of religion may introduce or intensify in a country that is pluralistic. Another point that must be added here is his attaching great value to fasting as a means of inner purification. But fasting may be paradoxical and morally ambiguous. Fasting figured prominently in the technique of nonviolent solutions of social and political problems. He used it constructively; but sometimes fasting amounts to coercion of a bad type. It can be positively obnoxious and used for narrow and selfish purposes without the requisite degree of inner purity that its use normally presupposes. Unscrupulous persons, Gandhi knew, have made fasting as a power technique almost a bad legacy from his use of it. Fundamentally, for Gandhi fasting was an instrument of maturity, part of his grand experiment with truth. Maturity in politics requires nonviolence within and without. We must note this also in Martin Luther King, Jr.

King's practical social ethics combined a nonviolent way of life with an appeal to the ideals of the American republic and a demand for

200

the enforcement of the Bill of Rights. Hence, his strategy walked on two legs, Christian faith grounded in metaphysical personalism, on the left, and, on the right, political commitment of law to freedom and justice for all. He appealed directly to the ecumenical conscience of the nation and to the federal government to enforce federal law above infringements of the constitution by state and local statutes. He understood the interaction of law and religion and the superior ultimate demands of religion over civil law. He did not hesitate to appeal to civic religion when it combined the best in political and religious heritage. On the one hand, he had a theological and philosophical position that synethesized the biblical prophetic tradition with personal idealism concerning God and the dignity of all persons. On the other hand, he had a social philosophy embedded in democratic values of the American Dream. He melded a strategy of nonviolent action and nonviolence as a way of life.

In offering King as an exemplar of maturity, though not of perfection, I wish to summarize relevant points from "Letter from Birmingham Jail," April 16, 1963, one of the great challenges to church and ministry in this century. Its significance lies in part in its being a reply to eight fellow clergymen from Alabama and a response to white moderates generally as well as to the evasions of the clergy on racial issues. He says:

> I have almost reached the regrettable conclusion that the Negro's great stumbling block in his stride toward freedom is not the White Citizen's Councilor or the Ku Klux Klanner, but the white moderate, who is more devoted to "order" than to justice; who prefers a negative peace which is the absence of tension to a positive peace which is the presence of justice; who constantly says: "I agree with you in the goal you seek, but I cannot agree with your methods of direct action"; who paternalistically believes he can set the time-table for another's freedom; who lives by a mythical concept of time and who constantly advises the Negro to wait for a "more convenient season." Shallow understanding from people of good will is more frustrating than absolute misunderstanding from people of ill will. Lukewarm acceptance is much more bewildering than outright rejection.[6]

King was not only disappointed in the white moderate in society, he was deeply grieved with the white church and its leadership.

Within his melioristic and comprehensive policy of social change, King elucidated four basic nonviolent steps: (1) collection of facts to determine whether injustice exists; (2) negotiation; (3) self-purification; and (4) direct action. His campaign went through all these steps. He appealed to the conscience of the community; he trained his followers in nonviolent techniques; he courageously created a crisis that made people confront the issues. Maturity, we may say, does not evade tension. "There is," he argued, "a type of constructive, nonviolent tension which is necessary for growth. It helps move the community from oppressive monologue to negotiating dialogue." In all this he was aware of Reinhold Niebuhr's thesis that groups tend to be more immoral than individuals and that freedom is never voluntarily given by the oppressor. It must be demanded by the oppressed. He refused to be intimidated by those who cried "Wait." He held that it is a moral responsibility to disobey unjust laws, appealing to St. Augustine that "an unjust law is no law at all." He defined an unjust law as "a code that a numerical or power majority group compels a minority group to obey but does not make binding on itself."

In breaking unjust laws, King abhorred evasion of law or defying law which would lead to anarchy. He said, "One who breaks an unjust law must do so openly, lovingly, and with a willingness to accept the penalty. I submit that an individual who breaks a law that conscience tells him is unjust, and who willingly accepts the penalty of imprisonment in order to arouse the conscience of the community over its injustice, is in reality expressing the highest respect for law. . . . The means we use must be as pure as the ends we seek." In this total letter he consciously walked on two feet, the prophetic Christian heritage and the ideal heritage of constitutional law of the nation. In his words: "We will win our freedom because the sacred heritage of our nation and the eternal will of God are embodied in our echoing demands."[7]

4.   The Moral Ambiguity of Politics

The spiritual stature of Gandhi and King rose above but did not dispel the ambiguity of political life. The educated, professional, ordained clergyperson will struggle both to embody a concern for the right in making personal decisions as well as to be responsible with respect to public consequences. Niebuhr once wisely commented: "Politics will, to the end of history, be an area where conscience and power meet, where the ethical and coercive factors of human life will interpenetrate and work out their tentative and uneasy compromise."[8] Having alluded to ambiguity earlier in this chapter, we should now explore it more fully. Some clergy refuse to acknowledge ethical ambiguity. Instead, such an admission for them represents, as summarized by Donald E. Messer, "an admission of character weakness, an acknowledgement of inadequate scriptural faith, and an unconscionable openness to the possibility of error."[9] Such is the posture of many in the Religious Political Right and most notably of Jerry Falwell. The appeal to the inerracy of Scripture, the conception of revelation as propositional, and the assumption that political action ought to be an unexceptionable deduction from literal biblical truths fall far short of responsible social ethics in a pluralistic, secular state. Reason, not such an interpretation of revelation, must be the guide. Reason opens the door to religious experience, revelation, and tradition but insists that they must establish their claims by the same norms as judge all counterclaims. In a pluralistic society, the democratic participation of all its members must be kept open in such a way that none is excluded from reasonable dialogue among competing interests. The mature religious leader knows, on the basis of church history, that the churches' positions have often been faulty and that, at best, the pure saintly position has seldom been the one that responsible ecclesiastics were able to take because the situation was too complex and the interests of the church were too diverse to permit a simple application of the saintly vision.

Messer cites four ingredients in the political process that highlight its ambiguity. They are: (1) the fact of coercion, (2) the reality of conflict, (3) the art of compromise, and (4) the complexity of political decisions and actions. The fact of coercion reflects the strain between passion and order and of means and ends. But not all coercion is justified, and at best, coercion must always *be* justified. The reality of conflict roots not only in sin but also in finitude. Even the clearest claims of rights or duties may be in contention with each other, as is evident in the debates about ecology, social security, and abortion. The art of compromise is required lest every conflict become an ultimate showdown and, hence, lest relativity and humaneness be lost. Those who appeal to the U.S. Constitution should recall that itself is a compromise and each amendment testifies to it. Finally, the admission of complexity recognizes that simplistic statements are errors which need correction. Indeed, some situations are so complex as to be perennially insoluble.

To speak of politics is to speak of power, the many forms and levels of power, and the taming of power. A religious leader may be called on to exercise coercive power, to seek earnestly for nonviolent power, and to shape the structure of power. Likewise politics is involved in ideology, in the task of embodying ideals into laws, and in the task of persuading others so as to win the consent of the governed. This century has seen the raging conflicts of ideologies defending capitalism, fascism, communism, national socialism, and democratic socialism. The century has witnessed the birth of mixed economies and pragmatic accommodations to revolution and liberation movements.

Ideology is a human invention. It may be the enemy of truth, whose criterion is the whole. Single-cause ideologies are a special menace to maturity. So also, law is a human invention, and conscience may appeal to a higher law. Thus, we may say that maturity in politics requires the constant struggle with ambiguity and the search for relevant discriminating judgment.

Reinhold Niebuhr has pointed out that even the most respected and courageous leaders of a previous generation like Bishop G. Bromey Oxnam, Karl Barth, Martin Niemoeller, Hromadka, and many others in one way or another failed at times to make the clearest discriminating judgments, though they were right in their commitments on major issues. Niebuhr admits himself to the company of those failing in correct discriminating decision-making.[10]

As a corrective to error and as a guide to constructive compromise, the ecumenical dialogue among churches and theologians has been a maturity-evoking element. The authority of the ecumenical dialogue is its merit. Participation in it assists the minister in politics in coming to grips with such particular challenges as nationalism, sectarianism, party loyalty, the separation of church and state, ideological folly, and relativism.

5. Challenges to Religious and Political Maturity
I shall now deal briefly with six particular challenges to maturity with special reference to religious leaders in politics. They are as follows:

1. The first is *nationalism*, humankind's other religion. Nationalism serves the function of unifying loyalty above the tribal and feudal level, but it tends to subordinate more universal values to itself. Specifically, it threatens the universality of the Gospel and of human rights. National sovereignty is a political dogma that in its extreme form defeats world government efforts, frustrates international law, and violates interdependent world order. Although patriotism and nationalism are indispensable for nation building, they are enemies of ecumenism in the churches and the foes of the practical unity of secular coparticipation.

2. Secondly, there is *communalism* or sectarianism in politics. Communalism violates the maturity of the nation-state by accenting loyalty to a single religious body above the rights and freedoms of competing religious groups or those with no religious loyalty. It intensifies the limited interest of a particular group and violates the principle of equal participation. Similarly, when sectarian interests concentrate on single-cause measures as the criteria of the social good, political maturity is strained. Moralistic and single-cause politics threaten full-orbed freedom by their divisiveness.

204

3. Closely related to the threats of sectarianism and communalism is the repudiation of the separation of church and state or the rejection of the *secular state*. The religiously neutral or secular state assures religious liberty for all groups in a pluralistic society. Separation of church and state is the best guarantee of the rights of religious minorities and of broadly conceived human rights in the political, social, and economic spheres. Maturity in ministry will accept the secular state.

4. Political *parties* constitute a challenge because they represent the ambiguity of the partial spectrum of concerns, a particular perspective, or a coalition of interests. A clergyperson in politics may hope to transcend partisan strife, but it is seldom possible to remain in politics without a party base. The issue of maturity is generally resolved by the quality of debate, dialogue, freedom of dissent, minority votes, and constitutional provision for reasonably frequent elections. The religious leader must face the reality of party strife prior to the decision to enter the arena of action. Maturity requires the relativizing of all political outcomes, lest injustice be done and idolatry be committed.

5. Once again we come to the issue of *ideology*. Conflicting interests bring with them defending ideologies. Some of these are very elaborate justifications and highly moralistic. The New Religious Right, Reaganomics, modern secularism, the Moral Majority, Pro-Life, and Pro-Choice are slogans that symbolize ideologies. The New Left also develops a dominant rationale. Such ideologies have varying degrees of inner consistency or coherence with empirical facts. They become special problems of maturity when they are adhered to in patent contradiction to the evidence or the level of emotion with which an opposing view is debated or tolerated. Sometimes ideologies become so dominant and rigid in government that they lead to national folly. The East-West conflict or the McCarthy Era are cases in point. Professor Barbara Tuchman's best selling history, *The March of Folly,* gives several instances of the conflict between maturity of judgment and ideology unexamined.

6. The opposite of ideology as a threat to maturity is extreme *pragmatism* or relativism. Americans often pride themselves on not being ideologues like the Marxist-Leninists or even like the Scientific-Creationists. Practical-minded persons are reputedly flexible in the face of rapid social change. Thus, though Americans supposedly hate communism, they are willing to do business with the Eastern Bloc and with China. One major problem with political pragmatism is its tendency toward short-range policy making. It is often difficult to obtain good ecological laws, for example, because these require short-range sacrifices and in the short range a legislator may be a very unpopular person in the polls. American politics is riddled with policies

205

that fail the generational test, i.e., they serve the present pressures so well that they fail to serve to future. Thus, the failure to find a solution for the problem of acid rain or the neglect of the nation's infrastructures highlights the evils of pragmatism.

6. Moral and Religious Maturity

There are levels of moral maturity. Levels and stages of maturity are evident both in individuals and groups, in pastors, and in people. The theory put forward by Kohlberg regarding stages has been criticized as being too individualistic, and I do not defend it as definitive, but in the present context, it is a useful reminder that a leader and those being led may be at great variance in these matters, thus complicating the other issues of political maturity. In Kohlberg's scheme an individual begins with a punishment-and-obedience orientation, grows to the reciprocity of "I'll scratch your back if you scratch mine," then to conformity and order, and on to autonomous and principled rule development, climbing then to the legalism of the social contract with utilitarian overtones. This is the alleged stage of the "official" morality of the Constitution. The sixth or highest stage is called the universal-ethical principle where right is defined by the decisions of conscience in accordance with self-chosen moral principles appealing to logical comprehensiveness, universality, and consistency. "At heart, there are," he says, "universal principles of justice, of the reciprocity and equality of human rights, and of respect for the dignity of human beings as individual persons."[11] Some have suggested that the level of the vast majority of the American people is one stage lower than the utilitarian and social contract ethic of the Constitution and that a person such as Nixon, for example, operated at the stages two and four, i.e., reciprocal back-scratching and principled rule development, but not at stages five and six. I have no intention of drawing up a balance sheet, but there is ample evidence that voters, by and large, are fearful of a truly principled idealist such as McGovern being president.

If the minister in politics goes beyond Kohlberg's Stage Six to an ethic of sacrificial love and servanthood, one must accept the dilemma of leadership, which means not to be so far ahead of the people as to lose them and not so close to them as to be their follower. What, then, are the moral traits of a mature leader in the political arena? In conclusion and summary I propose the following:

(1) A profound commitment to consistency of intention and communication.
(2) Sincerity and integrity, that is, autonomy.
(3) A holistic attitude that strives for coherence among policies and values.

206

(4) A critical inquiry into long-range as well as short-range consequences of proposed enactments.

(5) A concern for relevance to fit the specific situation at hand, not idealistic escapism.

(6) An equal concern for more inclusive ends that make for coherence on the domestic and international scene.

(7) A flexible approach to resolve competing interests, or a willingness to find constructive compromises.

(8) A determination to do the best possible in a compromise situation.

(9) A discernment and loyalty to a sound hierarchy of values that illuminates the best and the possible.

A morally mature religious leader will also balance:

(10) Legitimate self-interest (self-worth).

(11) Respect for all persons.

(12) A vision of what mature personality ought to be.

In one's loyalty to (13) the principle of the common good, such a person will combine a cooperative spirit and a (14) devotion that puts the welfare of the whole above personal gain and ambition, with a willingness to sacrifice. In all this a religious leader in politics ought to be humbly aware of the ultimate ground of personal, political, and social morality, that is, of the whole moral order. The leader will have a lively sense of what in ecumenical ethics is called the "idea of the responsible society," one that acknowledges justice, freedom, and order and that acknowledges on the part of all holders of power responsibility to God and to the people whose welfare is affected by the exercise of political and economic power.

There is, I conclude, a place for the educated, professional, and ordained clergyperson to take an active role in what Vatican II called the "different yet noble art of politics." Such a mature participant will seek to enhance the nobility of the quest for the unity of means and ends. Beyond just conflict, one will seek reconciliation. ?Those who do not now participate fully, or who are in any way disenfranchised and oppressed, will receive highest priority. The minister will be dedicated to the development of people to the highest stage of their possible maturity in community with all others.

Notes

1. Walter M. Abbott, ed., *The Documents of Vatican II* (New York: The American Press, 1966), par. 75.

2. John L. Kater, Jr., *Christians on the Right: The Moral Majority in Perspective* (New York: Seabury Press, 1981), pp.20–21.

3. Richard Hofstadter, *The Paranoid Style in American Politics and Studies* (Chicago: University of Chicago Press, 1979), p. 52.

4. Quoted in S. C. Tiwari and S. R. Sharma, eds., *Political Studies* (Agra: Shiva Lal Agaravala and Co., 1966), p. 52.

5. Ibid.

6. Martin Luther King, Jr., *Why We Can't Wait* (New York: Signet Books, 1963), ch. 5.

7. Ibid.

8. Quoted in Donald E. Messer, *Christian Ethics and Political Action* (Valley Forge, PA: Judson Press, 1984), p. 148.

9. Ibid.

10. D. B. Robertson, ed., *Reinhold Niebuhr: Essays in Applied Christianity* (New York: Meridian Books, 1954).

11. Thomas C. Hennessey, ed.,*Value/Moral Education: Schools and Teachers* (New York: Paulist Press, 1979), pp. 14–15.

Epilogue

The focus of this book is maturity in ministry, spirituality and theological reconstruction in the context of ever-changing technological culture for which the traditional static concept of maturity is no longer adequate. We need a better understanding of the concept of maturity to better equip us in ministering to others, either as laity or clergy, to vitalize our spiritual life and to enable us to construct a more mature theology in our struggle with meaning and identity as well as Christian ministry.

As previously discussed, maturity is to be seen not only as a state of being but also as a process of becoming. As a state of being, maturity signifies an ideal state, something like truth, beauty, and goodness to which one can aspire but seldom achieve, namely, perfection (*teleios*), whose prototype is divine perfection, which constitutes a vision for human becoming and fulfillment. When this vision dwindles, life loses its certainty, direction, and meaning. Maturity as a state of being has its goal-orientation, which provides a center for the development of cultural norms and wholeness as well as stability and cohesiveness of community. In the traditional static culture, the belief in the sacred is fundamental to maturity. In the Christian tradition, maturity is a vision of the kingdom of God, a vision of "the fullness of Christ," a vision of God's action in one's life and in history. However, maturity is also a dynamic process of becoming, here and now, existentially and experientially. It is a process of continual renewal of spiritual life and theological understanding; it is an ever-growing process.

Where are we going in this process? Religious authenticity is considered to be a vital concern for many professional clergy. In modern society, an authentic self is something many people want but few seem to have. They make a pilgrimage in search of religious authenticity to a sanctuary where they may find positive affirmation, unconditional acceptance, and guidance to restore their broken spirit through God's grace and healing power so as to enable them to live in the world with new meaning of life and sense of identity.

Cognitively, this process is a pilgrimage toward a mature theology. What is a mature theology? In an effort to find an answer to the question, it may be helpful to consider the following excerpts from the panel discussions on "Toward a Mature Theology" at the Symposium on Maturity, Spirituality, and Theological Reconstruction and on "Maturity in Ministry in Ecumenical Perspective" at the Symposium on Maturity in Ministry:

1.   "All of our thinking about what constitutes maturity is socially and culturally conditioned. It depends upon certain implicit *standards* by which we measure 'growth.' However, no 'objective' standards are available with regard to the difficult and profound questions about the ultimate foundations of human life or what is to be taken as truly meaningful or valuable or important in human affairs. Hence it is not at all clear what constitutes genuine 'growth' in these matters or what might properly be regarded as 'maturity.' It is only through ongoing free and open conversation among the many diverse views on these most fundamental questions about human life and its meaning that deeper perceptions and a more profound understanding of what is really important in human affairs may gradually be achieved.

"This observation can be taken as a summary of what may be regarded as theological maturity in our day. In view of the obvious religious and cultural pluralism in our world—with each of the great religious and humanistic traditions presenting profound insights and wisdom about human life, at least in some of its aspects and some of its important possibilities—theological maturity does not consist in the dogmatic insistence on the ultimate truth or rightness of one's own or one's community's moral or religious or political or economic convictions. It consists rather in a willingness to examine critically even one's profoundest convictions, to freely offer one's deepest insights to the wider human conversation about all such matters, and to keep oneself open to hearing and learning from those of other religious and cultural perspectives, especially those with whom we presently find ourselves to be in profound disagreement—for it is from these whom we may in the end need to learn the most." (Gordon D. Kaufman)

2.   "It is doubtful whether one can fruitfully discuss theology in the abstract, except to define the nature of the theological enterprise. Today there is lively disagreement as to whether theology should arise from commitment to a community's struggle or whether it is meaningful to begin with a formulation of faith and then translate that into practice. Our problem is difficult especially because we have not agreed on a definition of either *mature* or *theology*.

"Consider the question: would a pacifist Christian say that Reinhold Niebuhr had a mature theology? He might insist that Niebuhr in the epoch of his ministry was simply wrong, i.e., not empirically and rationally coherent. When Niebuhr derided sentimental, liberal pacifism, he meant, among other things, that it did not correspond to the 'real situation' respecting human nature, social responsibility, and the meaning of God's activity in history. A. J. Muste, who headed the Fellowship of Reconciliation, took the opposite view. Yet, pacifist Georgia Harkness and nonpacifist Niebuhr—along with a score of others—could agree on an important document in 1944 on "The Relation of the Church to the War in the Light of the Christian Faith." Is such a consensus document necessarily more mature than the theology of any or all the participants taken singly? When the Church and Society Conferences of the World Council of Churches in 1966 criticized American policy in Vietnam, Paul Ramsey wrote an indignant book called *Who Speaks for the Church?*

"Was Barth a mature theologian when he wrote his first commentary on Romans and announced the eternal qualitative difference between time and eternity? Was Heinrich Søe doing mature theology when he insisted still in midcareer that philosophy has no place in the Holy of Holies of theology, not in the forecourt of theology? Christian faith, he argued, means Christian love. . . . Is the Barthian method reliable when applied to the complex problems of contemporary bioethics?

"Does a judgment regarding maturity depend on theological outcomes? In this conference much is being said about spirituality and the development of mature Christian spirituality. Does a mature spirituality, assuming for the moment that we can define it truly, become the criterion of truth for mature theology? Jesus is held up as a model of maturity, but he was not a theologian and his teachings are widely regarded in the church as not adequate in dealing with the modern situation of revolution and war. On the other hand, some theologians regard his person and the narrative of his ministry as the essence of truth and maturity in ethics. Some would extol the virtues of Jesus for personal and interpersonal life but insist that modifying principles must be formulated or recognized in public theology.

"A close look at what I have stated would light up the ideas of particularity, reason, faith, relevance, spirituality, ethics, personal development, and group violence and nonviolence in a consideration of maturity in theology. Implicitly are also such ideas as transcendence, immanence, and the role of philosophy in theologizing. I wish to add another issue: *universality.* Is this a criterion of theological maturity? I would add a theology's compatibility with *dialogue,* dialogue with other living faiths and ideologies. It is significant that the Vatican has an ecumenical office dealing with non-Christian faiths and with Marxism. The World Council of Churches is also actively engaged with other living faiths and ideologies. . . .

"I personally believe that it has become a mark of universality and maturity when theology is dialogical. At the same time, to be dialogical it must be faithful to its own narrative. For me, it is also a mark of maturity for theologians to have a dialogue with persons of other disciplines. The enterprise of theology should be interdisciplinary and lead to synoptic and systematic formulations.

"All significant theology is both *creative* and *corrective*. On the creative side are fresh perspectives, new insights, needed emphases, and perhaps novel design. On the corrective side are criticism of error, neglected aspects of truth, and perceived immaturities. Thus neoorthodoxy was a corrective for a certain weakness in liberalism. But a corrective may itself be an overstatement and a heresy. A 'leap of faith' may go too far or in the wrong direction." (Walter G. Muelder)

3. "Theology has two poles: the subject as faith-person and God as Revealer. It is the maturity of the subject as faith-person that is decisive for a mature theology.

"While 'adulthood' denotes the endpoint of the process of growth and development or a fixed, plateaulike state of being, maturity on the other hand denotes the achievement of one's full potentialities, ripeness, self-actualization. Maturity connotes 'fulfillment' as non-quantifiable and cannot be measured with mathematical accuracy. A mature theology demands a mature faith. A mature faith is an authentic way of being-in-the-world, a creative integration, a developmental task, and a response to a primordial gift. Faith as such is an unending process that never reaches its ultimate goal—as a faith person no one can successfully terminate his/her search for self-identity; no one can ever find a final answer to the question, 'Who am I?'

"The achievement of mature theology is a never-ending task, an ideal which is always in the process of being realized—and a dynamic response to the inexhaustible gift to the divine logo." (Lucien J. Richard)

4. "A theological rationale for Christian ecumenism is the call for maturation into the 'fullness of Christ.' This word 'fullness' (*pleroma*) is known to have had a particular significance for the doctrine of Gnostics but was borrowed to give expression to Christian faith in the full meaning of Jesus Christ for humanity and cosmos.

"Meanwhile, there is a present, historical implication of 'fullness' as the goal of maturation. The remarkable developments in the twentieth century are indications of this process. For example, the 1982 agreement of the Commission on Faith and Order of the World Council of Churches on Baptism, Eucharist and Ministry is the result of a deliberate, painstaking movement away from the immaturity of church divisions to the maturity of an approximation to the fullness of unity in Christ." (J. Robert Nelson)